WALES
AND THE FIRST
AIR WAR 1914–1918

WALES
AND THE FIRST
AIR WAR 1914–1918

The Welsh Airmen and
Airwomen of the Great War

DR JONATHAN HICKS

First impression: 2017

The publishers wish to acknowledge the support of
Cyngor Llyfrau Cymru

Cover painting of Donovan Griffith: Chris Golds
Cover design: Y Lolfa

ISBN: 978 1 78461 462 1

Published and printed in Wales
on paper from well-maintained forests by
Y Lolfa Cyf., Talybont, Ceredigion SY24 5HE
website www.ylolfa.com
e-mail ylolfa@ylolfa.com
tel 01970 832 304
fax 832 782

Contents

Acknowledgements

I SHOULD LIKE to thank the following for their valuable assistance in producing this work:

My wife Wendy for her research and support.

The authors Norman Franks and Trevor Henshaw for sharing their vast knowledge of the air war.

Ed Griffith, himself ex-RAF, for permitting me to tell the story of his relation, Donovan Griffith.

Paul Kemp of the Western Front Association for giving me access to his private collection.

Gary Williams of the Western Front Association for granting me permission to use his photographs of the memorials.

All those relatives and archivists named in the endnotes for allowing me to include their previously unpublished information and photographs.

Eirian Jones and Carolyn Hodges of Y Lolfa for their work in editing my original typescript.

Jonathan Hicks
October 2017

Introduction

'The aeroplane is an invention of the devil
and will never play any part in such a serious business
as the defence of the nation.'
Sir Sam Hughes

WHEN GREAT BRITAIN declared war on Germany on 4 August 1914, the Royal Flying Corps (RFC) was just over two years old – the royal warrant establishing its existence having been signed by King George V on 13 April 1912. Until 1918, and the formation on 1 April of the Royal Air Force by the combining of the Royal Flying Corps and the Royal Naval Air Service, the Royal Flying Corps was part of the British Army and was divided into naval and military wings. The Corps was broken down into flying schools (the Central Flying School being at Upavon on Salisbury Plain), a recruit depot, a kite section, an aircraft park, an aeronautical inspection department and naval air stations. In August 1914 there were seven squadrons with an eighth being formed.

The naval wing saw the establishment of the naval flying school at Eastchurch, and naval air stations based at Calshot, Farnborough, Felixstowe, Fort George in Dundee, the Isle of Grain, Kingsnorth and Yarmouth. The military wing was comprised of its headquarters at Farnborough, the kite section at South Farnborough and the recruit depot, also at South Farnborough.

1 Squadron was based at South Farnborough, 2 Squadron at Montrose in Scotland, 3 and 4 Squadrons on Salisbury Plain, 5 Squadron at Gosport, and 6 and 7 Squadrons at South

Farnborough. The aircraft park and the aeronautical inspection department were also sited at South Farnborough.

In August 1914 Germany could muster 246 aircraft compared with Britain's 190. In terms of flying personnel, there were 254 pilots and 271 observers in the German Air Force, while the Royal Flying Corps comprised of 105 officers and 755 other ranks. The Germans also possessed seven Zeppelin airships.

Flying itself was very much a new pursuit. The first powered flight, made by the Wright brothers, had taken place in 1903. Louis Blériot's much-feted crossing of the English Channel had occurred just five years before the war began, but Welshmen had also taken a leading role in the development of aviation.

Charles Horace Watkins was born in Cardiff in 1884. Between 1907 and 1909 he designed and built a monoplane in his garage. He flew the machine over short distances in 1910, and then gradually increased the length of the flights. His aircraft, known as Robin Goch (Robin Redbreast), is now preserved in the National Waterfront Museum in Swansea.

Charles Watkins and the 'Robin Goch'

Watkins also designed the motor that powered the fuselage, which was made from wood, canvas and piano wire; the seat was a dining chair.

Charles Rolls, of Rolls-Royce fame, was from an aristocratic Monmouthshire family and he became the first man to fly non-stop from England to France and back before being killed in a flying accident a month later in July 1910. He was buried in Llangattock-Vibon-Avel and was the first Briton to die in a powered flying accident.

In September 1913, John Herbert 'Jimmie' James and his brother Henry Howard James became the first people in Pembrokeshire to build and fly their own aeroplane. During its first flight it fell 60 feet to the ground, without causing either of them a serious injury. The brothers rebuilt the machine following its initial mishap and on 22 November it flew perfectly. On 20 April 1914 they made their first successful flight over Narberth and Carmarthen. When war broke out, they abandoned their plans to build an aeroplane factory at Narberth and instead moved to Hendon, where they instructed pilots in their own aircraft.

After serving in the Great War, Jimmie James became a test pilot for the British Nieuport Company and in 1921 he held the British speed record of 196.6 mph. After 1918, Howard James never flew again.

Wales also provided a pioneer of airship design. Ernest Willows from Cardiff was the first man in Britain to be granted a pilot's licence and, on 28 December 1910, he made the first cross-Channel airship flight from England to France. Born in July 1886 and educated at Clifton College in Bristol, he trained as a dentist. He built his first airship when he was just 19 and, after flying across the Channel, he moved to Birmingham to build his next airship, which was sold to the Admiralty. During the Great War he built kite balloons in Cardiff, and was a temporary honorary lieutenant in the Royal Flying Corps. After the war ended, he continued his pioneering work until he was killed in a balloon accident in August 1926.

'Jimmie' and Howard James and their aircraft

Ernest Willows

Two air stations were constructed in Wales to house the new airships: one at Llangefni on Anglesey and the other at Milton in Pembrokeshire. These were comprised of iron hangars for the airships, hydrogen gas storage tanks, huts, workshops and accommodation. Royal Naval Air Station (RNAS) Llangefni was commissioned on 26 September 1915, and the airships stationed there were to protect sea traffic from attacks by German U-boats – in particular, the convoys headed for Liverpool and the ferry that ran between Dublin and Holyhead. RNAS Pembrokeshire did not become operational until January 1916, but the airships from both stations offered effective protection to the convoys, and no ships were lost when airships were present, though no U-boats were sunk by the airships either.

The first aircraft arrived at Milton in April 1917 and these were Sopwith 1½ Strutter fighter-bombers which could patrol over 100 miles offshore. Six Airco DH.4 fighter-bombers were sent to RNAS Llangefni in November 1917, but it was 1918 before a purpose-built landing strip was constructed in north Wales. Fishguard became an Royal Naval Air Service seaplane base on 1 March 1917 and initially six aircraft were based there, but as the U-boat menace grew, a further six aircraft were added to that number.

The aircraft supplied for use at the beginning of the war were the B.E.2, Avro 504, Airco DH.2 and aircraft built in France – the Blériot airplanes and the Maurice Farman MF.11.

The Royal Flying Corps saw its first action on 19 August 1914, six days after leaving the UK for its base in France. Just 37 aircraft were available to depart for the front, none of which possessed fitted armament. They had flown from Dover to Boulogne and along the coast to the mouth of the River Somme. From here they had followed the course of the river to Amiens. Two aircraft took off on a reconnaissance mission, intending to take photographs of the German advance, but the weather was so poor that one pilot lost his way and was unable to complete his mission.

Officers of the Royal Flying Corps in 1914

The role of the Royal Flying Corps for much of the Great War was seen primarily as taking photographs for intelligence analysis and spotting for the artillery, and less as taking part in dogfights with the German air service. Over the next four years huge advances were made in aircraft design and pilot training, and Welshmen volunteered for the new service arm in large numbers. Weaponry evolved from pistols, rifles and shotguns carried by the pilot or observer, to interrupter gear mechanisms which allowed a machine gun to fire directly through the rotation of the propeller. Fighter pilots became the knights of the air, the notion of the 'ace' was born and newspapers clamoured for photographs of them and information on their deeds.

The first fighter was the Vickers F.B.5 'Gunbus', which arrived in France in February 1915. A two-seater biplane, with the engine located behind the pilot and the observer out in front, was armed with a single .303 Lewis machine gun and it was the first aircraft designed for air-to-air combat. This now meant that squadrons could be equipped with a small number of these 'scouts' to protect the reconnaissance aircraft.

The German air service reacted by introducing two-seater

biplanes with armed observer/gunners. These were aircraft such as the Albatros C.I, the DFW C.V, Rumpler C.IV and Halberstadt C.V. There were also to be four classes of aircraft to fulfil the roles of bombing, aerial fighting, ground support, and reconnaissance and artillery spotting.

Their next move was to introduce the first true single-seat fighter – the Fokker E.I. This was a monoplane or Eindecker, armed with single 7.92mm machine gun which fired through the rotating propeller, giving the pilot enhanced sighting capability. During the 'Fokker Scourge', from the summer of 1915 to the spring of 1916, these aircraft were perceived to dominate the skies. By March 1916, the introduction of the Nieuport and Sopwith 1½ Strutter aircraft much reduced German air activity over the British front line.

The Germans responded by introducing the Fokker D.II and Halberstadt D.II, and the Eindeckers were withdrawn from front-line service by September 1916. In addition, that autumn the Germans rolled out the Albatros D.I and D.II. Autumn 1916 also saw the formation of the *Jagdstaffel* (*Jasta*) fighter squadrons, and by April 1917 no fewer than 37 were operational.

A Nieuport fighter

April 1917, or 'Bloody April' as it became known, meant huge losses for the Royal Flying Corps. The Battle of Arras began on 9 April and was a large-scale offensive from Bullecourt in the south-east to Vimy in the north-west. By the time it was called off on 16 May, the Allies had made advances but no breakthrough.

In the air, it was a disaster. Casualties have been estimated at a third of the strength of the Royal Flying Corps, with the German aircraft adopting a passive defence of the skies above their lines. They climbed high and waited with the sun behind them for the Allied reconnaissance and artillery observation aeroplanes to appear below them. At this period, the average life span of a newly-posted subaltern was something approaching three weeks. This period also saw the loss of many experienced pilots and the Royal Flying Corps took some time to recover from these dreadful losses.

As the casualties mounted during this period, the Royal Flying Corps requested the assistance of the Royal Naval Air Service, which was operating mostly along the Channel coast. These squadrons were equipped with the new Sopwith Triplane, the 'Tripehound', which, although underarmed compared with the German machines, was nevertheless a huge improvement in terms of its agility and rate of climb. However, they were built and supplied in insufficient numbers to affect the balance of the air war during this period. What was required was a new generation of fighters to overcome the menace of the German Albatros fighters. This came with the arrival of the S.E.5, a faster, more heavily-armed machine than the previous British fighters. In July 1917, the most successful fighter used by the Allies began to be deployed – the Sopwith Camel. Armed with two Vickers machine guns and superb aerobatic performance, it meant the Germans had to produce a riposte. In August 1917, the Fokker Dr.I triplane was introduced and used to great effect by the German aces.

Many of the aces on both sides of the war are still

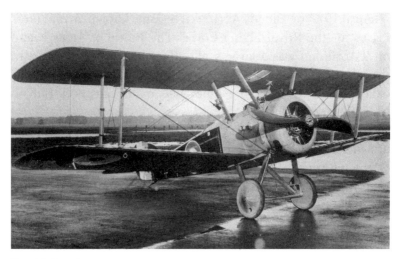

Sopwith Camel

household names even now. Some fighter pilots amassed enormous scores of victims before they met their own fates in the skies above northern France: German pilots Manfred von Richthofen (the 'Red Baron'), Oswald Boelcke and Werner Voss; French airmen Georges Guynemer and René Fonck; and British aces Edward 'Mick' Mannock, Albert Ball and James McCudden.

Yet Wales produced its own aces, and these men are worthy of remembrance for their heroism in fighting a war high up in the air, where the chances of survival, if aircrew or machine were hit by enemy bullets or shrapnel, were slim.

Fire was the constant concern. To be thousands of feet above the Earth with a fire breaking out would usually mean a terrifying death long before the safety of the aerodrome could be reached. Parachutes were not issued to pilots of the Royal Flying Corps, though the question was considered many times. It was felt that doing so might impair the fighting spirit of the pilot or that the speed of a descending aircraft would not permit proper deployment of the parachute. Thus, when an engine stopped some 8,000 feet from the ground, all most pilots and observers could do was wait for the five minutes it took to fall in a near-vertical spin towards the ground and hope that a miracle would occur.

CHAPTER ONE

1914 and 1915

'When once you have tasted flight, you will forever walk
the earth with your eyes turned upward, for there you have been,
and there you will always long to return.'

Leonardo da Vinci

ELEMENTS OF THE Royal Flying Corps began arriving in France
on 13 August 1914 to support the British Expeditionary Force.
The first clash with the German Army occurred on 23 August at
Mons in Belgium. Fighting continued at Le Cateau three days
later, and after the German advance was halted at the Battle of
the Marne, the British Army fought another rearguard action to
defend the Belgian town of Ypres in October and November.
In September, the *Llanelli Star* carried the following story:

German airmen rescued. A British submarine arrived at Harwich
yesterday bringing a German naval lieutenant and a mechanic,
who were captured in the North Sea. They were found clinging
to an aeroplane which had broken down and was floating on the
sea. The two men were rescued and made prisoners, and after
some bombs had been taken from it, the aeroplane was sunk.
The airmen were sent to the centre where German prisoners are
detained. They were conducted by a military escort and walked
unconcernedly to the fort, smiling and smoking cigarettes, in the
presence of a large crowd.[1]

The first Welsh Royal Flying Corps casualty of the Great
War was not a flier, but one of the invaluable teams of men

John Harrington

who kept the airmen flying. Air Mechanic 1st Class John Joseph Harrington from Newport was 26 when he was killed on 13 November 1914. Educated at St Mary's Roman Catholic School in Newport, he joined the Royal Monmouth Engineers in 1905 as a sapper, and obtained his discharge in 1908. He was then employed in driving the mail between Tredegar and Newport, and subsequently worked at the British and Colonial Aeroplane Company at Filton, Bristol. In 1912 he joined the Royal Flying Corps, giving his trade as that of a motor mechanic, and landed in France on 12 August 1914. He was killed by shrapnel in the fighting around Ypres in Belgium. Originally buried at a farm just north of Zillebeke, he was later reburied in Birr Cross Roads Cemetery, east of Ypres.

At the end of November, a remarkable story broke of the conduct of a Welsh airman:

According to the official story, the daring raid by British airmen upon the Zeppelin construction sheds and factory at Friedrichshafen on Saturday was successful, serious damage being done to the Zeppelin factory. The following is the statement issued by the Secretary of the Admiralty on Monday night:

'On Saturday a flight of aeroplanes under the command of Squadron-Commander E.F. Briggs, of the Royal Naval Air Service, with Flight-Commander J.T. Babington and Flight Lieutenant S.V. Sippe as pilots, flew from French territory to the Zeppelin airship factory at Friedrichshafen.

'All three pilots in succession flew down to close range under a heavy fire from guns, mitrailleuses, and rifles, and launched their bombs according to instructions. Commander Briggs is reported to have been shot down, wounded and taken to hospital as a prisoner. Both the other officers have returned safely to French territory, though their machines were damaged by gunfire. They report positively that all bombs reached their objective and that serious damage was done to the Zeppelin factory.'

This flight of 250 miles, which penetrated 120 miles into Germany, across mountainous country in difficult weather conditions, constitutes with the attack a fine feat of arms.

The Daily Mail Copenhagen correspondent says the British airman at Friedrichshafen went about their work with great courage and coolness. Squadron-Commander Briggs had his petroleum tank pierced and was compelled to descend, but he volplaned down in such a way as to pass directly over the airship shed and dropped several bombs as he did so, eventually landing within 100 yards of it.

When he was surrounded by the guards and Lanstrurm, he resisted arrest with his revolver and had to be overpowered and dragged from his seat. He was injured about the head and was taken for first aid to a neighbouring café, where he fainted. Then he was taken to hospital, and it is now reported that his wound is comparatively slight. His Avro aeroplane was undamaged.

The *Chronicle* special correspondent, wiring from Basle, says: 'I learn that after Commander Briggs, the naval aviator captured in the Friedrichshafen raid, had been overpowered by German soldiers, following a desperate resistance, an officer struck him across the face with a riding-whip. Commander Briggs then said, "Leave me alone; I only did my duty." In hospital in declared, "Wait, this is only the beginning."'[2]

Further details emerged the following month:

Memorandum by the Director of the Air Department. Admiralty, 17 December, 1914. On 21 November, 1914, Squadron Commander E.F. Briggs, Flight commander J.T. Babington, and Flight Lieutenant S.V. Sippe, Royal Navy, carried out an aerial attack on the Zeppelin airship sheds and factory at Friedrichshafen on Lake Constance.

Leaving French territory shortly after 10 a.m., they arrived over their objective at about noon, and, although under a very heavy rifle, machine-gun and shrapnel fire from the moment they were sighted, they all three dived steeply to within a few hundred yards of the sheds, when they released their bombs – in all eleven. Squadron Commander Briggs was wounded, brought down, and made a prisoner, but the other two officers regained their starting point after a flight of more than four hours across hostile country under very bad weather conditions.

It is believed that the damage caused by this attack includes the destruction of one airship and serious damage to the larger shed, and also demolition of the hydrogen-producing plant, which had only lately been completed. Later reports stated that flames of considerable magnitude were seen issuing from the factory immediately after the raid.[3]

Edward Featherstone Briggs was a surveyor at the Great Western Colliery, Pontypridd, and played rugby for Clifton before he joined the Royal Flying Corps in 1912. He had gained his pilot's certificate in July 1912 at the Naval School, Eastchurch. His connection to Wales was made clear a week after the raid took place:

Squadron-Commander E.F. Briggs of the Royal Naval Air Service, whose wonderful raid on the German Zeppelin Factory at Friedrichshafen last Saturday is on everybody's lips, is a Pontypridd hero. Although not a native of the town, he spent many years there, and he is regarded by the residents as one of themselves. During his residence at Pontypridd, he was an active member of the Church Guild, whose members continue to take a keen interest in his career.

Commander Briggs, who is a native of Bristol, for some time held a colliery appointment at Pontypridd, which he resigned not more than two years ago to enter the Royal Naval Air Service, in which his promotion has been singularly rapid. He is the holder of the British height record, having on 11 March at Eastchurch, while flying a Blériot monoplane, reached an altitude registered by his barograph of 14,920 feet.[4]

With a view to the contradicting statements that had been made in the French newspaper *Le Matin* in late November 1914 regarding the treatment meted out to Briggs when he was captured, the Berlin *Tageblatt* published a statement purporting to have been made by Briggs himself:

> In accordance with orders, I appeared on 21 November over
> the Zeppelin sheds at Friedrichshafen in a two-seated aeroplane
> without a companion. About noon, when at a height of about one
> hundred metres, my petrol tank was pierced and I was forced to
> descend immediately. My right ear was also slightly grazed by a
> bullet and was bleeding. I was obliged to come to the ground quite
> near the airship hangars. I landed on the flat surface near these,
> my aeroplane suffering no damage.
>
> After landing, the aeroplane remained on the ground.
> Immediately after landing, a German soldier from the direction
> of two hangars about forty metres away fired five shots at me in
> succession, but I was not hit. Then I held up my hands, and several
> people, military and civilians, rushed upon me and my machine, in
> which I sat, bound by a belt. The belt was then undone and I was
> torn from the aeroplane. While I was bending down, I received on
> my head a heavy blow which I felt powerfully through my thick
> airman's cap. I lost, however, neither consciousness nor blood
> through this blow. I presume the blow, judging by its force, was
> dealt by the butt end of a rifle. This blow obviously was struck by
> a German private, since I only saw such with rifles in their hands.
> Judging by his sword, a German officer was also among those
> who rushed up, but I remember to have seen him last about forty
> metres away.
>
> When I was completely pulled from my machine and was
> standing up, I found myself between two soldiers, who held me
> fast. Behind me was a crowd, which, judging by their behaviour,
> apparently wished to spring upon me. I was then forthwith led
> away by two soldiers to the guardhouse a few minutes distant.
> There I remained half an hour and got a drink of water from a
> German who spoke English. He then, with two soldiers, took me in
> a motor car to the hospital at Friedrichshafen, where the following
> day an English-speaking German informed me that the German
> officer who arrived on the scene when I landed had probably

saved my life, because he placed himself between me and the crowd when I was led away from the machine, and that the officer threatened to shoot down anyone who attacked me.

No German officer at any time attacked me nor, as has been alleged by the *Matin*, struck me with a whip after I was taken from the aeroplane. Before that, I received only one blow as mentioned and did not see who delivered it, since I had to hold my head down while being dragged from the machine, but I declare that for the above reasons it is entirely improbable that the officer gave the blow. Besides, it is my personal opinion that a German officer or an English officer would consider it beneath his dignity to commit such an act as the *Matin* of 27 November alleged.[5]

On 1 January 1915 the announcement was made of the award of a Distinguished Service Order to Briggs:

He carried out an aerial attack on the Zeppelin Airship sheds and factory at Friedrichshafen on Lake Constance. Although under a very heavy rifle, machine-gun and shrapnel fire from the moment they were sighted, they all three dived steeply to within a few hundred feet of the sheds, when they released their bombs. Squadron Commander Briggs was wounded, brought down, and made a prisoner, but the other two officers regained their starting point after a flight of more than 4 hours across hostile country under very bad weather conditions. It is believed that the damage caused by this attack includes the destruction of one airship and serious damage to the larger shed, and also demolition of the hydrogen producing plant.[6]

The bomb racks for the aircraft piloted by Briggs and his fellow pilots were designed and made by Charles Horace Watkins (see page 9). This setback could have been the end of Briggs' wartime contribution but, in 1917, he escaped captivity and made his way back to Britain. This was again reported in the newspapers:

How Commander Edward Briggs, the famous Pontypridd airman, escaped from captivity is told by the London correspondent of the *Manchester Guardian*. Following his achievement in leading the attack on the Zeppelin shed at Friedrichshafen, Commander Briggs was a prisoner in Germany for twenty-nine months, and he arrived in England after an exciting escape at the beginning of April. With him on the same boat was another escaped officer, whose adventures had not ended when he passed the frontier, as he was unaware that he was in Holland until some hours afterwards, and after enduring such unnecessary discomfort, I understand (adds the writer) that Commander Briggs and another officer were being transferred from one fortress to another by train, and at one of the stations when the carriage was unguarded, they slipped out on the far side, and after two days' hiding and cautious travelling reached the Dutch frontier, which was not far distant. The fact that he escaped at all through the German frontier guards and the wire fences shows that the coolness and resources which distinguished his air career had not been weakened by long confinement. He was an engineer officer in the Navy, and took up flying – he was indeed the first officer to join the new flying wing of the Navy – at the beginning. He was assistant to Commander Sampson when he had charge of the training establishment at Eastchurch, and did much fine work with the Dunkirk air squadron.[7]

At the end of 1919 he received a bar to his DSO in recognition of his conduct while a prisoner of war:

His Majesty the King has been pleased to approve of recognition being accorded, as indicated below, to Officers and other ranks of the Royal Air Force, for gallantry whilst Prisoners of War in escaping, or attempting to escape, from captivity, or for valuable services rendered in the Prison Camps of the Enemy.[8]

Edward Briggs

Briggs was also awarded the OBE for his war service. His son Michael served as a pilot with the RAF during the Second World War and was killed while flying a Spitfire in poor conditions over Richmond in Yorkshire in April 1941. Edward Briggs died in 1963.

*

On 20 December 1914, Captain Wilfred Picton-Warlow took off from the Air Park at St Omer in France in a Blériot XI two-seater monoplane. He was on his way back home on leave, and it was the custom under such circumstances to allow pilots to fly a redundant aircraft back to Britain. The Blériot XI was being taken out of service at this time as it was found to be too slow in climbing with a full military load.

Picton-Warlow was born at Laleston in Bridgend on 6 April 1884. He was the younger son of Colonel John Picton Turbevill of Ewenny Priory, Bridgend, and a relation of General Thomas Picton of Waterloo fame. Educated at Clifton College and Elizabeth College, Guernsey, he had joined the Guernsey

Blériot XI

25

Wilfred Picton-Warlow

Militia and subsequently the Welsh Regiment in January 1903. He served with the battalion in India and South Africa before joining the Royal Flying Corps in August 1913.

He was last seen flying over Calais, but he never arrived in England and was presumed dead, aged 30. Although the visibility from Calais to Dover was clear, there were some high banks of cloud and it was assumed that Picton-Warlow had flown into these, lost his bearings, become disorientated and crashed; perhaps even running out of fuel beforehand.

He left behind a widow, Eleanor, and is commemorated on the Arras Flying Services Memorial. Ivor, his brother, served with the 1st Gordon Highlanders and was taken prisoner in September 1914, spending the rest of the war in internment. Ivor's twin brother Arthur joined the East African Rifles and died of malaria on active service on 8 November 1917.

In February 1915, a letter was published in a Welsh newspaper conveying the excitement felt by one young man who experienced this new form of transport:

An interesting letter has been received from Second Aerial Mechanic J.J. Cox, son of Mr and Mrs J. Cox of Port Talbot, who is in the Flying Corps now stationed at Salisbury Plain. Writing home after his first flight in the air he says: 'Last Thursday I had my first ride in the air; it's grand: it's absolutely great. I only wish you could have a ride. It's a lovely sensation when you are coming down to earth nearly perpendicular at the rate of 75 to 80 miles an hour ...

Well, Jack Cox and Serjeant Turner sat in the aeroplane and gently moved along the ground. Eventually we increased speed, and when reaching about forty miles an hour we started rising from the ground, and to express my feeling better the ground started dropping from underneath us. That is the sensation which tickled our ribs in climbing up. When we reached the height of 1,500 feet from the earth, we travelled level or thereabouts and made a great circle of the aerodrome. The camp looked like a little doll's house, sheep looked like young mice. It's a feeling which I cannot express, but it has a great fascination for some people. When you are up that height you can see for miles. I almost thought I could see Port Talbot! There is little flying, for the weather is terribly rough. The sea winds cannot touch those here.'

The writer proceeds to say he has very little time off and continues: 'In the summer months they start flying at three, four, and five o'clock in the morning, and do not finish up till nearly eight or nine o'clock at night. There is a lot of overtime, but we are paid by the day in the Army, and a day is twenty-four hours.'[9]

In March 1915, Major Tom Ince Webb-Bowen assumed command of 2 Squadron. Born in Tenby in January 1879, he was commissioned into a militia battalion of the Middlesex Regiment and later served pre-war as a captain in the Bedfordshire Regiment, serving in India. He learned to fly in a

Farman Biplane at Brooklands, Surrey, in 1912, and joined the Royal Flying Corps. During his time with 2 Squadron, one of his pilots became the first airman to be awarded the Victoria Cross; William Rhodes-Moorhouse completed his bombing mission and returned to base despite terrible injuries which caused his death the following day.

Tom Webb-Bowen

27

Webb-Bowen commanded Number 3 Wing from May 1915 and, as Brigadier-General, subsequently led II and VII Brigades of the Royal Flying Corps in France and Italy. After retiring from the Royal Air Force in September 1933, he was recalled during the Second World War and served as Duty Air Commodore in the operations room at the headquarters of Fighter Command. He was later knighted and died in 1956.

April 1915 saw the announcement of another promotion for a Welsh officer:

> Captain G.E. Todd of the Welsh Regiment, who has been promoted from flight-commander to squadron-commander in the Royal Flying Corps, and has been given the temporary rank of major, is one of the most daring and popular officers in the Welsh Regiment.
>
> Born in 1881, he served for a time in the old Royal Glamorgan Militia, and obtained his first commission as a second-lieutenant in the Welsh Regiment in July 1903. Four years later he obtained his second star, and was raised to the rank of captain on August 14, 1913, upon which day he was attached to the Military Wing of the Royal Flying Corps. He served with his regiment in the late South Africa [Boer] war, for which he holds the Queen's medal with five clasps. From 26 August 1911, to 25 November 1912, he was employed as a staff officer with the West Africa Frontier Force.
>
> He has done some remarkably good work in connection with the present war. He is one of three officers of the Welsh Regiment now serving with the Royal Flying Corps, the others being Captain C.A.H. Longcroft and Captain W. Picton-Warlow, of Ewenny Priory near Bridgend.[10]

Two Welshmen died in 1915 while serving with the Royal Flying Corps. The first was Air Mechanic 2nd Class William Williams, aged 21, who had lived with his parents at Penybwlch, Llechwedd, Conwy. He had been attached to the Recruits Depot in Farnborough, but died of tuberculosis at Aldershot on 18 May 1915. His body was taken home and he was buried in Llechwedd Tabernacle Cemetery.

A day later a lucky escape for another airman was reported:

> One of our airmen had a thrilling experience, says 'Eye-Witness', in pursuit of a German machine. While trying to reload his machine gun, he lost control of the steering gear and the aeroplane turned upside down. The belt round his waist happened to be loose, and the jerk of the turn almost threw him out of the machine, but he saved himself by clutching hold of the rear centre strut – the belt slipping down round his legs. While he hung thus, head downwards, making desperate efforts to disengage his legs, the aeroplane fell from a height of 8,000 ft to 2,500 ft, spinning round and round like a falling leaf. At last, he managed to free his legs and reach the control lever with his feet. He then succeeded in righting the machine, which turned slowing over, completely 'looping the loop', whereupon he slid back into his seat.
>
> This constitutes a record even in a service where hairbreadth escapes are of daily occurrence. There have been many duels in the air, which have invariably resulted in our favour, several German machines having been brought down either by our aeroplanes or anti-aircraft guns. A few of our machines have also been hit and forced to descend, though this has not been brought about by the enemy's airmen, but by gun and rifle fire from the ground.[11]

It is often noted that of the poetry of the Great War, not a great deal was written by or about airmen. An exception was this poem written in June 1915 and published in a Welsh newspaper in response to the death of Lieutenant Reginald Warneford, who, after being awarded the Victoria Cross for shooting down a Zeppelin airship on 7 June 1915, died of injuries received in a flying accident on 17 June 1915.

In Memoriam
Lieut. Warneford, V.C., Chevalier

In the grey light of early morn,
He notes a speck against the sky;
Death and destruction therein borne,
A Zeppelin goes sailing by.

Eager he marks the ship of prey,
Nor heeds the odds, though great they be;
Strong-nerved hand, unfaltering eyes,
A doughty son of Britain He.

With speedy wing, he goes through space,
Nearing the speck, now grown so great;
Yet moving with an eagle's grace,
But filled with spleen and deadly hate.

He soars aloft, attains his aim,
Above the monster – soul elate.
His lightning looses, not in vain,
Unequal combat – unrivalled feat.

A mighty roar, the airship's burst,
Flames lighten up the morning sky;
The dreadnought vanishes in dust,
Its crew no more will sail on high.

But now alas! in peaceful flight,
The conqueror too has passed away,
His fame well earned – intensely bright,
Aye, brilliant as the diamond's ray.

Long will his memory cherished be,
For deeds like his will never die;
Hallow'd the spot where resteth He,
And thoughtless ne'r will man pass by.

C.S. Llandilo, June 21 1915[12]

The second Welsh airman fatality of 1915 was Captain Arthur Henry Leslie Soames from Bryn Estyn, Wrexham. He was killed on 7 July 1915, aged 28, and was buried at All Saints Church, Gresford. Soames had taken his Royal Aero Club Aviator's Certificate in a Vickers monoplane at the Vickers School, Brooklands, on 26 November 1912.

Captain Soames had served as a second lieutenant with the Royal Welsh Fusiliers and then in the 3rd King's Own Hussars, before being transferred to 4 Squadron Royal Flying Corps and being posted to France. He was transferred to the Central Flying School in February 1915.

The Soames family lived at Bryn Estyn Hall in Rhosnesni and his father, Frederick, ran the brewery in Wrexham. A cousin had married Lord Baden-Powell, the founder of the Scouts movement. Soames was mentioned in dispatches in October 1914 and was awarded the Military Cross in January 1915 for his work in aerial reconnaissance.

His brother William was killed in May 1916 in Egypt and another brother, Julian, who served with the Royal Welsh Fusiliers, was wounded and subsequently had a leg amputated. His sister's husband had been killed on active service in October 1914.

A national newspaper carried an account of his death:

Army Airman Killed Testing an Explosive Bomb. An inquest was held by Mr Sylvester, Coroner for Central Wiltshire, at Netheravon Military Hospital yesterday on the body of Captain Arthur Henry Leslie Soames, 3rd Hussars, attached to the Royal Flying Corps. On Wednesday, Captain Soames, who was the head of the experimental section of the flying school at Upavon, was experimenting with a bomb. It was placed on its nose in a wood near Netheravon Hospital, and was fired by an electric wire, 100 yards long, which was carried through a thick clump of trees. After the bomb had been fired, Captain Soames was found on the ground severely injured. A tree near him had been cut through by part of the exploded bomb. The officer's injuries were very severe, but he was still conscious. He died the same night.

Evidence was given by Colonel Pitcher, Central Indian Horse, who said that another officer, Major Boase, was also knocked over and too badly shaken to attend the inquest. The bomb was of a new type and was tested under these conditions for the first time, but 100 yards' distance was considered sufficient. The jury returned a verdict of 'Accidental Death'. Captain Soames was one of the most daring airmen of the Royal Flying Service, and at the beginning of the war he served at the front for some time, and gained the French Medal for Valour.[13]

Soames was one of the first pilots to fly in attacks on the Western Front in 1914 and the impact of his death was such that King George V wrote to Soames' commanding officer asking about the circumstances of the incident. Captain Paine, Commandant of the Central Flying School at Upavon, received a letter from Buckingham Palace, dated 10 July 1915:

> The King is greatly distressed to hear of the death of Captain Soames through an accident, and I am commanded to convey to you the expression of His Majesty's sympathy in the loss of a gallant comrade and experienced flier. His Majesty well remembers Captain Soames, having decorated him some time ago with the Military Cross and also having seen him give an exhibition on bomb throwing on the occasion of his visit to Upavon. The King would like to know further details of the incident by which Captain Soames lost his life.[14]

Second Lieutenant Alfred Vivian McKiever reported to 1 Reserve Air Training Squadron at South Farnborough on 11 August 1915. Born in November 1890 in Pontypridd, he had

Arthur Soames   Alfred McKiever

returned from Johannesburg, South Africa, to serve the country of his birth. After enlisting in the Seaforth Highlanders, he gained his flying certificate on 9 September and, as an Observer with the Royal Flying Corps, he joined 26 Squadron and served in German East Africa from 23 December 1915. This squadron was formed of personnel from the South African Air Corps.

They were charged with assisting ground forces against the Germans, who were led by the formidable Colonel Paul Emil von Lettow-Vorbeck. Arriving in Mombasa on 31 January 1916, they were equipped with B.E.2.cs and some Henri Farman aircraft that had been flown during the previous campaign in South West Africa. Conditions were extremely difficult, with heavy rain and mountainous topography; disease was also rife. Emergency landings were impossible owing to the dense bush, which also meant difficulties in constructing new airfields as the British forces advanced. Consequently, flight times were long, taking a toll on the aircrew, who were mostly engaged in reconnaissance, bombing and spotting work for the artillery.

In July 1918, the squadron returned to Great Britain and was disbanded. Alfred McKiever was promoted to lieutenant and transferred to 33 Squadron of the Royal Air Force. He survived the war, and continued to serve in the RAF. On 16 January 1922, he was killed in a flying accident in Egypt.

CHAPTER TWO

1916

'Airplanes are interesting toys but of no military value.'
Marshal Ferdinand Foch

AFTER THEIR FAILURE to achieve a breakthrough on the Western Front in the autumn of 1914, the German strategy was to hold the ground they had taken and to allow the Allies to waste their resources in futile frontal attacks on well-prepared defensive positions. Allied aircraft were used primarily for observation and reconnaissance, and the German pilots were charged with shooting them down.

After the catastrophic battles of 1915 – most notably Neuve Chapelle, Second Ypres and Loos – which attempted an infantry breakthrough on a narrow front after an artillery bombardment, by the winter of 1915–16 Allied strategy switched to a war of attrition, with attacks planned along a wide front to wear down the German Army. When the Germans surprisingly attacked the French Army at Verdun in February 1916, it became clear that the British and their Allies from the British Empire would be responsible for the bulk of this offensive, and so they were – on the Somme from 1 July to 18 November 1916.

The first Welsh airman to be killed in 1916 was Second Lieutenant Richard Borlase Jenkins, who died of his wounds on 17 January. Born in Bishopston near Swansea on 21 August 1896, he was educated at Llandrindod Wells and Sherborne School, where he was a member of the Officer Training Corps and played rugby for the first team for three years. Jenkins

Richard Jenkins had intended to be an engineer but, when the war started, he volunteered for the Army. He was gazetted a second lieutenant in the 6th South Wales Borderers on 19 September 1914 and sent to Sandhurst. On 16 June 1915, he joined the Royal Flying Corps and trained as a pilot at Farnborough and Upavon. He obtained his wings in September and joined 9 Squadron in France in December.

On 17 January 1916, he took off in a B.E.2c on a bombing mission. His aircraft was attacked on its way back by a Fokker aeroplane. Jenkins was struck on the head in the incident, but he made a perfect landing and appeared only slightly wounded. He was admitted to a casualty clearing station, where he died of a brain haemorrhage a few hours later. He was buried at Terlincthun British Cemetery, Wimille in France.

Second Lieutenant Ernest John Radcliffe, who was born in Mumbles, Swansea, died on 20 February and was buried at St Pancras Cemetery in London. The newspaper report of his death read:

Army Airman's Death at Brooklands
An inquest was held at Byfleet yesterday on the body of Second Lieutenant Ernest John Radcliffe of the Royal Flying Corps, who was killed while flying at Brooklands on Sunday.
    The Officer commanding at Brooklands said Mr Radcliffe, who was 21 years of age, was gazetted on January 15. He had passed the elementary flight under dual control, and had flown alone for an hour. Evidence was given by a flight commander to the effect that when completing a second circuit of the aerodrome

the biplane, which was a new one, 'banked' on the right wing. In order to rectify matters the pilot increased the 'banking', and this resulted in side slip. The biplane struck a house outside the aerodrome. The petrol burst into flames, igniting and destroying the biplane. Mr Radcliffe's body was badly burned.

A verdict of 'Accidental Death' was returned. Mr Radcliffe was the only son of Mr and Mrs H.E. Radcliffe of Muswell Hill.[1]

Corporal William George Morgan, aged 28, died of illness on 30 March and was buried in Llantwit Fadre (Salem) Welsh Baptist Chapel cemetery. His parents lived at Tonteg, Pontypool, though he was a native of Pontypridd. He was serving at 1 Training Centre.

Second Lieutenant Norman William Thomas was killed on 8 April, aged 28, while serving with 27 Squadron and was buried at Écoivres Military Cemetery, Mont-Saint-Éloi. His parents lived at Croeswylan, Oswestry, and he was a director in his father's contracting firm. He had joined the Montgomeryshire Yeomanry as a trooper in September 1914, and was promoted to serjeant despatch rider in December of that year. In June 1915, he was commissioned into the Shropshire Light Infantry and took his flying certificate at Hendon the following month. Educated at Wellingborough, he was a good cricketer

and hockey player, frequently representing Shropshire.

Thomas was flying a Martinsyde G.100 when his aircraft crashed near Mont-Saint-Éloi and was wrecked at 9 a.m.

In May 1916, a British aircraft failed to return from its mission to bomb the aerodrome at Ostend. A pilot flew over the German

Norman William Thomas

aerodrome and dropped a message asking for information about the pilot's fate, to which the Germans replied. William David Sambrook, from Cilgerran in Pembrokeshire, took up the story in his diary:

> They said attempts had been made at rescue, but when the machine was brought in the pilot was already dead. He was buried with full military honours alongside two comrades at Marrakerke cemetery, Ostend. The message was accompanied by two photos of the funeral and the grave. There was also a message in German stating the name and place in German territory where our machines could land if they had engine trouble.[2]

Sambrook took part in bombing raids on aerodromes and docks, as well as the Zeppelin bases at Bruges and Zeebrugge. He survived the war, being awarded the Distinguished Service Medal in 1917.

In June 1916, a young Welshman named David Ivor Davies enlisted in the Royal Naval Air Service, aged 23, as a probationary flight sub-lieutenant. After twice crashing

William Sambrook   Ivor Novello

37

aeroplanes, he moved to the Air Ministry office in central London and performed clerical duties for the remainder of the war. As Ivor Novello, he had written the music for the song 'Keep the Home Fires Burning' in 1914, which had brought him money and fame. He also wrote the music for *Theodore & Co.*, a wartime musical comedy which was hugely successful.

William Warren Carey-Thomas was born in Penarth in 1885. He gained his Aero Club Certificate at the Military School, Norwich, in October 1915 and was promoted to pilot in the Royal Flying Corps in January 1916. He served with No. 26 (South African) Squadron in East Africa where he flew B.E.2cs and, later, Henri Farman aircraft.

In June 1916, he had a lucky escape from predators:

> It was while they were at Palms (airfield) that one of the pilots, Lieutenant Carey-Thomas, a fiery little Welshman, took off for a solo reconnaissance. As he flew back and darkness was falling, he realised that he had flown too far and had missed the aerodrome. As his fuel was getting low he looked for somewhere to land and saw a clearing he recognised as being a vacated airfield and landed there. The airfield was the notorious 'Daniel's Den', with a large number of lions roaming in the vicinity. All night Carey-Thomas huddled in the cockpit of the plane hoping the lions which he could hear would not be able to get at him. He was found by a search party next day but never wanted to repeat the experience.[3]

His observer, Lieutenant Leo Walmsley, described flying with Carey-Thomas on a bombing raid in August that year:

> My pilot lost no time in getting to work. Throttling down the engine, he pushed the joy-stick forward, and we dived at the (railway) station at a speed of something like 100 miles an hour. It was a very thrilling sensation. This engine of ours had an awkward habit of refusing to open out again after being throttled down, and I heaved a sigh of relief when, at 800 feet from the ground, we flattened out, and it burst forth once more into a comforting roar. We now had an excellent view of the station ... We circled round and round for a minute or two and then, flying immediately

over the trains, the pilot released the first bomb. I watched it
leave the machine and sail swiftly down towards the ground:
then with a greenish flash and a puff of black smoke it burst on
the embankment side, a yard or two from the centre of one of
the trains. The Huns looked now as though they were feeling the
strain. The second bomb was an infinitely better shot, but a trifle
short, bursting in the centre of the track ten yards behind the
guard's van of the second train. The third was obviously a dud, for
neither of us saw it; but the fourth and last made a direct hit on a
large station building, which was evidently being used as a store.
Following the first flash of the explosion, the whole roof seemed
to rise slowly up, until its rafters showed like the teeth of a comb,
then it sank earthwards in an immense cloud of dust and smoke.[4]

Later that month, Carey-Thomas went missing. The engine
of his aircraft failed and he crashed, fortunately on the British
side of the lines. He and his observer were lost in the bush for
three days without food or water, being constantly attacked by
tsetse flies which caused their arms and faces to swell, before
they were eventually found.

Carey-Thomas was awarded the Military Cross in June 1917.
He was mentioned in despatches in March 1918 and survived

the war. After returning home
he sailed back to Cape Town
from Southampton in October
1920 on the *Carisbrooke Castle*
and joined the South African
Air Force.

He was killed on 10 March
1922 in the air over Benoni in
the Transvaal while serving
as the adjutant of his unit. He
was acting as observer in an
aircraft being flown by Colonel

William Warren Carey-Thomas

Sir Pierre van Ryneveld in action against striking miners. His death was reported in a magazine:

> Two or three machines were sent off to Benoni with instructions to use their machine guns on the Trades Hall, which was the Headquarters of the rebels. Another machine was sent to the Brakpan mines.
>
> The observer in this machine was Capt. Carey Thomas, who will be remembered by many officers and men of the RAF. In the course of the reconnaissance, Capt. Carey Thomas was killed. The manner of his death was reported by his pilot as follows: 'Saw a commando of about 200 men in the trees near east corner of Brakpan. Dived low down, nothing happened. Captain Carey Thomas instructed me to go lower. I dived again, still nothing happened so far as I could make out. I looked round, however, saw Captain Carey Thomas all crumpled up and it was found that Capt. Thomas had been shot through the heart.'[5]

William Warren Carey-Thomas was buried in Thaba Tshwane (old No. 1) Military Cemetery, Pretoria.

The success of one Welsh pilot was reported on 6 July:

> A Carmarthenshire airman has distinguished himself in France by bringing down two Fokkers. Some time ago the British official dispatch from France reported 27 air combats on Whit-Sunday. 'Two of our fighting aeroplanes encountered two Fokkers in the vicinity of Lens,' it added, 'and one of the hostile machines was driven down damaged. The other was shot down, and crashed to earth from a height of 4,000 ft.'

J.N. Morley

The person responsible for this fine achievement is Chief Artificer J.N. Morley, son of Mrs M.J. Jones, Penymynydd, Gorslad [Gorslas], Llandebie. At the time Chief Artificer Morley was in the Naval Air Service, but was recently transferred to the Anti-Aircraft Corps. Writing home, he states: 'I brought down two Fokkers on Whit-Sunday: that was my holiday, as you will see by the British official report.'[6]

Morley survived the war.

Lieutenant Reginald Burgess of 22 Squadron died of his wounds on 7 July 1916, aged 24, and was buried in Douchy-lès-Ayette British Cemetery. His parents lived in Narberth, Pembrokeshire. Burgess set off on a patrol at 6.38 a.m. as the observer in an F.E.2b. Over Clery-Longueval, east of the lines, they were attacked and shot down. The Canadian pilot, Lieutenant J.H. Firstbrook, was wounded and captured.

Lieutenant Martyn Tulloch Vaughan-Lewes was the only son of Captain Price Vaughan-Lewes. He died of his wounds on 22 July 1916, aged 21. His grandfather was Colonel J. Lewes

F.E.2b

of Llanllŷr, Talsarn, Cardiganshire, who was known locally as the 'Hero of the Redan'. Born in Marylebone in London in June 1895, Martyn Vaughan-Lewes was educated at Harrow and then at the Royal School of Mines at Camborne, Cornwall. After qualifying as a mining engineer he emigrated to Canada.

When war broke out, he was gazetted to the 3rd Welsh Regiment and landed in France the following May, and was then attached to the Monmouthshire Regiment. He went through the heavy fighting of the spring of 1915 around Ypres, and was wounded in the engagement at Andverous, part of the Second Battle of Ypres. He refused to be sent back to base and returned to duty as soon as possible.

After a short leave at home, he was attached to the Royal Flying Corps and trained as an observer before being engaged in reconnaissance work with 25 Squadron from February 1916. A talented pilot, he brought down three enemy aircraft during the week before his death. It was while engaged in a flight over the German lines, on 15 July, that he received the injuries to which he succumbed. He lost his way in dense fog and remained for many hours in the air, unable to land for fear of descending behind the German lines. When at last he did descend, he was severely wounded by shrapnel and the aircraft's landing gear was badly damaged. After reaching Bailleul, he decided to jump from the machine before it crashed, sustaining a shattered leg and internal injuries. He was taken to the hospital but died a week later and was buried in Bailleul Communal Cemetery Extension in France. His father had died of illness in November 1914 while on active service.

On 27 July, it was announced that Flight Lieutenant Walter Travis Swire Williams had been awarded the Distinguished Service Cross for services rendered during an attack on a railway bridge. He was on service with the Royal Naval Air Service in the Mediterranean. Williams had gained his pilot's qualification at the Royal Navy Flying School in Eastchurch on 7 September 1915. Born in Porthmadog in May 1897 and

Martyn Vaughan-Lewes   Walter Williams

the son of a doctor, Williams survived the war and remained in the RAF. He served during the Second World War, rising to be a squadron leader, and died on active service, aged 50, on Christmas Day 1947. He is buried in Cambridge City Cemetery.

An airman's view of the battlefield appeared in the press on 9 August:

> Lieut. G.M. Garro-Jones 10th SWB, is now attached to the Royal Flying Corps as observation officer. Writing home on the 20 ult., Mr Garro-Jones says:
> 'I have been up several times now in different kinds of machines and have flown right across the trenches over territory occupied by the Germans. From a height of ten or twelve thousand feet, one would not believe that the scarred and spotted and smoke-puffed area below was the scene of long-continued and deadly strife. From a great height one can distinguish the trenches and mine craters, shell holes and burst, etc., if one knows from

previous experience what they are, but to a novice it would look as if the earth in the afflicted area had been smitten with some terrible blight and was being eaten up. Behind the trenches on your left stretches our territory – on the right is the German portion. One is surprised to find that it looks the same whether it is German or British occupied land. From all heights up to 15,000 ft, on a clear day the main roads are easily distinguishable because they are white. Other things that stand out prominently are the woods, because they are darker than their surroundings. But more prominent than anything is a sheet of water when it reflects the sun up to us. At other times it is almost invisible.

'On one occasion I went as observer in a machine which was detailed to drop bombs on a railway siding behind the German line. Fortunately it was pretty cloudy, and we ascended right up above the clouds and the pilot brought the machine down just enough to see the objective and, at the moment required, he pulled the lever which released the bombs. We had a few anti-aircraft shells ... (I forgot they no longer drop on me) bursting at us, but they were not too close, and the weight of the bombs being disposed of we simply soared up into the clouds again and by a bank of the planes and slight turn of the rudder we were again making for the aerodrome.

'If I tried to describe what everything looked like from above and what one's feelings are from the time when the propeller is started by the mechanic to the time when the landing is complete and the plane is taxi'd (i.e. propelled along the ground or rather pulled by the tractor) into the shed, I should be writing all day, so you must be content with these few of my impressions which I have written today.'

The gallant young officer is the only son of the Rev. D. Garro-Jones.[7]

George Morgan Garro-Jones was born on 14 September 1894 in Zion Hill House, Trefgarn, in Pembrokeshire. Educated at Caterham School in Surrey, he served with the Denbighshire Yeomanry from 1913 to 1914. When the war began, he enlisted in the 10th South Wales Borderers and was sent to France in 1915. Commissioned Second Lieutenant with the SWB in November 1915, he then joined

George Garro-Jones

the Royal Flying Corps. He was promoted to Captain in December 1917, and in 1918 went to America as an advisory officer to the United States Air Service. When the war ended, he worked as the Private Secretary to the Chief Secretary for Ireland and was responsible for producing anti-Sinn Féin propaganda. Later an MP, he wrote a book on his war experiences and practised as a barrister. He died in 1960.

*

The First World War was fought on many fronts across the globe. Air Mechanic 2nd Class Sidney George Butler, of 30 Squadron, died of illness on 10 August, aged 22, and lies in North Gate War Cemetery, Baghdad. Born in Leeds, he was living with his family in Cadoxton in Barry, where his father was a teacher, when the war broke out.

Lieutenant Eynon George Arthur Bowen was from Newcastle Emlyn. Born in 1893, he was educated at Stoke Bishop in Bristol and then at Sherborne School. He entered Woolwich in January 1912 and was gazetted in December 1913 to the Royal Garrison Artillery. Sent to France in June 1915, he joined the Royal Flying Corps in August and flew as an observer. He passed his pilot's training in May 1916 and returned to France with 22 Squadron.

Bowen was reported missing on 8 September 1916, aged 23. His F.E.2b had taken off at 4.15 p.m. on a photographic patrol.

It was last seen falling in flames at 5.29 p.m. north of Le Sars. The victory was claimed by *Hauptmann* Oswald Boelcke of *Jasta* 2. Bowen and his observer, Lieutenant Robert Macallan Stalker from Wick in Scotland, are commemorated on the Arras Flying Services Memorial. Their commanding officer wrote: 'He was a very valuable officer, both on account of his extensive knowledge of flying and also the manner in which he always performed his duties. He was an officer in whom I had complete confidence, and I feel his going very much.'[8]

Oswald Boelcke was born in Saxony on 19 May 1891 and was the son of a schoolteacher. After leaving school he joined the Prussian Cadet Corps, and became a pilot in 1914. By February 1915 he had been awarded both classes of the Iron Cross, the Knight's Cross with Swords in November 1915, and the *Pour le Mérite* (Germany's highest military honour of the Great War, sometimes referred to as the 'Blue Max') in January 1916. Between July 1915 and October 1916, he shot down 40 enemy aircraft before being killed on 28 October 1916, when his machine collided with that of another German pilot. In August

Eynon Bowen   Oswald Boelcke

1915, this deadly killer dived into a French canal to rescue a drowning French boy and was described as a gentleman in everything he did.

Captain Oliver Hugh Ormrod was killed in a flying accident on 12 September 1916. He was born in Holt, Denbigh, on 3 October 1885 and educated at Sandroyd and Eton, where he was captain of his house football team for two years. After leaving school, he studied farming and land agency, and joined the Denbighshire Hussars. He emigrated to Canada and went into business in Vancouver. When war broke out, he returned home and obtained a commission in the Royal Field Artillery. Ormrod was gazetted Lieutenant in October 1914 and Captain in February 1915. He served as Adjutant to the 87th Brigade from July 1915, but contracted enteric fever in December of that year and was invalided home in February 1916. When he recovered, he transferred to the Royal Flying Corps in May 1916, obtained his wings and was about to return to France when he was killed at Gosport. He took off in an FE8 of 41 Squadron but was too slow in the take off. The engine stalled, and the aircraft nosedived and crashed into the ground.

His commanding officer wrote: 'He was a very able and  plucky pilot, and to be relied on in everything.'[9] His commanding officer in the Royal Flying Artillery wrote: 'He was a smart officer and a good fellow all round.'[10]

His younger brother, Lawrence Moreland Ormrod, was to die of his wounds on 25 August 1917 while serving with the Royal Welsh

Oliver Ormrod

47

Fusiliers and after having won the Military Cross. Another brother, Lionel James, had died at Boreatton Park, Baschurch in Shropshire on 3 May 1915 while serving with the 12th Lancers. All three brothers are buried in St Dunawd Church cemetery, Bangor Monachorum.

On 15 September, Captain Alfred Spencer Mason Summers was killed, aged 30. He had been mentioned in dispatches and was serving with 60 Squadron. His parents lived in Emral Hall, Worthenbury, Flintshire, which his father, a Liberal MP, had purchased in 1903. He was educated at Eton and served with the Montgomeryshire Yeomanry and the 19th Hussars before volunteering for the Royal Flying Corps. He married in 1914 and obtained his Royal Aero Club Certificate in November 1915 at Beatty School, Hendon, in a Beatty-Wright biplane.

Summers was flying a Nieuport 16 and had destroyed a kite balloon near Bapaume before becoming the 11th victim of *Leutnant* Wilhelm Frankl of *Jasta* 4. He was shot down over Ligny Beaulencourt on the Somme and died of his wounds as a prisoner of war. He was buried in Beaulencourt British Cemetery, Ligny-Thilloy.

Frankl was to record 20 kills and be awarded the *Pour le Mérite* before, while in a dogfight with Bristol F.2B fighters of 48 Squadron near Vitry-Sailly in France on 8 April 1917, the lower wing of his Albatros D.III collapsed and the aircraft fell 2,600 feet to the ground. Frankl was buried in Charlottenburg, Berlin.

Two days after Summers' death, on 17 September, Captain Tom Rees of 11 Squadron was killed, aged 21. Buried in Villers-Plouich Communal Cemetery, he was an observer in the first Royal Flying Corps aircraft to be shot down by Baron Manfred von Richthofen.

Rees was born to a Welsh-speaking family at a farm near Sennybridge, some ten miles west of Brecon. He was educated at Brecon Boys County School and later at University College of Wales, Aberystwyth. Here he joined the Officers' Training

Alfred Summers   Wilhelm Frankl

Corps, and upon graduating joined the Army and was commissioned into the Royal Welsh Fusiliers in January 1915, joining the 14th Battalion. He volunteered for the Royal Flying Corps in November 1915.

On 17 September, Rees was the observer in an F.E.2b of 11 Squadron, one of six aircraft charged with protecting eight B.E.2c bombers on a mission to bomb Marcoing railway station. The aircraft was being flown by Lieutenant Lionel Bertram Frank Morris from Richmond, Surrey. On their return flight they were attacked by aircraft from *Jasta* 2, under the command of Oswald Boelcke.

The engine and propeller of an F.E.2b were mounted behind the pilot and observer, which meant that the observer at the front of the aircraft could fire forwards and backwards. The observer was not strapped in.

Morris and Rees' aircraft was set upon by Manfred von Richthofen, newly assigned to the German squadron, in his Albatros D.II. Morris took evasive action but eventually von

Richthofen fired from underneath, and the propeller stopped turning. The aircraft then flew unsteadily, indicating that both men had been hit. Morris managed to land at a nearby German airfield at Flesquières but by now Rees was dead. Morris died later the same day. In a tragic coincidence, Tom Rees' brother, John, was struck by lightning on the same day and killed.

A local newspaper conveyed the uncertainty of the original information received by Rees' parents:

> On 20th of last month, news reached Mr and Mrs Rees, Cefn Brynich, Sennybridge, from the War Office that their youngest son, Lieut. T. Rees of the Royal Flying Corps, had been reported missing since 17 September. Subsequently, the following letter has been received by them concerning him. Since then nothing is known of his whereabouts. Hope is entertained that he is alive and that in due time he will be, as a prisoner of war, allowed to write home himself. Lieut. T. Rees is an old UCW and Brecon County School boy.
>
> The following letter has been received by Mr Rees: 'My dear sir, I much regret to have to inform you that your son is, in all probability, a prisoner. He and his pilot, Lieut. L.B.F. Morris, were on escort duty in company with other of my machines yesterday and failed to return. A machine, which may have been theirs, was seen to go down under control after a fight, so it is believed that the engine was shot through, compelling them to land. It may be some few weeks before you hear from him, but the Germans always treat RFC officers very well. He was the best observer and is a great loss to the squadron. I had never had a braver or keener officer. I sincerely hope

Tom Rees

50

you may soon hear from him. Yours very truly, T.O.B. Hubbard, Major No. 11 Squadron, RFC, BEF, 10/9/16.'[11]

In his combat report, von Richthofen wrote:

When patrol flying, I detected shrapnel clouds in the direction of Cambrai. I hurried forth and met a squad which I attacked shortly after 1100. I singled out the last machine and fired several times at closest range (ten metres). Suddenly the enemy propeller stood stock still. The machine went down, gliding, and I followed until I had killed the observer, who had not stopped shooting until the last moment. Now my opponent went downwards in sharp curves. At approximately 1,200 metres, a second German machine came along and attacked my victim right down to the ground and then landed next to the English plane.[12]

Manfred Freiherr von Richthofen was born in Breslau in May 1892. He served on the Eastern Front as an infantry officer, and then on the Western Front, where he was awarded the Iron Cross Second Class. He joined the Imperial German Air Service in May 1915 as an observer. He completed his pilot's training at Döberitz the following year and, from 17 September 1916 until his death on 21 April 1918, he accounted for 80 Allied aircraft, making him the highest-scoring fighter pilot of the Great War. He was awarded both classes of the Iron Cross, the Knight's Cross with Swords, and the *Pour le Mérite*.

Manfred von Richthofen

Hugh Tower

On the early evening of 19 September, Captain Hugh Christopher Tower of 60 Squadron was killed, aged 30. Educated at Sir Anthony Browne's School, Brentwood, and abroad, he passed the Surveyors' Institute examination and his first post was as sub-agent on the estates of Lady Heytesbury in Wiltshire. He then worked as a land agent in Wales. On the outbreak of war, he volunteered for the Special Reserve of the Royal Flying Corps and joined at Farnborough in August 1914. Awarded his Aero Certificate in April 1915, he arrived in France in April 1915 and returned to England in November 1915 on his promotion to Flight Commander. He returned to France in May 1916, 'where his skill and fearless bravery were well-known'.[13]

On 19 September, Tower was flying a Morane-Saulnier, part of a fighter escort for F.E.2bs of 11 Squadron. The aircraft was shot to pieces in the air by *Hauptmann* Oswald Boelcke, and fell in flames into Grévillers Wood. His grave was lost and he is commemorated on the Arras Flying Services Memorial.

His parents lived at Weald Hall, Essex, and his brother, Lieutenant Christopher Cecil Tower, had been killed on 2 October 1915 while serving with the Essex Yeomanry as aide-de-camp to Major-General F.D.V. Wing, 12th Division.

Lieutenant John Stephen Windsor of Barry Dock was awarded the Military Cross for conspicuous bravery whilst night flying in Mesopotamia, and was also recommended for promotion as Captain and Flight Commander.

Windsor had served his apprenticeship as an engineer

A Morane-Saulnier

with the Barry Railway Company before war broke out. He entered for the Sandhurst Royal Military College examination and gained admission. Upon passing out, he was gazetted to the South Wales Borderers in November 1915 and was later attached to the Royal Flying Corps, leaving for Mesopotamia in June 1916.

The action for which Windsor won the MC occurred on 23 September 1916, when he started out before dawn and flew for 60 miles to an enemy aerodrome to destroy it. Despite heavy anti-aircraft fire, he bombed the target and returned safely to base. It was then discovered that he had 70 bullet holes in the wings of his machine, his service petrol tank was shot through, and one bullet had passed just over his knees.

He went through all the fighting at Kût and Baghdad, being one of the first aviators to drop bombs on Baghdad and one of the first to fly into the ancient city on 10 March 1917, when the Turks evacuated it. Windsor also flew 150 miles from Baghdad to the location of the Russian forces, but as the ground was very rough for landing, the undercarriage of his machine was damaged and he was compelled to wait with the Russians for three weeks until a spare set of gears arrived.

On another occasion, he was detailed with another officer to fly to a railway bridge 60 miles behind the enemy's lines beyond Baghdad. When he landed to make an examination of the bridge with a view to blowing it up, 50 mounted Arabs were seen galloping towards him. He just had time to return to his machine and fired 100 rounds from his machine gun at them.

In May 1917 he was wounded in the wrist whilst flying in France and was hospitalised in Devonport. He had only been in France for three days, but had served in Mesopotamia for 15 months, and had been an instructor for six months. His brother, Lieutenant D. Reginald Windsor, was attached to the South Wales Borderers and would be captured by the Germans at Cambrai in December 1917; he was released from a prisoner of war camp at Heidelberg in Germany in December 1918.

Allan Chapman was born in Aberavon in March 1897, and matriculated at Edinburgh University. Commissioned into the 2nd Battalion of the East Surrey Regiment, he learned to fly and gained his pilot's certificate on 28 September 1916, then transferred to the Royal Flying Corps as a pilot. He was seriously injured in an aeroplane crash when on a test flight with Albert Ball, who was later to become a famous First World War fighter ace before being killed in May 1917.

John Windsor   Allan Chapman

After he had recovered from his injuries, Allan Chapman became a flying instructor to the Night Flying Squadron and served in the night aerial defence of London. While studying at Queen's College Cambridge, he was a prominent member of the Union Debating Society and this grounding came in useful when he was elected as Member of Parliament for the Rutherglen Division of Lanarkshire in 1935. Two years later, he became Parliamentary Private Secretary to Colonel Walter Elliot, Secretary of State for Scotland. Chapman was then appointed as Assistant Postmaster-General before becoming Under-Secretary for Scotland during the Second World War.

Second Lieutenant William Henry Irvine, from Southerndown, was killed in a flying accident on Salisbury Plain on 25 October 1916, aged 19, and was buried in St Bridget's Church cemetery in St Brides Major. An only son, he was educated at the Old Hall, Wellington, Shropshire and at Malvern. He matriculated at London University, after which he was employed at a munitions factory. Joining the Royal Fusiliers in May 1916, he was commissioned into the Royal Flying Corps in July and received his wings on 28 September.

Second Lieutenant Willie Jordan, an observer with 45 Squadron, was killed while flying on 8 November and was buried at St Omer Souvenir Cemetery, Longuenesse. He was born in Newport, Monmouthshire, though the family later moved to Newcastle-upon-Tyne, where his father was an iron founder and he was employed in the General Post Office. Jordan was in a Sopwith 1½ Strutter, piloted by Second Lieutenant H.G.P. Lowe which was on a practice observation flight. The aircraft was later found wrecked near Adsoit, with both men dead. They share the same grave.

Second Lieutenant Cyril Edward Morgan, aged 29, was killed in an accident on 4 December and was buried in Cairo War Memorial Cemetery. His parents lived in Tredegar, Monmouthshire. He had arrived in Alexandria in December 1914 and served as a serjeant in the Royal Flying Corps before being commissioned in July 1916. At the time of his death he was serving with 'X' Aircraft Park in Cairo as an equipment officer, and died in an accident at the park.

Lieutenant Edmund Llewelyn Lewis was shot down on 26 December 1916, while flying with 24 Squadron. He was born to Welsh parents in Birmingham on 5 October 1915 and, after leaving Marlborough College, he attended King's College, London. He was older brother of the Welsh ace Gwilym Lewis (see page 280) and was killed on their father's birthday. His body was never found and his name is recorded on the Arras Flying Services Memorial.

His obituary read:

Lieutenant Edmund Llewelyn Lewis, Essex Regiment and RFC, who was killed by the fall of his machine over the German lines on December 26th after a single-handed fight with five enemy machines, in which he brought down one of them, was the eldest son of Mr Hugh Lewis of St David's, Templewood Avenue, Hampstead, London manager of the Liverpool and London and Globe Insurance Company Limited, and was 21 years of age. Educated at Marlborough and in Germany and France,

Edmund Lewis

Dieter Collin

he had returned home to take up a career at Lloyds, when, on the declaration of war, he was appointed to a commission in the Essex Regiment. In July 1915, he left for the Dardanelles, but was invalided home in the following November. During his convalescence he learned to fly, and was seconded to the Royal Flying Corps in March 1916. Within three months he was at the Front and, after being engaged in many combats, was wounded while fighting single-handed six enemy machines. On this occasion, with controls shot away, he managed to land safely on our side of the lines. After two months' sick leave he was again at the Front. He was gazetted Lieutenant on the day after his death.[14]

He was shot down over Beaulencourt on the Somme by *Leutnant der Reserve* Dieter Collin of *Jasta* 2, his second victory. Collin was shot down on 13 August 1918 and died in hospital later the same day. Born in Lüben on 17 February 1893, he had been wounded in September 1917 and achieved 13 victories in total.

CHAPTER THREE

1917

'The purpose of the propeller is to keep the pilot cool.
If you think not, stop the propeller and watch him sweat.'

Anon.

IN EARLY 1917, having learned the lessons of the Somme, the German Army withdrew to the prepared positions of the Hindenburg Line in order to shorten its front and to make maximum use of the high ground it had captured earlier in the war. The British launched the Battle of Arras, which lasted from 9 April to 16 June, and achieved success at Messines in June and July before the enormously costly battle of Third Ypres, often referred to as Passchendaele, from 31 July to 10 November. The fighting that year ended with the partially successful deployment of tanks at Cambrai in November and December. For the Royal Flying Corps, April 1917 was to be its most tragic month.

Air Mechanic 2nd Class Tom Dicken, of 30 Squadron, died of natural causes on 4 January 1917 and was buried in St Cynbryd Church cemetery, Llanddulas, aged 30. Air mechanics were sometimes trained as observers, but it seems Tom Dicken fell ill while serving with his unit and died in a military hospital in Grantham.

On 13 January this report appeared in a Welsh newspaper:

Air Mechanic Thomas Morris, Royal Flying Corps, of Quarry
House, arrived home on Saturday night for ten days' leave, this

being his first leave since he enlisted. He joined the Royal Flying Corps 14 months ago, being the first local recruit to join this corps. He was in England for the first week after enlistment, after which he was transferred to Ireland, and thence to France, where he has been for 13 months. He is now serving with the Advance Echelon of the Flying Corps, and during his time in France has had many thrilling experiences. He returns on Monday next.[1]

In June 1917, Morris was promoted to Air Mechanic 1st Class and served as a wireless mechanic. Prior to enlisting, he was employed in the lamp room at the Penrhiwceiber Colliery.

Captain David Roy Jenkins died on 21 January, aged 28, and was buried in St Mary Church cemetery in Nolton, Bridgend. His parents lived nearby in Brackla. A local newspaper reported his death:

Sad End to Promising Career
We deeply regret to announce the death, as the result of a flying accident on Salisbury Plain, of Captain D. Roy Jenkins, RFC, son of Mr Jacob Jenkins, Bridgend, head of the firm of Messrs Charles Jenkins and Son, timber merchants. The intimation reached

Thomas Morris   David Jenkins

Bridgend on Sunday last through a wire from a brother officer,
Lieutenant Eric Hughes (son of Sir Thomas Hughes, Cardiff).

The accident occurred on Sunday morning. Lieutenant Jenkins
seems to have gone up about midday, alone. He was up about a
couple of hours, when it [is] surmised that something went wrong
with the mechanism of the machine, and he fell. He was found
some three miles from the camp. It is a strange and melancholy
coincidence that the last flying accident on Salisbury Plain resulted
in the death of another Bridgend officer, Lieutenant W. Irvine. [See
Chapter 2]

Captain Jenkins, who was the younger son of Mr Jacob
Jenkins, was for several years a lieutenant in the RFA (Territorial
Force), under Colonel Gilling. About eighteen months ago he was
promoted to the rank of captain. After training in England, he
went with his brigade to France. He was only two months in that
country, being then drafted out to Egypt, where he remained for
nine months. At the end of that time he volunteered for the Flying
Service in France, and came home for the necessary instruction.
He had only been at the camp on Salisbury Plain since a fortnight
last Monday.

Captain Jenkins was 27 years of age [*sic*], and before the war
managed for his father the Tunnel Works at Fforest Fach, near
Swansea. A brilliant hockey player, he was captain of the Bridgend
Hockey Club. He was educated at Christ College, Brecon, and
Clifton School.[2]

The Bridgend platoon of the Glamorgan Volunteers
provided a firing party at the head of the funeral procession
from his home to the church in Nolton. Mrs Jenkins, who was
an invalid, suffered heart problems after receiving news of her
son's death and died in April 1917.

Air Mechanic 2nd Class William Elwyn Evans died in
Aylesbury Military Hospital on 9 February, aged 21, while
attached to the Recruits Training Centre at Halton in Cheshire.
He was buried in Manor Park Cemetery in Essex, but his family
lived in Barry.

Second Lieutenant Elwyn Roberts, of 10 Squadron, died on
10 February, aged 22. Before the war he had been a surveyor

with the Commercial Union Assurance Company and lived in Llanllyfni in Caernarvonshire, where his father was a church minister.

He was the observer in a B.E.2g piloted by Lieutenant W.A. Porkess, which took off at 2.12 p.m. on an artillery observation sortie. The aircraft was hit by anti-aircraft fire at 3.45 p.m. and crashed in flames. Both men were killed. Roberts has no known grave and is commemorated on the Arras Flying Services Memorial.

Lieutenant George Trevor Brown was killed on 12 February and was buried in Oystermouth, Swansea. He met his death in a flying accident, after seeing service in France with the 6th Welsh Regiment. A newspaper account stated:

> Mr J.S. Brown, a well-known Swansea ironmonger and motor engineer, has received information that his youngest son, Second Lieutenant George Trevor Brown, was killed on Monday while flying on Salisbury Plain. It is understood he met his death while engaged in testing a machine. He only left home for duty last Saturday. He joined the Glamorgan Yeomanry at the outbreak of the war, and later obtained a commission in the Welsh Regiment. He afterwards joined the Royal Flying Corps. He was 23 years [sic] of age.[3]

On the same day, Second Lieutenant Gordon Ivor Wilson, from Presteigne in Radnorshire, was killed in a flying accident, aged 20. He was buried at Upavon Cemetery, Wiltshire. He had been commissioned in March 1915.

A newspaper reported how the two men's fates were linked:

> Two airmen have been killed as the result of a collision while flying in Wiltshire. They were Sec-Lieut. Gordon Ivor Wilson, aged 20, whose home is at Bridgwater, Somerset, and Sec-Lieut. George Trevor Brown, aged 25, Wiltshire Regiment, Blackwood, Glamorganshire. Both were attached to the Royal Flying Corps.
> At the inquest it was stated that each airman was flying

unaccompanied. One aeroplane fell to the earth, and directly afterwards the other came down, and, while nobody saw them come into contact, it was assumed that there had been a collision. The jury returned a verdict that the officers met with accidental deaths, due to collision.[4]

On 2 March, Second Lieutenant Cyril Stephen Cravos of Cardiff was killed, aged 20. Cravos was educated at Ampleforth College in York and the college's journal for 1917 stated:

He joined the Honourable Artillery Company in February 1915. In the following August he obtained a commission in the 21st Battalion, Welsh Regiment, and last summer joined the Royal Flying Corps. He got his wings in December, and went to the front in January. In a letter written to Mr Cravos, his commanding officer wrote: 'I regret his loss immensely as he was very keen and could always be relied upon to carry out his duties with courage and cheerfulness. He was a very clever pilot.'

That is precisely what we at Ampleforth would have expected of him. He was courageous to recklessness and buoyantly cheerful. Qualities he displayed not only in the Rugger XV but also in the boxing ring.

Cravos entered the School in May 1908, and left in April 1913. By nature he was a singularly generous and kindly boy. He was ever ready to play his part in every department of the school life, shirking nothing and always giving his best. Of such a character it goes without saying that he developed into a fine specimen of young manhood, notable for his upright and faithful adherence to all duties, among which he counted not least his religion. May he rest in peace.[5]

Having joined the Honourable Artillery Company in February 1915 and the Welsh Regiment the following August, Cravos joined the Royal Flying Corps in the summer of 1916 and, having been commissioned Flying Officer in November 1916, served as a pilot with 5 Squadron in France from 24 January 1917. Carrying out mainly artillery observation patrols with 5 Squadron, he took off with his observer, Flight Serjeant

A.G. Shepherd, in a B.E.2c. They left the aerodrome at 2.30 p.m. and called the aerodrome by wireless at 2.40 p.m. They were never heard from again. They were reported missing over the Gommecourt area, and were later recorded as killed in action. Both men were buried by the Germans in Moyenneville German Cemetery, south of Arras, before being relocated to Douchy-lès-Ayette British Cemetery, France.

Two days later, on 4 March, Second Lieutenant Brinley Arthur Morgan was killed, aged 24. From Sketty in Swansea, he was educated at Arnold School in the town. After he left school he was employed by his father, assisting him with shipping management. He joined the Glamorgan Yeomanry on 12 September 1914, transferred to the Royal Field Artillery and was commissioned on 5 May 1916.

He joined the Royal Flying Corps on 16 January 1917. Lieutenant Colonel Hall Pringle, DSO, of the Royal Field Artillery wrote to the parents: 'I was sorry to lose your boy from my brigade, but he will do very well in the Royal Flying Corps I am sure, and there is a great future in front of that corps. I hope he may have the best of luck; I know he will be a credit to his profession.'[6]

Morgan was an observer with 53 Squadron when he was killed in aerial action. Hall Pringle wrote again to say: 'Your

son's death will be a great loss to the country; he showed great promise, and with his abilities and keenness he would have done very well.'[7] Another officer wrote: 'He was a very excellent fellow, keen, and a good pal, and I was very much cut up to hear of his death.'[8]

Brinley Morgan

Another wrote: 'I was told by an officer who saw your son's machine come down how it all happened; his death was the cause of much sorrow throughout the whole division. Officers and men loved him; he was a fellow one could do nothing else but like and respect.'[9]

Brinley Morgan was buried at Bailleul Communal Cemetery Extension, with the original cross marking his grave being made from the propeller of his aircraft.

Second Lieutenant Arthur Leslie Constable, from Arthog in Merionethshire, was killed in aerial combat on 17 March, aged 25, while serving with 43 Squadron, and was buried in Cabaret-Rouge British Cemetery, Souchez. He obtained his commission in July 1916 and his wings the following August, before arriving in France in February 1917. Educated at Liverpool Institute, at the time of his enlistment he was employed by the British-American Tobacco Company Limited of London and the provinces as a pupil-manager.

Constable was the pilot of a Sopwith 1½ Strutter which took off at 9.10 a.m. on an offensive patrol to Beaumont. The aircraft was attacked by *Leutnant* Kurt Wolff of *Jasta* 11 and shot down. The observer, Second Lieutenant C.D. Knox, was also killed. They were the third of Wolff's victories.

Kurt Wolff was born in February 1895 in Greifswald, Pomerania. He had served as an infantry officer in the early part of the war and then joined the German Air Service as an observer in July 1915. He received his pilot's certificate that December and joined *Jasta* 11. When von Richthofen took command, he began his sequence of victories. Awarded the Knight's Cross and the *Pour le Mérite*, he was eventually shot down and killed on 15 September 1917 after scoring 33 victories in just four months.

Corporal Arthur William Evans, from St Fagans near Cardiff, was killed while flying on the same day. Aged 20, he was serving with 21 Squadron and was buried in St Omer Souvenir Cemetery, Longuenesse. He was the observer in an R.E.8 being flown by Lieutenant F.O. Baxter, which failed to

Arthur Constable   Kurt Wolff

pull out of a practice spin and crashed. Baxter was also killed.

Also killed on 17 March was Second Lieutenant Aaron Appleton, aged 20, from Glan Conway in Denbighshire, who was serving with 6 Squadron. He had previously served in the Royal Field Artillery before training as a pilot. Flying a B.E.2e, he and his observer, Corporal Joseph Cooper were shot down in flames at 12.05 p.m. over Polygon Wood by *Oberleutnant* Griessenhagen of *Jasta* 18. Appleton is remembered on the Arras Flying Services Memorial, and Cooper is listed on the Arras Memorial.

Second Lieutenant Guy Everingham was killed on 8 April, aged 22. Serving with 16 Squadron, he was buried alongside his pilot, Second Lieutenant Keith Ingleby MacKenzie, in Bois-Carré British Cemetery, Thelus. Everingham was born in Barry, privately educated, and was living in Colwyn Bay when war broke out. Enlisting in the 13th Royal Welsh Fusiliers, he was commissioned in February 1915 and arrived in France in March 1916, serving as signalling officer. He later served as a bombing officer with 113th Trench Mortar Battery before applying to join the Royal Flying Corps, training as an observer. Everingham married in February 1917 and set up home with his wife in Llandudno, but was ordered to return to the front after just two days of marriage.

His B.E.2g was photographing the village of Farbus, northeast of Arras, just a day before the Battle of Arras began. It was shot down at 4.40 p.m. over what was to become the battlefield, so the crew were not buried for a week until the ground had been taken by British troops. Their attacker was Baron Manfred von Richthofen – the two airmen were his 39th victory and his second of the day. The pilot, Keith MacKenzie, was von Richthofen's youngest victim, at 18.

Von Richthofen wrote in his combat report: 'I was flying and surprised an English artillery flyer. After a very few shots, the plane broke to pieces and fell near Vimy ... Remnants distributed over more than one kilometre.'[10]

Everingham's brother Robin had died on active service on 10 December 1915, serving with the Welsh Horse Yeomanry at Gallipoli.

Aaron Appleton   Guy Everingham

Lieutenant Alfred John Hamar, from Knighton in Radnorshire, fell on the same day, while serving with 55 Squadron. He was buried in St Pierre Cemetery, Amiens. His death was reported thus:

> Lieutenant Alfred John Hamar, of the Royal Flying Corps, son of Mr and Mrs William Hamar, Hill Crest, Knighton, has died of injuries, the result of a flight in France. The sad intimation reached the parents when they were both indisposed. Lieutenant Hamar had been in the RFC for eighteen months.[11]

A local newspaper added the following information:

> Knighton Airman's Sacrifice
> As announced in our last issue, Lieut. A.J. Hamar, Royal Flying Corps (55 Squadron), son of Mr and Mrs W. Hamar, Hill Crest, Knighton, gave his life for King and country on the 8th inst. We are now in a position to give the following telegram and letters, referring to the gallant young officer's heroism and death:
> 'To W. Hamar, Hill Crest, Knighton. – Deeply regret to inform you that Lieut. A.J. Hamar, Royal Flying Corps, 55 Squadron, was admitted to New Zealand Stationary Hospital, Amiens, 8 April, dangerously ill, and died result of compound fracture arm and leg, 8 April. The Army Council express their sympathy – Secretary, War Office.'
> '55 Squadron, RFC, BEF, France, 9 April 1917. – Dear Mr Hamar, – It is with the deepest feelings of sorrow that I write to you to express my sympathy on the death of your son. I have been his observer since we landed in France, during which time I have been in the closest touch with him, and I can say most sincerely the Army has not lost a braver soldier, or a man of a more staunch friend. He was buried on Monday the 9th at Amiens, where I attended his funeral. I have personally seen to his kit, and it will be forwarded to Messrs Cox and Son, 16 Charing Cross. Again assuring you of my sympathy. – Believe me, yours sincerely, J.L. Trulock (Lieut.).'
> 'New Zealand Stationary Hospital, BEF France, 10/4/17. – Dear Mr Hamar, – I expect that long before this note reaches you, you will have received the sad news of the death of your son, Lieut.

WALES AND THE FIRST AIR WAR 1914-1918

A.J. Hamar, RFC 55 Squadron, 9th Wing. On Sunday afternoon, 8/4/17, your son and his mate, Lieut. Myburgh, were both admitted to this hospital. It seems that three of our machines had gone out on Sunday to do some bombing. They were successful and were returning when they were attacked by a German formation of picked men and machines who act as patrols along their front lines. In the encounter, both your son and his companion were wounded, but managed to bring their machine to earth somewhere near here. They were not able, however, to make a good landing, and the two brave men sustained further injuries from their fall. Your son was not conscious all the time he was here. Nature was kind enough to deaden consciousness, so I had not an opportunity to talk to him. He died at 9.30 p.m. the same day. I buried him yesterday in the new Military Cemetery, Amiens. (The location of the grave is – Officers' Section, 2nd row left, grave 8.) Major Baldwin and three other officers of the squadron were present. The Graves' Registration Unit will erect a simple cross of identification, and Major Baldwin said he would see that one was erected from the squadron. Your grief must be great, but may you be richly comforted. Your son was brave, and he gave a man's life in a man's service. – I am, yours sincerely, R.S. Watson (Presbyterian chaplain).'

'10 April, 1917. – Dear Mr Hamar, – I do not know how to express my sympathy with you in this great loss. Your son put up a magnificent show. He was very badly wounded, indeed, and must have remained conscious to pilot his machine by pure will power. He brought his machine, one of three, through a hostile formation of 30 machines. He was the only one to get back, and he brought it nearly 25 miles back over our lines in his attempt to get back to his own aerodrome. He apparently lost consciousness just before he reached the ground and received the additional wounds in the smash landing. He landed at about 3.30 to 4 o'clock, and never recovered consciousness up to the time he died, at about 10.30 that night. Unfortunately, his passenger has since died from the wounds he received, although your son managed to get him back to ground without any further mishap to him. I am endeavouring to obtain fuller details from the doctors who spoke to your son's observer, as it was one of the finest acts of endurance that I have heard of during the whole war. He had important information which his observer managed to give, and, if it had not been for your son, we should never have obtained it, as neither of the other machines managed to get back. I will forward you the fuller details as soon as I can obtain the same. He was buried the day after his death, i.e., the 9th inst., at 4 p.m. The service was held by the Presbyterian minister from the 1st New Zealand Hospital. The minister will write and inform you when he was buried and where the grave is, as I am not allowed to say. I can only close by saying that he has set a wonderful example to us all, and we hope that sufficient evidence will be obtained to place his act on record among the other outstanding acts of bravery in this war, none of which, to our minds, surpass it. I have lost a really good and useful officer, and we all, officers and men, have lost a friend, and offer you and your wife our deepest sympathy. – Yours sincerely, (Major) Jack E.A. Baldwin.'

Last Tuesday would have been Lieutenant Hamar's 27th birthday. A service to his memory was held at Knighton Wesley Church on the previous Sunday, the Rev. A.D. Baskerville officiating. Mr and Mrs William Hamar (Hill Crest, Knighton) wish to thank all the kind friends for their letters of sympathy in their recent great sorrow.[12]

Alfred Hamar was born in Knighton in 1890. He and his three brothers were all keen motorcycle enthusiasts, known locally as the 'Mad Hamars'. One female passenger of Alfred

was left sitting in the air after he made a sudden take off. Before the war he ran three cinemas in Knighton, Presteigne and Rhayader. After the outbreak of war, he qualified as a pilot, serving on the Western Front. After one leave of absence, he returned to the front with his mother's fur coat, so cold were the open cockpits of the

Alfred Hamar

biplanes. His younger brother, Clarence Richard Hamar, also served in the Royal Flying Corps and was killed in 1918 (see page 181).

The third Welsh Royal Flying Corps casualty of 8 April was Second Lieutenant Thomas John Owen of 29 Squadron, from Pwlhelli in Caernarvonshire. Aged 25 when he was killed, he was buried in Boyelles Communal Cemetery Extension. He was flying a Nieuport 23 single-seater fighter, which took off at 6.35 p.m. on an offensive patrol. At 7.10 p.m. he was shot down over Croisilles by *Leutnant* Georg Schlenker of *Jasta* 3. This was the seventh of Schlenker's 14 eventual victories before he was so badly wounded that he could not return to duty before the war ended.

Second Lieutenant Hugh Howells died in a flying accident at Spittlegate in Lincolnshire on 10 April, aged 26. Born at Bedlinog in Glamorgan, where his parents ran the Railway Hotel, he was married with a young child and had lived on Barry Island. Before the war he was an electrician with the Rhymney Iron Company. A flying magazine carried an account of his death:

> 2nd Lieut. Hugh Howells, RFC, was flying an aeroplane at rather low altitude in an Eastern County on 10 April, when the machine fell, struck a corner of a building, and burst into flames. The officer was so badly burned that he died in a neighbouring military hospital during the night.[13]

Hugh Howells was buried at Soar-y-Graig Cemetery in Llechryd. In 2005 the chapel and cemetery were sold for development and the ground was no longer maintained. The area now lies abandoned to Japanese knotweed and bluebells. The names of the war dead were then recorded on Cardiff Western Cemetery Screen Wall.

On 13 April, James Allen Cunniffe, of Port Tennant, survived an attack by the Red Baron. A pilot with 11 Squadron, he took off at 11.25 a.m. in an F.E.2b on an observation patrol with his

Thomas Owen   Hugh Howells

observer, Air Mechanic 2nd Class W.J. Batten. Their aircraft
was shot down between Monchy and Feuchy at 12.45 p.m.
They were von Richthofen's 42nd victory.

The aircraft crashed to the ground, but both men were
saved when an observer in a balloon, who saw the plane
come down, rescued them from the wreckage. Cunniffe
was seriously wounded and spent two years in hospital in
Spalding, Lincolnshire, before returning to his post at the
Public Analyst Laboratory in Swansea. He had learnt to
fly at his own expense after serving as an observer with 23
Squadron for six months. He was awarded the Bronze Medal
for Military Valour by the King of Italy on 26 May 1917 for an
action which had taken place on 3 April 1917, ten days before
his encounter with von Richthofen. On that occasion, during
another dogfight, his observer was wounded and Cunniffe had
part of his nose blown away when a machine gun exploded
in his face.

Allen Cunniffe

Von Richthofen wrote in his combat report: 'Together with *Leutnant* Simon, I attacked a Vickers two-seater, coming back from German territory. After a rather a long fight, during which I manoeuvered in such a way that my adversary could not fire one shot, the enemy plane plunged down to the ground between Monchy and Feuchy.'[14]

During the Second World War Cunniffe worked for the Swansea Gas Light and Coke Company and was awarded the British Empire Medal for his work in maintaining the gas supply to Swansea during the German air raids. He died in Pembrokeshire in January 1959, aged 64.

On the same day, another Swansea pilot, Second Lieutenant Allan Harold Bates, aged 20, of 25 Squadron, was shot down and killed. He was buried in Noyelles-Godault Communal Cemetery. His parents were shopkeepers, selling hardware and electrical goods. After leaving school, he studied engineering at Swansea Technical College and worked in an aeroplane factory before enlisting in the Royal Flying Corps. He had only arrived at the front a week before.

Bates and his observer were the 43rd victory of Manfred von Richthofen. The German's combat report stated: 'With three planes of my Staffel, I attacked an enemy bombing squadron consisting of Vickers (old type) above Hénin Liétard. After a short fight, my adversary began to glide down and finally plunged into a house near Noyelles-Godault. The occupants were both killed and the machine destroyed.'[15]

Lieutenant Charles Herbert Morris was also killed on 13 April. He was 25 and from Welshpool in Montgomeryshire. His grave was lost and he is remembered on the Arras Flying Services Memorial. His brother, Joseph, was also a lieutenant in the Royal Flying Corps.

Charles Morris was the observer in an R.E.8 of 59 Squadron piloted by Captain G.B. Hodgson. They were attacked by aircraft from *Jasta* 11, which shot down five of the six British aircraft at 8.55 a.m. north-east of Blache, and were the 4th victory of Lothar von Richthofen. The R.E.8s were reconnoitering the railway line which ran from Quiéry-la-Motte to Étaing, and *Jasta* 11 was based nearby at Douai. Their fighter escorts were delayed, so they were very much exposed when the German aircraft attacked.

Lothar Freiherr von Richthofen was the younger brother of the Red Baron. Born in Kleinburg near Breslau in September 1894, he was serving with the German Dragoons at the commencement of the war and followed his older brother into aviation late in 1915, joining him in *Jasta* 11 on 6 March 1917.

He was awarded the Knight's Cross and the *Pour le Mérite* and both classes of the Iron Cross. Wounded several times, he heard of his brother's death while he was in hospital. He returned to active service and was wounded yet again. Surviving the war, with a total of 40 victories, he was killed in a flying accident on 4 July 1922.

Lothar von Richthofen

Captain Lionel Sydney Platt was born on 1 October 1885. The family lived on the 150-acre estate of Bryn-y-Neuadd, Llanfairfechan, Caernarvonshire, until 1898, when they moved to Wargrave Manor in Berkshire. Educated at Eton and Magdalen College, Oxford, he was commissioned into the 17th Lancers in 1905 and served in India. He was appointed as Adjutant in the Denbighshire Yeomanry and served in Egypt in 1916 before joining the Royal Flying Corps in September 1916. Gaining his wings in November, he joined 57 Squadron and became a flight commander on 6 March 1917. On 5 April, while piloting a F.E.2d, he and his observer, Second Lieutenant Thomas Margerison, shot down an Albatros scout over Arras. They had taken off at 7 a.m. on 13 April on an offensive patrol, but were shot down at 9.05 a.m. by *Leutnant* H. Gontermann of *Jasta* 5. An only son, Platt left a widow and young daughter. He and Margerison are buried in Copse Cemetery, Roeux.

Heinrich Gontermann was born in Westphalia in February 1896. He enlisted in the 6th Uhlan Cavalry Regiment in August 1914 and was wounded the following month. In the spring of 1915, he was promoted to *leutnant* and awarded the Iron Cross Second Class. He joined the German Air Service in 1916 and began a run of victories on his first combat patrol. Awarded the Iron Cross First Class in March 1917, the Knight's Cross with Swords followed on 6 May, and eleven days later the *Pour le*

Lionel Platt and his crashed aircraft

Mérite. By October 1917, he had 39 victories – 21 aircraft and 18 balloons.

On 30 October he took off in a new Fokker Dr.I. After a few minutes' flying, while trying a left turn, his upper wing collapsed and broke off. The stricken aircraft crashed to the ground. Gontermann survived the impact but died of head injuries a few hours later. He was 21.

On 13 April, Lieutenant Arthur Watson was reported missing. He was a pilot in an R.E.8, one of a patrol from 59 Squadron which took off just after 8.15 a.m. on a photographic mission over Étaing. The six R.E.8s were all shot down in a matter of minutes by pilots of *Jasta* 11 – Manfred von Richthofen's 'circus'. Watson and his observer, Lieutenant Law, were both wounded and captured, Watson suffering four machine-gun bullet wounds in his left shoulder. They had been shot down by *Vizefeldwebel* Sebastian Festner.

Festner recorded 12 victories before his aircraft was shot down and he was killed on 25 April 1917. His body was never recovered and he therefore has no known grave. He was 22.

Heinrich Gontermann   Sebastian Festner

Watson survived his injuries and was repatriated the following year. A local newspaper carried the story:

> The many friends of Flight Lieutenant Arthur Watson RFC of Lammas Street, Carmarthen, who has been a prisoner of war in Germany for twelve months, were glad to learn that he had arrived unexpectedly in London on Sunday evening with other released officers. He arrived in Carmarthen on Tuesday night and was extended a hearty welcome. Lieut. Watson was reported missing in France on 13 April 1917, when he descended behind the German lines in the course of an aerial attack.
>
> He enlisted as a private in the Public Schools Battalion. He was then granted a commission in the Royal Welsh Fusiliers, and later transferred to the Royal Flying Corps. Daring and intrepid, he established a fine reputation as a flight-lieutenant, and was the first St Peter's boy to secure his wings. His only brother, Leading Mechanic R.H. Watson, Royal Naval Air Service, was killed in France in May [*sic*], 1917.[16]

Arthur Watson's service pay had accumulated in his bank account during his captivity, so he put it to good use by later training to be a doctor at St Mary's in Paddington.

His brother, Richard Henry Watson, was the gunlayer in the crew of a Handley Page bomber, one of several from 7 Squadron, Royal Naval Air Service, which took off from Koudekerke for a daylight raid on Ostend on 25 April. The aircraft was shot down by a German seaplane near Nieuport and landed in the sea three miles north of Nieuport. Two French seaplanes tried to assist the stricken crew. One managed to rescue one survivor, but the other was captured by German vessels. Watson was a strong swimmer and set off to swim to the shore, but was shot dead in the water, aged 22. His body was never recovered and he is commemorated on the Chatham Naval Memorial.

On 15 April, Second Lieutenant Neville Dudley Budgen gained his pilot's certificate at the Military School, Shoreham, in a Maurice Farman biplane. He lived with his

Arthur Watson   Richard Watson

parents at Victoria Road in Penarth. He was to survive the war.

His brother, Second Lieutenant Henry Kenneth Budgen of the South Wales Borderers, also joined the Royal Flying Corps and was wounded in the forearm by anti-aircraft fire during an artillery observation patrol in an R.E.8 on 31 July 1917. Before enlisting, he was articled to a solicitor at Cardiff Docks, and joined the University and Public Schools Corps at the outbreak of the war. After transferring to the Royal Flying Corps he trained as an observer. He also survived the war.

Although the war was to be won or lost on the Western Front, campaigns were still being fought on many other fronts. Captain Francis Harry Vaughan Bevan, of 14 Squadron, was killed on 19 April, aged 22, while serving in Palestine.

Neville Budgen

Henry Kenneth Budgen

A resident of Newcastle Emlyn in Cardiganshire, he is remembered on the Jerusalem Memorial. Originally with the 8th South Wales Borderers, he was flying a Martinsyde G.100 aircraft that day and had shot down an enemy two-seater over Sihan before himself being attacked. He appears to have fallen out of the aircraft, as when it was found (and then burnt) by soldiers of the Australian and New Zealand Army Corps Mounted Division, his body could not be located. The aircraft which attacked him was also shot down. In January and February that year, Bevan had taken part in bombing raids in support of T.E. Lawrence – the famous 'Lawrence of Arabia'.

Second Lieutenant Alan Bertram Morgan, of 29 Squadron, was killed on 21 April, aged 20. He was buried in Douai Communal Cemetery. A native of Caerphilly, he took off in a Nieuport 17 on an offensive patrol at 4.30 p.m., and was initially reported as missing until his body was found the following day. His death was reported thus:

Alan Morgan

Caerphilly Gentleman's loss. Mr Morgan, relieving officer, Caerphilly, has been informed by the War Office that a report has been received from the German Government, through the Netherlands Legation, that his son, Second Lieutenant A.B. Morgan, Royal Flying Corps, was admitted dead into the Kriegs Gefangenenlager Nazarette at Douai on April 22 last. He had been reported missing on April 21. On that date, he and two others went up on an offensive patrol, and nothing further has been heard of one of them beyond the report of Second Lieutenant Morgan's death. The young officer was twenty years of age and previous to enlistment was a student at Reading University.[17]

The following day Lieutenant John Rhys Joseph died, aged 18. He was buried in Edinburgh's Comely Bank Cemetery. His parents lived in Llanelli and his death was reported thus:

With full military honours, the funeral took place at Edinburgh on Friday of 2nd. Lieut. J.R. Joseph, son of Mr and Mrs Wm. Joseph, 60 Ann Street, Llanelli. This promising young officer was an old Intermediate School boy, having served as private secretary to the late Mr Wm. Lewis for some time. He left the school to take up a position at Lloyds Bank, Yeovil, and was then selected to be private secretary to a gentleman at Bournemouth out of 550 applicants. When the war came, young Joseph volunteered for service and joined the Artists' Rifle Corps, and later on he was selected as one of six for a special course of training at Reading for the Royal Flying Corps. He passed the examination with credit and having been granted a commission, he proceeded to Edinburgh. While preparing for his first flight in an aeroplane in company with his captain, a distressing accident occurred, another aeroplane descending and crashing into it. The result was that Lieut. Joseph sustained fatal injuries, death taking place a few hours later. Thus a promising career has been cut short. The deceased was the only son of his parents with whom the deepest sympathy is expressed.[18]

On 22 April, Second Lieutenant Kevin Robert Furniss took off in a Spad 7 of 23 Squadron on a bomber escort to F.E.2b aircraft of 18 Squadron. He was last seen over Cambrai where his aircraft was shot down by *Offizierstellvertreter* Nathanael of *Jasta* 5.

Kevin Furniss was born in Llanelli on 11 March 1898, but by 1910 the family had moved to the vicinity of Wolverhampton and he was attending Wolverhampton Grammar School. When Furniss was 17 in 1915, he applied to join the Royal Engineers but failed the examinations. It was suggested that he join his local regiment, the Staffordshire Territorials, instead, which he did, and was commissioned as a second lieutenant. In early 1917, he transferred to the Royal Flying Corps and trained as a pilot at Upavon. He was then posted to France on 7 April 1917.

Despite being shot down, Furniss survived the crash and was taken prisoner by the Germans. He did not recover from his injuries, however, and died seven days later on 29 April in German hands. He was 19 and now lies in Cambrai East Military Cemetery.

Edmund Nathanael was born on 18 December 1889 in Dielsdorf in Switzerland. He shot down 15 Allied aircraft before he was killed on 11 May 1917 west of Bourlon Wood, when his Albatros D.III was destroyed in flames by the Scottish ace, Major William John Charles Kennedy Cochran-Patrick.

Air Mechanic 2nd Class Cyril J.E. Jones, a former student at the School of Mines, Treforest, died of illness on 28 April. He was serving with the Royal Naval Air Service at HMS President II, a shore base. He was buried at Blaenau Gwent Baptist Chapel cemetery, Monmouthshire.

Kevin Furniss   Edmund Nathanael

LIEUT. JOHN HAYDN DAVIES.
PTE. DAVID EVANS.
LT. E. LINDSAY PRITCHARD EVANS.
CADET CYRIL J. E. JONES.
LIEUT. WILLIAM KNOX.
CAPT. E. A. MORGANS.
CAPT. T. G. L. PHILLIPS. M.C.
2ND LIEUT. E. J. PHILLIPS.
PTE. T. R. D. RAY.
2ND LIEUT. ERIC M. REES.
PTE. LEO P. WILLIAMS.
CAPT. FRANK E. WILLIAMS.

School of Mines Memorial

Second Lieutenant George Beaumont Bate was born into a family of brewers in Bersham, near Wrexham, in 1896. The family later lived at Rhyddyn Hall. Educated at Downside College in Somerset, he had obtained a commission in the Loyal North Lancashire Regiment and spent two years in the trenches. After joining the Royal Flying Corps he trained as a gunner/observer and arrived back in France in 1917, serving with 18 Squadron.

He made his first operational flight on 28 March 1917, and on 23 April he and his pilot, Second Lieutenant Edmund Leonard Zinc, were attacked by enemy aircraft over Barelle. Bate shot down one of the attackers but their F.E.2b was then attacked by a second aircraft and were themselves shot down. Bate was unharmed but a machine-gun bullet had passed through his flying jacket.

Their attacker was Hermann Göring, and they were the fourth of his eventual 22 victories. Göring was to become infamous during the Second World War as Commander-in-Chief of the Luftwaffe. Born in Upper Bavaria in 1893, Göring was commissioned into the German infantry in March 1912. After being hospitalised with rheumatoid arthritis, he was persuaded to train as an observer and was awarded the Iron

Hermann Göring

Cross Second Class in March 1915. He then trained as a pilot and achieved his first victory in June 1915. Shot down and wounded in November 1916, he later received the *Pour le Mérite*, the Iron Cross First Class and the Knight's Cross with Swords. Captured by the Allies in May 1945 and tried at Nuremberg, Göring committed suicide on 15 October 1946.

On 29 April, Bate was the observer in an aircraft piloted by Second Lieutenant G.H.S. Dinsmore when they were attacked south of Pronville by an Albatros D.III flown by Kurt Wolff (see page 64). Dinsmore recorded an account of what happened:

> My machine engaged three of the enemy. One circling in front, one coming from top and rear and one from beneath to the rear. My observer (Bate) fired about thirty rounds at the front. He motioned to me to pull up the nose of the machine and then engaged the top rear machine. This was evidently hit and dropped out of the fight. At the same time, the bottom rear machine fired a heavy burst from below. My observer fell over and the rear gun, instruments, etc., were all hit. The left aileron control snapped at the control lever and I dived for our lines, side-slipping to avoid further shots. I crossed the Hindenburg Line at 500 feet and landed. I was followed down by the remaining hostile aircraft to within 100 feet of the ground, but it was driven off by rifle and machine-gun fire from our lines. The machine was at once brought under enemy machine-gun and artillery fire, but a detachment of the Border Regiment secured the body of my observer, who had been killed instantaneously.[19]

Dinsmore also wrote to the bereaved father:

> Dear Mr Bate,
> It is with the deepest regret that I have to inform you of the circumstances under which your son met his death. I was the pilot of the machine in which your son was, and whilst engaged in work over the enemy lines on 29/4/17, our formation was attacked by superior enemy forces. Our machine was attacked by three of the enemy at once. Your son put up a wonderful fight, and brought an enemy machine down in flames, and drove another off, evidently

hit. Unfortunately, whilst engaged with the second machine, we were attacked by a third from below, which poured a murderous fire into us. I saw your son fall, and with some of my controls broken, dived for earth. Notwithstanding the fact that the third machine followed, I was fortunate enough to just make the British lines, and a party of soldiers got your son out.

To my deep regret I found that he must have been instantly killed: a bullet had passed through his heart. All his personal belongings, including his rosary, are being returned to you, and a Roman Catholic priest was secured to conduct the funeral service. A cross has been erected and the exact location of the spot is being ascertained. The whole squadron extends its deepest sympathy to you and mourns the loss of a very popular and gallant soldier and gentleman.

Yours very sincerely,

Geo. H.L. Dinsmore.[20]

Bate lies in Quéant Road Cemetery, Buissy.

The previous day, 28 April, another Welsh airman had been shot down by Hermann Göring. Second Lieutenant Clifford Mansel Reece was born in November 1894 at Nantclwyd House in Ruthin, where his father was a clergyman. He was the pilot of a Sopwith 1½ Strutter of 43 Squadron that was downed south of Saint-Quentin at 6.30 p.m. Reece and his observer,

Aircraftsman 2nd Class William E. Moult, were taken prisoner.

Reece was educated at Rossall School, Fylde, Lancashire, and went to Magdalene College, Cambridge, in 1913, but his studies were interrupted by the outbreak of war. He was commissioned into the Cheshire Regiment in October 1914. He joined the Royal Flying Corps

George Bate

in November 1916 and was wounded in action on 13 January 1917. He was held prisoner at Gustren in Silesia and was repatriated in January 1919. Later a Queen's Counsel, Reece died in Devon in November 1973.

Air Mechanic 2nd Class James Henry Wynn, of 18 Squadron, died of his wounds on 30 April, aged 24, and was buried in Grévillers British Cemetery. His family home was in Coedcae, Pontypool, and pre-war he had worked in a coal mine in Hafodyrynys. He had enlisted in the 2nd Battalion of the Monmouthshire Regiment on 1 November 1914. Joining the Royal Flying Corps in February 1917, he was stationed at Bertangles as an observer. His pilot was Serjeant Tom Whiteman, an ex-collier from Abertillery, who had gained his Aviators' Certificate on 6 October 1916.

They took off on 30 April 1917 in an F.E.2b of 18 Squadron on a photographic reconnaissance mission and were attacked some 12 miles behind the German lines, possibly by *Leutnant* Hans Klein of *Jasta* 4. Both Welshmen were initially wounded in the combat that followed.

It was said later that Wynn gave a good account of himself, firing his Lewis gun even after he was hit in the hand, until his machine gun jammed. Another bullet hit Whiteman under the left ear before breaking some of his upper teeth and becoming lodged under his right eye. Blinded for some minutes, Whiteman managed to keep flying towards the British lines. He took the craft down from 12,000 feet to 2,000 feet, where they were met by ground fire from the Germans below.

James Wynn

The aircraft was badly shot up and Whiteman crashed on landing at Ribécourt when the undercarriage collapsed. A report on the condition of the aircraft stated: 'Steel framework of nacelle shot through. Tail plane shot through main spars. Tail booms badly strained and shot through. Undercarriage completely crushed. Engine shot through in many places.'[21]

A newspaper report the following month gave more details:

> Flight-serjeant Tom Whiteman, of the Royal Flying Corps, who previous to joining the Army in June 1915 was employed in the lamp-room at the Vivian Colliery, Abertillery, has had some thrilling experiences in France. Whilst out with his squadron on 30 April, about twelve miles over the German lines, Whiteman's observer, a Pontypool man, was shot in the left hand. The gun became jammed, and then the engine failed. Presently Whiteman himself was shot under the left ear and the bullet destroying his teeth and appearing just beneath the skin over the right eye. He was blinded for some minutes, but giving directions to the observer, they made for the British lines, and when over No-Man's-Land, after descending from a height of 12,000ft to 2,000ft, encountered a fusillade from the German field guns. Eventually they landed safely, only to find that his gallant observer was quite dead, absolutely riddled, whilst the machine was in a similar condition, and Whiteman's clothing also contained many bullet holes.
>
> Flight-serjeant Whiteman is the son of Mr and Mrs J. Whiteman, now of Usk, who have two other sons serving in his Majesty's forces. He is now in hospital at Wandsworth. The bullet has been extracted, and the young airman when visited by his brother-in-law, Mr David Parsons, 58 Newall Steet, Abertillery, cheerfully remarked that, though he had lost the sight of the right eye, he would be glad to have another cut at the enemy.[22]

Serjeant Whiteman was discharged from the Royal Flying Corps on 10 August 1917 as a result of his wounds. Wynn's parents were sent a letter calling their son 'a very good gunner observer', and adding, 'He is missed very much by all in his squadron, as he was such a game, cheerful little fellow.'[23]

They were Hans Klein's eighth victory – his seventh in 26 days. Born in Stettin on 17 January 1891, he had volunteered for the Army at the start of the war and fought on the Western Front. He joined the Air Service in the spring of 1916 and amassed a total of 22 victories before being grounded as the result of having his right thumb shot off. He was awarded both classes of the Iron Cross while serving in the Army, and the Knight's Cross and the *Pour le Mérite*. He joined the Luftwaffe in 1935 after obtaining an engineering degree, and served until he died on 18 November 1944 of injuries received in a car accident, though his family suspected he had been murdered.

Second Lieutenant Rhys Beynon Davies was 20 when he was killed on 1 May, south-west of Lens and was buried in Monchy-Breton Church cemetery. His parents lived in Henllan, Cardiganshire, and he was their only child. Educated at Aberbanc Elementary School in Llyngwern, Henllan, at Llandysul County School, and St George's College, London,

Tom Whiteman   Hans Klein

Rhys Davies

he joined the Inns of Court Officers' Training Corps in May 1915. He was commissioned into the 4th (Territorial) Battalion of the Northumberland Fusiliers in August and promoted to lieutenant in July 1916. Davies served with the British Expeditionary Force in France and Flanders from March to October 1916, commanding a Trench Mortar Battery from 15 September. He was then attached to the Royal Flying Corps as an observer and was wounded over Hulluch Wood in December and invalided home. After returning to France in February 1917, he was appointed as a flying officer in March.

His commanding officer wrote to the parents: 'Your son was doing so splendidly, and was one of our best observers. His loss is very great to us.'[24] His pilot officer wrote:

> I write to tell you in what high regard he was held by those of us in his flight, and what splendid courage he possessed. As an observer your son was tremendously valuable to the squadron, and as a friend he meant so much to us all. At the time he was hit he was handling his gun with all possible coolness and courage. His death was a very sad blow to us indeed.[25]

However, this was not the whole story of his demise. His aircraft was actually shot down by a French pilot who claimed he was blinded by the sun and unable to identify the aircraft properly. Davies and his pilot were on an artillery registration sortie, having taken off from their aerodrome at Hesdigneul at 5.30 a.m. The shots from the French pilot hit their aircraft's fuel tank, causing a fire to break out. The pilot landed the aircraft near Arras, whereupon it exploded, killing Rhys Davies but leaving the pilot uninjured.

Second Lieutenant Iorwerth Roland Owen was the son of a Welshman. His father was a physician and surgeon who was born in Holyhead, Anglesey. Educated at Mill Hill School in London, Iorwerth Owen was a medical student when the war broke out. On 7 May 1917 he was the pilot of a B.E.2c of 13 Squadron which left its aerodrome at 10.40 a.m. on a photographic patrol over XVII Corps' front. It was attacked over Arras by enemy aircraft and shot down by *Leutnant* Karl Allmenröder of *Jasta* 11. Owen had been shot in the head and chest but remained conscious and was able to land his machine safely. He then passed out and died, aged 20, in a field ambulance without regaining consciousness. His observer, Air Mechanic 2nd Class Reginald Hickling from Malvern, who had been a gardener before enlisting, was also killed.

Avro B.E.2c

A tribute to Owen appeared in Liverpool's Scroll of Fame:

Among the many new aspects of the art of war, none are more
worthy of Britain's pride than the splendid work of the members
of the Royal Flying Corps in winning the mastery of the air. They
were all heroes, and nearly all were boys, and many of them,
when life still lay before them fair and untried, died willingly for
their country in a service as romantic as it was hazardous. To this
splendid company of eager young patriots belonged 2nd Lieut.
Iorwerth Ap Roland Owen, son of Dr and Mrs Roland Owen, of
Arley House, Seaforth. He was born on July 22nd 1896, and his
bright young life ended when only twenty years of age, in a death
of honour in his country's service.

Educated at Merchant Taylors' School, Crosby, and at
Mill Hill, under Sir John McClure, he became an enthusiastic
member of the latter school's OTC [Officers' Training Corps].
In August 1915, he matriculated at London University with a
view later of entering the medical profession, but he postponed
his further course of study, and immediately joined the Inns
of Court Officers' Training Corps. His first intention was to
accept a commission offered him (after twelve months' infantry
training) in the Royal Welsh Fusiliers, but, having for some
years taken an intense interest in aviation and the making of
aeroplanes, his earlier predilections induced him instead to
apply for a commission in the Royal Flying Corps, which was
granted him in September 1916. He was sent to the Flying
School at Oxford until November 8th, when he was posted to
the Reserve Squadron at Netheravon, Salisbury Plain, until
December 6th, 1916. Then he was transferred to 17 Squadron,
at Croydon, where he remained until he received his wings, on
March 31st, 1917, after only six months training, during which
he never had an accident in landing, a fact of which he was
justifiably proud.

After only four days' leave, and ten days after gaining his
pilot's certificate, he was sent to France, and less than a month
later, on May 7th, 1917, he was killed in action, while engaged
in an unequal contest with five German planes. During his brief
period in France, he won for himself a fine reputation for daring
and nerve, and succeeded in bringing down more than one
hostile machine. Boy though he was in years, he proved himself

a man in courage, steadfastness of purpose, and reliability. Physically he was a fine specimen of young manhood, standing 6' 2" in height. He was a keen lover of sport of all kinds, a great reader, a good musician and chess-player, and a dead shot with the rifle, and, possessing in addition a generous and happy disposition, he made friends wherever he went, who will long cherish the recollection of his cheery, whimsical personality.[26]

His commanding officer, Major Powell, wrote to the parents:

He left the aerodrome about 11 a.m. and was out on photography with our best gunner observer, and, as far as we can hear, was attacked by five hostile machines. His observer was shot dead, and your son was shot in the head and chest. He seems to have remained conscious long enough to land his machine without an accident, when he landed just inside our lines about two o'clock. He died very soon after in a field ambulance, without suffering any pain or recovering consciousness. The following day, he was buried with military honours at the British cemetery at St Catherine's outside Arras, near to where his machine came

down, having drifted some distance during the fight. He will be an awful loss to the squadron, as he was such a good fellow, and had made a particularly good beginning, and was a great favourite. Every officer in this squadron (the 13th) unites with me in sending our sincere sympathy to you in your time of sorrow.[27]

Iorwerth Owen

91

An observer in his squadron paid this tribute:

I have not been up myself with your son, but all the observers in
his flight said the same thing: 'Owen is a jolly good pilot,' and I
am sure he was by the way he handled his machine. He was very
much liked in the mess, and we are all very sorry to have lost him,
as he was one of the right sort. His observer was killed instantly
and your son died on reaching the field ambulance after, I think,
remaining conscious long enough to land his machine, as during
the fight he must have drifted some distance away, but coming
down just within our lines.[28]

Ironically, Karl Allmenröder was also a medical student
before the war began. Born in Wald in May 1896, he served as
an artilleryman on the Eastern Front, where he won the Iron
Cross Second Class. Joining the Air Service in March 1916,
he joined von Richthofen's *Jasta* 11 in November of that year.
In February 1917 he achieved the first of his 30 victories. He

was awarded the Iron
Cross First Class, the
Knight's Cross in June
1917, and a few days
later the *Pour le Mérite*.
He rose to command
the *Jasta* before being
shot down and killed on
27 June 1917, possibly
by Raymond Collishaw
(see page 302), who was
of Welsh descent.

Karl Allmenröder

Air Mechanic 3rd Class James Harold Jones, aged 25, died of natural causes on 16 May and was buried in Cathays Cemetery, Cardiff. His widow lived in Cardiff.

Two days later it was reported that one Welsh airman had had a very lucky escape: 'Mr W.D. Jones, Bodfor, has received information from Lieut. Thomas Bowen, RFC, that he has been seriously hurt while testing a new aeroplane. He fell from a height of 1,500 feet and fractured his skull. He has undergone an operation and is now progressing favourably.'[29]

A story of extraordinary derring-do appeared in the press the following week:

> One of the newest – and most daring – of the Welsh aviators in France has just flown home in a captured German aeroplane. Before he had been long in France, he brought down a German machine, blew up a German observation balloon and was himself brought down between the British and German lines. His machine was shelled to bits, but he and his observer took shelter in a shell-hole, and got back to our lines at night, both unhurt.[30]

Captain John Richard Anthony of 1 Squadron died of his wounds on 25 May and was buried in Mendinghem Military Cemetery in Belgium. He was from Pwllheli. Originally a lieutenant with the 6th Battalion of the Royal Welsh Fusiliers, he was appointed Flying Officer in June 1915 and Flight Commander in May 1917. On the morning of 25 May, the German *Jasta* 18 were patrolling in their Albatros D.IIIs at 1,600 feet when they were attacked by Nieuport 17s of 1 Squadron from above. *Leutnant* Strähle attacked Anthony's plane and forced it down, with Anthony making a good but rough landing in a meadow near to Morveaux. Strähle's fire had damaged the engine cowling behind the propeller and wounded the pilot. Captain Anthony was treated at the nearby Flak Battery and then taken to hospital where he died the same evening.

A local newspaper carried an account of his death:

The Late Lieutenant Anthony

It now appears that Flight Lieutenant J.R. Anthony, son of the late Alderman Anthony JP, ex-mayor of Pwllheli, died of wounds within 24 hours after he was shot in an aerial engagement with the Germans. An officer who was with him in the fight and taken prisoner at the same time has written to his brother, Mr Isaac M. Anthony, stating that the young lieutenant was taken by a German officer named Muller to the latter's own hut and that he was attended by six German doctors. A surgical operation was necessary and it was successfully performed. The patient was bright and cheerful after the operation, but had a relapse during the night and passed away next morning. Lieut. Anthony was an officer in the Territorial Force when war broke out, but in a few months was transferred to the Royal Flying Corps. During operations in this country, he met with a serious accident and it was some months before he was able to resume his duties. Eventually he crossed over to France, where he proved himself in numerous engagements an able and gallant officer. He was brought up as a solicitor and was with the firm of Messrs Picton Jones and Roberts at Pwllheli and frequently appeared as an advocate in the local courts. He had a winning personality and

John Anthony's crashed Nieuport

a wide circle of friends who feel deeply for the family in their double bereavement, for only a few months previous, his younger brother (Pte. Willie R Anthony) formerly a bank clerk, fell in action in France.[31]

Air Mechanic 1st Class Harold Tolson Vaughan was born in Cardiff in December 1893 and had joined the Royal Flying Corps in July 1914, being among the first to go to France the following month. Before enlisting, he had been employed by Commercial Cars Limited in Luton. He married in June 1916 in Doncaster and died in Luton in 1948, aged 55. Vaughan is pictured below with the peaked cap, holding the propeller of his aircraft in May 1917.

Lieutenant Gwyn Arthur Griffiths was killed on 2 June, aged 24, and buried in Mons-en-Chaussée Communal Cemetery. His family home was in Golden Grove, Carmarthenshire. Commissioned into the 15th Welsh Regiment in March 1915, he volunteered for the Royal Flying Corps in the summer of 1916. He trained as an observer and was posted to 35 Squadron.

Harold Vaughan

On the day he was killed, he was flying an artillery observation sortie over Vermand in an Armstrong Whitworth F.K.8. The aircraft was hit by anti-aircraft fire and forced down behind the German lines. Griffiths was initially taken prisoner but was so badly wounded he died the same day.

Serjeant William Charles Turner, of Brecon, died on 3 June. He was serving with 38 Training Squadron and was buried in Brecon Cemetery. A local newspaper carried an account of his death:

> The greatest regret is expressed amongst their numerous friends, and the deepest sympathy extended to Mr and Mrs Turner, formerly of the County Club, Brecon, now of Southampton, at the loss they have sustained by the death of their eldest son, Sgt. Wm. Turner, of the Royal Flying Corps, who met with a shocking fatality on Sunday. At the inquest held at Cirencester on Monday, a verdict of 'Accidental Death' was returned. The accident took place near North Cerney. As deceased, aged 26, was taking a flight, while at a height of about 1,000 yards, his machine was observed to be in flames, and, on reaching the ground, Turner was so badly burned as to be unrecognisable. Young Turner entered the Government Air Service before the outbreak of war, and in the early days of the struggle saw much service in France. He often crossed the Channel in his machine. Latterly he had been attached to the service at home, and it was probably in the work of machine testing that he met his sad end. His brother Fred is serving with the Brecknocks in India. The funeral, we understand, takes place at Brecon on Thursday.[32]

William Turner was born in 1893, the eldest son of Charles and Sarah Jane Turner of the Brecon County Club, where his father was the steward. Educated at Brecon County School, he trained in the motor trade and was for a short while in business in Brecon. He was training for a First Class Pilot Certificate when accidentally killed while flying at Rendcombe Aerodrome in Cirencester.

His obituary read:

The long association of the parents with Brecon and district, and the popularity of the deceased himself in the county town where he was brought up, sufficiently account for the deep regret and sympathy shown here at the tragic death of Sgt. W.C. Turner of the Royal Flying Corps (son of Mr and Mrs C. Turner, of Hamble, Hants, formerly of Brecon), who was killed whilst flying at an aerodrome in England on Sunday, the 3rd instant. Sgt. Turner, who was 26 years of age, was the first Breconshire man to join the Royal Flying Corps. He enlisted in January 1914, and his squadron was the first to go to France, crossing on 8 August. He served 16 months in France, having many exciting experiences; was then sent home to act as an aero engine mechanic. He had been trained as a motor engineer at Cardiff, serving an apprenticeship with Messrs Sully, and was consequently specially fitted for this new work. In January last, he was sent to a military aero-nautical school to qualify for a first class pilot's certificate in theory, including aerial gunnery, wireless observation, and aerial photography, formation of troops, and rigging. From this school he was sent to an aerodrome, where he passed his examination in practical flying, and about six weeks ago he was transferred to the aerodrome where he was killed, and where his duty was training on battle planes preparatory to receiving his commission and going to the Front. He was due to go to France, in fact, a few days after the date of his death. On Sunday, the 3rd instant, he had been flying for some time most successfully. Then he was observed to be in difficulties, and his machine came down in a spinning nosedive, and he was instantaneously killed. Mr and Mrs Turner received a telegram from the office commanding the aerodrome, which read as follows: 'The officer commanding expresses his deep sympathy and regrets to inform you that Sgt. W.C. Turner was killed instantaneously in an aeroplane accident this morning.'

THE INQUEST. The inquest was held at Cirencester on the 4th inst, before Deputy Coroner, Mr R.H. Smith. Second Lieutenant Leonard Arthur Rivers stated that deceased came to the Aerodrome on 10 May. On Sunday morning witness sent him on a flight at 6.20. He flew satisfactorily for a time, and then, in attempting to land, he overshot the mark and switched his engine on again. He mounted to an altitude of 1,000 feet, and then appeared to be in difficulties. The machine made a spinning nosedive to the ground in a field adjoining the Aerodrome. From

the injuries to the body, witness concluded that deceased must
have been killed at the moment the machine struck the ground.
The machine caught fire after it fell. In reply to the Coroner,
witness said, as deceased had overshot the mark, it was quite the
right thing for him to do to start the engine again. If he had not
done so he would have gone straight into a wood. Witness had
examined the machine carefully and flew it in the company of
the deceased for half an hour prior to the accident, finding it in
perfect order. He was giving deceased his last tuition, though he
was quite fit to go alone. Replying to further questions, witness
gave the opinion that in some way deceased lost control of the
machine. When it made the dive the engine was on, which is
pretty conclusive proof that deceased had lost control, or he
would have switched the engine off. The fall resulted in the tanks
bursting, which immediately enveloped the whole machine in very
explosive gas. It was quite a standard type of machine. Witness
had flown it himself on various occasions and always found it easy
to control. Previous to deceased going up alone, witness asked
if he felt perfectly confident or if he would like him (witness) to
go up just once more. Deceased replied that he never felt more
confident, and he was quite certain that he had nothing to learn
by witness going. Captain David John Lewis, RAMC, medical
officer in charge of the Aerodrome, said he saw the body shortly
after the accident, and either of the two principal injuries would
account for an immediate fatal result. There was no suffering, and
the doctor added that perhaps it would be just as well for the jury
to know that he made frequent examinations of the staff and men,
and 10 days ago he examined the deceased, who was in perfect
physical condition in every way. The jury returned a verdict of
'Accidental Death', and attached no blame to anyone.[33]

William Turner had written home in October 1914 and his
letter was published:

An airman with the British force in France, Mr W.C. Turner, son
of Mr C. Turner of the County Club Brecon, who is serving in
No. 5 Squadron of the RFC, has sent a very interesting letter to
his parents. The only Breconshire man known to be in the Flying
Corps, Mr Turner sailed from Newhaven for the front on 10

August. At the time of writing (17 October) he was preparing for a hurried journey to England to take back a new Blériot aeroplane. He says:

'This last fortnight I have flown a distance of 1,100 kilometres over the German lines. My planes have been riddled by bullets several times, but they have not been sharp enough to bring me down. The worst misfortune I have had is a bullet through my petrol tank, and I managed to plane down to our lines with my finger on the hole. I went over Antwerp early yesterday morning. The Germans are strong round there.

'Last Thursday I went over to Paris by air and got 900 newspapers. Since then I have been called the 'paper boy'. On the Wednesday I came down with engine trouble and was surprised to find – works close by. They actually gave me a new engine to come away with in the machine. I don't know how to praise the French for the reception we have had. Last evening, when we descended on an aerodrome belonging to the ------ people, a German came over and dropped four bombs on us, but did not succeed in doing anything to satisfy himself. Then he went over the town of St Omer, dropped one bomb, and killed a woman and a baby boy. Several went up to circle him, but could not get near.'[34]

On 5 June, Captain William Thomas Lloyd Allcock of Knighton in Radnorshire was killed, aged 21, while serving with 40 Squadron. Following his secondary schooling at Bourne College, Birmingham, he left home for Canada in 1913. Having travelled across Canada without really settling and with the outbreak of war, he returned to Great Britain via New York and arrived home in January 1915.

Allcock set his sights on joining the Royal Flying Corps, and his parents arranged for him to go to Hendon Flying School on 22 February 1915 to train privately for his pilot's certificate. It was normal at this time for military pilot candidates to sponsor their own initial training. Allcock applied to join the Royal Flying Corps, and while at Hendon he was interviewed at the War Office and told that his application would be subject to successful qualification for his pilot's certificate, which he completed with six hours flying at the Beatty School, Hendon.

He qualified for his Royal Aero Club pilot's certificate on 16 May 1915.

Appointed as a probationary Second Lieutenant Special Reserve in the Royal Flying Corps on 12 June 1915, he was posted to the Central Flying School to undertake his military flying training. Having completed this, he was confirmed in his rank on 22 September 1915 and appointed to No. 2 Squadron in France.

Allcock left behind a diary of his time in the Royal Flying Corps. This is his entry for 5 October 1915:

Artillery observation with Lt. Brown. While so doing we were hit at 8,000ft by shrapnel over Hulluch. My engine gone dud, I turned for our lines, when just crossing them the machine caught fire at 6,300 feet. I immediately put her nose down; the flames burst out and spread along the fuselage behind the pilot's seat. Brown threw the ammunition overboard and climbed along back nearly into my cockpit as the whole front of the machine was a blazing mass. In the meantime, we were speeding to earth at 120 mph. Brown was trying to keep the fire down from burning his clothes, while I kept my eye on the pitot tube, the ground and the flames, pushing the joy stick further forward until we were nearly nose diving. Every minute I thought would be the last, for I expected the whole machine to collapse from strain as a number of wires were broken. Eventually, I saw the ground not far below and found myself going straight at a village, so I turned to the right and spying a ploughed field decided to land there, cutting through telephone wires and a tall hedge, missing a horse and plough by inches. A few feet from the ground I levelled out and the machine took the ground at 70 mph. A perfect landing but, the undercarriage being burnt, the machine ran a few yards and collapsed, digging her nose into the plough, and turned over. I was thrown right out 10 yards ahead, putting out my hands saved me but I lay dazed a little; in the meantime the tail came down and hit me on the head. Staggering round to find Brown, I found him hunting for me. He had fallen under the engine and just managed to crawl out a few seconds before the bearings broke and the engine fell on the spot. Looking on the wreckage we saw a mass of flame with every few seconds shots going off from the revolvers. A huge crowd collected but, putting a Serjeant in charge with some

men, we left in a tender for our aerodrome and reported to the
officer commanding, Major Becke. From the wreckage we got a few
souvenirs – revolver, compass and a piece of the engine bed which
had been melted by the heat.[35]

A further report of his work was carried in a newspaper:

Second-Lieutenant and flying officer William T. Lloyd-Allcock,
Royal Flying Corps, Knighton … has had some thrilling
experiences at the front in France. On one occasion he met two
German machines in the air: an 'Albatros' coming up in front of
him, and a monoplane in the rear. The fire from his observer's
machine-gun must have been effective, as after a contest lasting
some five minutes, the two enemy machines made off and went
to ground as they generally do when they come in contact with
British airmen. When patrolling over our lines, he could not get his
machine (which he piloted for the first time) to climb above 2,500
ft, and a 'drift' caused him to pass over the lines. As he approached
the German trenches, the enemy opened fire with machine-guns
and rifles. Some damage was done to his petrol tank, but he
succeeded in getting away safely.

All previous experiences were eclipsed last week when his
duties took him some four miles behind the enemy lines on a
cloudy and misty day. When at a height of 8,000 ft, coming towards
his own lines, there was a big explosion, a column of smoke rising
to a height of 500 ft. The Germans evidently thought a bomb from
the British machine had caused the explosion, and they opened
a severe shell fire. After he had just registered a shot from a
battery, two shells burst simultaneously under the front part of his
aeroplane, blowing his and his observer's cockpits to pieces. The
engine was hit, bullets passed through his clothing and splinters
were flying in all directions, but, fortunately, he so far escaped
serious injury, only, as he put it, being 'touched' on the leg and arm.
With great presence of mind, he put the nose of his machine down
gradually until she was almost in a vertical position. Travelling at
great speed, he had just passed over the German lines when his
machine caught fire. He made straight for home, and succeeded
in making a landing in a ploughed field behind the British lines.
Airman and observer had to be pulled from under the burning

wreckage. Lieutenant Allcock was advised to take a flight the next day for the benefit of his nerves, and after bringing a new machine up from the base to the firing lines, he was granted a week's leave.[36]

On 11 November 1915 Allcock wrote in his diary:

Escort to long reconnaissance machine. Observer 1AM Bowes District Valenciennes, Douai etc. Three machines crossed the line at eight thousand feet. Kept together until we turned to come back when we had a very strong head wind. My machine was slightly slower, so I got left behind. Over Douai a Fokker attacked us over my tail; he dived at us and fired through his propeller. The first thing we heard was the rattle of the machine gun, then the thud of bullets hitting. I managed to put in a drum from the back gun bracket as he crossed behind my machine. He then cleared off. In the meantime, an Albatros attacked from underneath but at fairly long-range. My observer did some long potting and we kept him at a good distance under. We got to Lens when 'Archie' started shelling us and tore gaping holes in my planes. Fortunately, we arrived home safely, but much dilapidated.[37]

On 2 December:

Bomb raid on Don. Three squadrons, No. 2, No. 10, and No. 16 rendezvous over No. 2 at 7,000 feet carrying 2 one hundred pound bombs. Crossed the lines north of La Bassée. I went over a little in front of the others and was attacked as I was fixing my bomb sites. Thud, thud as the bullets hit. Getting my machine into the Hun line of fire, I poured into him a drum at 800 feet; he dived steeply, apparently hit. After the excitement I surveyed the damage. His first burst had riddled the passenger's seat. Lucky no Observer as he would certainly have been killed. His second burst hit the wing and riddled it, while 2 glancing shots hit my cockpit two inches below my right arm. Having dropped my bombs with good effect I returned, getting Archied terribly but fortunately pulling through all right.[38]

On 5 June 1917 Allcock took off in his Nieuport 17 at 7.22 p.m. for an offensive patrol, and never returned. He is commemorated on the Arras Flying Services Memorial and was mentioned in dispatches on 7 November 1917.

Second Lieutenant Gwynonfryn Albert Haydn Davies, of 45 Squadron, was killed two days afterwards on 7 June, aged 23. From Abertillery in Monmouthshire, he is also commemorated on the Arras Flying Services Memorial as he too has no known grave. The Battle of Messines commenced on this day and he was the observer in a Sopwith 1½ Strutter piloted by Lieutenant A.E.J. Dobson when it went missing west of Deûlémont. Davies was a teacher at Bryngwyn School, Six Bells, when he enlisted in the 3rd Battalion of the Monmouthshire Regiment before later volunteering for the Royal Flying Corps.

Also killed on the same day was Lieutenant Bernard Sanderson Marshall, aged 22, who had previously been awarded the Military Cross. From the Mumbles area in Swansea, he is remembered on the Arras Flying Services Memorial. Flying with 20 Squadron, he was the pilot of an F.E.2d which took off at 3.17 p.m. on patrol and was shot down by enemy anti-aircraft fire. His body was never identified but his observer, Private C. Lloyd, was found alive and served out the war as a prisoner of the Germans.

William Lloyd Allcock

Gwynonfryn Davies

Marshall was educated at Abingdon School and left in July 1912. He had decided on a career in engineering and was reading for a degree. Just prior to the outbreak of war he took his Inter B.Sc. (Engineering) in London. In September 1914 he volunteered for service in the Royal Engineers but in December of that year was gazetted to the 5th South Wales Borderers (Pioneers). After the usual period of training he was ordered out to France in 1915 and spent the winter of 1915/16 at the front.

On 13 May 1916, he was wounded on the Vimy Ridge and was recommended by his commanding officer for a Military Cross for gallant conduct in capturing and holding a crater under a hurricane of fire, and, although wounded, stuck to his post for three hours before returning to the dressing station to have his wound dressed (the bullet having passed right through the right shoulder). He then insisted on returning to his men through a heavy fire and held on again until relieved the next morning. He was invested with the Military Cross by King George V at Buckingham Palace in October 1916.

The circumstances leading to the award of his MC were as follows:

MARSHALL – 2nd Lieut. Bernard S. Marshall. His Colonel, in a letter to his parents, says, 'He distinguished himself by rallying the men and leading them to the crater's edge, there digging themselves in under a heavy flanking fire chiefly from machine guns. Although the doctor and others tried to discourage him (after being hit), he insisted upon returning to his men, and continued to work with them until all were re-called.' He later obtained the Military Cross.[39]

Temp. 2nd Lt. Bernard Sanderson Marshall, 6th (S) Battalion, South Wales Borderers. For gallant conduct and devotion to duty when consolidating a crater. Though badly hit in the arm he carried on till exhausted. He had his wound dressed and returned to superintend his working parties.[40]

After recovering from his wound, he applied for transfer to

the Royal Flying Corps and was gazetted in December 1916. After about six months' training, he took his wings and was immediately ordered to France again (June 1917). His career as a flying officer was a short one, for on 7 June, while on his second flight that day, he failed to return and was reported missing. Some months later, his observer reported that, while on an offensive patrol, they had attacked a flight of enemy machines and an anti-aircraft shell had burst near them. Marshall was hit in the head and killed as a result. The aircraft was also hit and put out of action, plunging down into a canal near Lille. The machine sank and his body was not recovered. The observer, although injured by the fall, managed to reach the bank and was immediately taken prisoner.

Second Lieutenant Archibald Vincent Shirley, of 66 Squadron, died on 8 June, aged 30. Born in Penarth but a resident of Leckwith in Cardiff, he was educated at Llandaff Cathedral School and Rugby School before studying at Exeter College, Oxford. A prominent local sportsman, he represented Cardiff Polo Club. He enlisted in the Welsh Horse Yeomanry

Bernard Marshall   Archibald Shirley

on the outbreak of war and served as a despatch rider. Shirley served in the ranks and then obtained a commission in the spring of 1915, fighting at Gallipoli and in Egypt before transferring to the Royal Flying Corps in October 1916. He was flying a Sopwith Scout in action against German machines when he collided with an aircraft piloted by Second Lieutenant Archibald Garden Robertson. Declared missing in action, his death was reported by the Germans on 1 September 1917. Both men are commemorated on the Arras Flying Services Memorial.

On 12 June, Lieutenant William Bertram Protheroe was killed. Aged 26, he was a native of Llanelli and was serving with 53 Squadron. He had enlisted with the 15th Welsh Regiment before volunteering for the Royal Flying Corps. Flying as observer in an R.E.8 piloted by Second Lieutenant William Turnbull on a photographic mission, they were attacked by enemy aircraft over Oosttaverne at 8.20 a.m. and fell in flames. A local newspaper carried an account of his death:

> As announced in the later edition of *The Star* last Saturday, Lieut. Bert Protheroe, of the Royal Flying Corps, has been killed in action. This gallant young officer was formerly attached to the 15th Welsh, where he did excellent work. At his own request, he was then transferred to the RFC and quickly qualified as a daring and skilful flyer. It appears that Lieut. Protheroe, who was senior observer, was in an aeroplane with Turnbull, the famous Rugby international. They were attacked by five German machines. When the British machine was forced down behind our lines, it was discovered that both the pilot and observer were killed. Lieut. Protheroe, whose bravery and daring were proverbial, was to have come home next week for three months for further training to qualify as a pilot. Prior to this he was employed by Messrs Thomas and Clements, and took a keen interest in sport, being a good Rugby player.
>
> A few months ago we forwarded to Lieut. Protheroe a consignment of cigarettes from the *Star* Cigarette Fund with the

request that he would see to their distribution among the Llanelli boys of the Carmarthenshire Battalion. Writing to us later on, Bert described the gratitude with which the smokes were received by his fellow townsmen.[41]

Both men are commemorated on the Arras Flying Services memorial as neither has a known grave. They were shot down by *Vizefeldwebel* Wittekind of *Jasta* 28.

Lieutenant David Rhys Cadwgan Lloyd was killed in action over Marquion on 16 June 1917, aged 20. Born in 1897 in the Tendring district of Essex, his parents lived in Kirby-le-Soken, but Lloyd was a direct male descendant of Bleddyn ap Cynfyn, Prince of Powys and Wales in the eleventh century. Lloyd served with the 10th Loyal North Lancashire Regiment and was wounded in 1916, whereupon he transferred to the Royal Flying Corps, obtaining his pilot's certificate in February 1917. On the afternoon of 11 May, he destroyed an Albatros in the Écourt-Saint-Quentin commune and, on 15 June,

again flying a Nieuport 17, he destroyed another Albatros. The following day, while on observation patrol, he was seen to follow an enemy aircraft down to 2,000 feet and collided with an Albatros flown by *Vizefeldwebel* Robert Riessinger of *Jasta* 12. Both men were killed. Lloyd was buried in H.A.C. Cemetery, Écoust-St-Mein.

David Lloyd

Lieutenant Harold Carver Barlow was reported missing on 18 June:

> Lieutenant Harold C. Barlow, reported missing, is the only son of Mr and Mrs Barlow of Woodville, Marple, Cheshire, and Ystymcolwyn Hall, Montgomery. Lieut. Barlow was born in 1891, educated at Sywell House School, Llandudno, and Leighton Park, Reading, and, before joining the Lancashire Fusiliers was a partner in the firms of Messrs Thomas Barlow and Brother, Manchester and London, and Messrs Barlow and Co., Calcutta, Shanghai, Singapore and Kuala Lumpur. He obtained his commission in 1915 and his first lieutenancy in 1916, and was attached to the Royal Flying Corps in February 1917.[42]

Barlow was the observer in an R.E.8 of 9 Squadron that left the aerodrome at Proven at 11 a.m. on a photographic patrol. The pilot was Lieutenant Ralph Walter Ellis. The aircraft was then either shot down by anti-aircraft fire, according to the casualty report at the time, or was the 53rd victory of Baron Manfred von Richthofen. Ellis' body was found in the aircraft and buried, but the grave was lost. Barlow's was so badly burnt it could not be identified. He was 27. The two airmen are commemorated on the Arras Flying Services Memorial.

Harold Barlow

The announcement was made on 21 June of a gallantry award to a Welsh airman:

Lieutenant Howell Arnold Evans, Welsh Regiment, son of Mr T.D. Evans, rate collector, Mountain Ash, has been awarded the Military Cross and promoted to the rank of captain for distinguished conduct in Palestine. Captain Evans, who is only 21 years of age, was articled to Mr William Thomas, solicitor of Aberdare. He has served in Gallipoli, Egypt, and latterly in Palestine.[43]

He survived the war, dying in 1972.

Second Lieutenant John Wathen Eyton-Lloyd from Rhyl, aged 22, died in a flying accident on 24 June while serving with 10 Squadron and was buried in Chocques Military Cemetery. He was flying a B.E.2g on artillery observation when he hit a kite balloon cable and nosedived to the ground. His observer, Serjeant F.G. Matthews, was also killed.

Eyton-Lloyd's obituary appeared in a local newspaper:

News was received last week that Flight Lieutenant John Eyton Lloyd, younger son of Dr and Mrs Eyton Lloyd, Rhyl, has been killed. He was educated at Colet House, Rhyl, and Epsom College. From Epsom he was articled to the Shotton Engineering Works, where he soon showed extraordinary aptitude and was making rapid progress. When the war broke out, he at once joined the Army, and after a time received his commission. He was transferred to the Royal Flying Corps, and at once proved that he had found his job. He passed the several stages of his training with ease and distinction, and was given his wings. He was a bold, intrepid airman. He knew no fear; his courage was without limit. His Flight-Commander, speaking to a friend a few days ago, said of him: 'He was a born pilot; he had already done much excellent work on his own and was likely to do extremely well.' The following extract from a letter written to his father by his Commanding Officer says: 'It is with the deepest regret that I have to tell you that your boy was killed on duty today, 24 June ... Only today I recommended that your son should be promoted to Flight Commander (Captain), as he had done extraordinarily well since he has been here. I was very fond of him, as were all the other officers and men of the Squadron. He will be buried near our Squadron on Tuesday, in the Cemetery.'[44]

Air Mechanic 1st Class Montague Vincent Pocock was born in Cardiff in 1895. His actions on 25 June led to him being awarded the Military Medal. His citation read:

For conspicuous gallantry and devotion to duty on 25 June 1917. Whilst receiving wireless signals from an aeroplane for a siege battery, which was carrying out a shoot with aeroplane observation, his wireless aerial was cut by hostile shell fire. Pocock mended his aerial under heavy fire and continued receiving the signals with only a slight interruption to the shoot. On several other occasions he has repaired his apparatus under heavy fire.[45]

Pocock had joined up in the summer of 1915. He left a record of his service describing the hazardous nature of his work:

Towards the end of June we were completely wiped out, all of the guns were destroyed and the ammunition blown up. We suffered very heavy casualties, only 28 men left unwounded out of the total complement of the battery. I was wounded the next day and taken to the casualty clearing station, after to hospital at Étaples.

Montague Pocock

After a month recovering, he was posted back to his battery where he witnessed more of the horrors of this dreadful war: 'We passed over a considerable portion of the Somme battlefield, and dead bodies were still lying about in goodly numbers, and of course the shell holes were there in abundance.'[46]

Montague Pocock survived the war, and during the Second World War he served in the Home Guard and rose from corporal to second lieutenant.

On 26 June, Captain George Walter Thomas Lindsay was killed in a flying accident near Bristol, aged 26. He was buried in a family vault in Holy Trinity Church cemetery, Ystrad Mynach. Educated at Wellington College, where he was a good all-round athlete, and after passing out from the Royal Military Academy in Woolwich, he joined the Royal Artillery in 1911 and fought in France from August 1914, being wounded in November of that year. He subsequently commanded a battery in France and in Salonika before joining the Royal Flying Corps in November 1916. Lindsay was posted back to Britain in 1917 to test newly-built and repaired aircraft from the Rolls-Royce factory adjacent to Filton Aerodrome in Bristol. His B.E.2c aircraft was seen to be in a spinning nosedive before crashing near Chipping Sodbury.

His death was reported in a newspaper: 'An aeroplane fell from a considerable height into a field in South Gloucestershire on Tuesday. The aviators, Captain G.W.T. Lindsay, who comes from a

George Lindsay

South Wales family, and first Air Mechanic, C.E. Sharman of Sheffield, were killed instantly.'[47]

Both of his brothers were killed during the conflict, within a week of each other. Lieutenant Archibald Thurston Thomas Lindsay was killed, aged 20, on 26 March 1918 while serving with the 7th Army Troops Company, Royal Monmouthshire; Major Claud Frederic Thomas Lindsay was killed on 31 March, aged 26, serving with 33rd Battery of the Royal Field Artillery.

Second Lieutenant John Wesley Howells was born in Tenby, Pembrokeshire, on 26 October 1887 and was educated at the Wesleyan Day and Council Schools in the town. He subsequently attended the Westminster Training College, where he trained to be a teacher. After qualifying, he taught at the Seacombe Wesleyan School and was a Wesleyan Minister in charge of Victoria Hall, Ancoats, Manchester. He enlisted on 14 May 1915, and was commissioned into the 7th Battalion of the Lancashire Fusiliers the following August and served in Egypt and Mesopotamia. He then transferred to the Royal Flying Corps and served in Palestine with 14 Squadron. Howells was killed in action in Gaza on 23 July 1917 while acting as an observer/gunner. His machine was brought down into the sea by anti-aircraft guns and his body was not recovered. He is commemorated on the Jerusalem memorial.

In 1917 he wrote: 'We don't know much about how the war is going, but we'll do our bit by doing our best.'[48]

A fellow officer wrote of him:

It struck us as strange that a clergyman should be in a fighting unit, particularly one of such scholarly attainments. But the fact that he had chosen and taken the path of exceeding danger increased our respect tremendously, and made us realise how burning the conviction was that made him lay aside the duties of his office for the rough work of the field. He met his death, as he would have wished had he known – doing what he counted the prime duty of British manhood today, and in a country which, from his previous knowledge of it and its association with his faith, meant more to him than to most. We grieve at the loss of a good comrade and a plucky soldier.[49]

Also killed on 23 July was Captain Robert Newton Thomas of 14 Squadron. He was serving with the Egyptian Expeditionary Force and had served in France for 11 months. He was 26 years old and had recently been awarded the French *Croix de Guerre*. Robert Thomas is commemorated on the Jerusalem Memorial. His younger brother, Second Lieutenant Trevor Thomas, had been killed in action on 10 January 1916 while serving with the Royal Welsh Fusiliers. His remaining brother, Captain Owen Vincent Thomas, was to be killed in a flying accident on 29 July 1918. Their father, Brigadier-General Owen Thomas, had been in charge of recruiting in Anglesey.

The three Thomas brothers (standing) with their father

Ivan Hart-Davies

Lieutenant Ivan Beauclerk Hart-Davies was 39 years of age when he died on 27 July while flying a Bristol F.2B. He was laid to rest in St James Church cemetery, Southam. His parents were both Welsh but he was born in Huntingdon. He took flying lessons and qualified as a pilot on 6 October 1913. His obituary stated:

> Lieutenant Ivan Beauclerk Hart-Davies, RFC, who was killed in an aeroplane accident in England, was the son of the late Rev. John Hart-Davies of Southam Rectory, Warwickshire, and was 39 years of age. He was educated at a school at Maidenhead and at King's School, Canterbury, and began life as a schoolmaster at New Beacon, Sevenoaks. Afterwards, however, he worked up a wide life insurance and motor insurance business in the Midlands. He held the 'end-to-end' record for motor cycles and light cars, and in 1913, with three other motorcyclists, won the Murren Cup, though none of the four had done any bobsleighing before. He took to flying before the war as an amateur, but last year he obtained a commission in the RFC and was on the eve of going to the front. A brother officer writes: 'A gallant fellow who we all liked immensely, and are deeply grieved that he should have been fatally injured when he so much wished to go to France, where doubtless he would have won honours.'[50]

Major Owen Mostyn Conran was killed returning from a night sortie with 10 Squadron in July 1917. Conran was born in Brondyffryn, Denbigh, on 1 April 1881. Educated at Shrewsbury, he was commissioned into the 3rd South Lancashire Militia on 4 April 1900. He joined the Royal Lancaster Regiment from the

Militia in 1901 and was promoted to Lieutenant in February of that year. Conran served in the Boer War with the regiment. He was promoted to Captain in July 1907 and in June 1913 was seconded for service with the Egyptian Army, being attached to the 14th Sudanese Battalion from June 1913 to June 1916. He was appointed *Bimbashi* (Major) in the Egyptian Army in June 1913.

Conran learned to fly with 3 Squadron, gaining his wings flying a Maurice Farman biplane in France on 14 August 1913. He was promoted to Major in September 1915 and took part in the Darfur campaign of 1916. In July 1916, he was sent to England on sick leave and while at home he obtained permission to become attached to the Royal Flying Corps. On 23 April 1917 he went to France and was posted to No. 10 (Bombing) Squadron Royal Flying Corps, being made a Flight Commander in November 1916. As a pilot flying Armstrong Whitworth bombers, Conran took part in the battle of Messines, the planes of his squadron being mostly engaged in bombing and artillery observation.

On 28 July 1917 Conran took off on a night mission as observer with Lieutenant H. Mitton over Carvin, flying an

Armstrong Whitworth bomber. They dropped two 112 lb bombs on Carvin and four drums of ammunition were fired by Conran. Following a failed attempt to land, their aircraft crashed near Marle-les-Mines church, and both Conran and Mitton were killed. Conran was buried in the Chocques Military Cemetery.

Second Lieutenant Ralph Lionel James was killed in a flying accident on 3 August, aged 24, and was buried

Owen Conran

in Weybridge Cemetery. Born in Penarth, Glamorgan, he obtained a B.Sc. from Cardiff University before enlisting in the 7th Royal Welsh Fusiliers. He volunteered for the Royal Flying Corps and was training with 53 Training Squadron, attached to the Wireless and Observation School. He was an only son.

Taliesin Mordecai was born in Pontypridd in 1891 and worked in the Gwalia Stores in Ogmore Vale (now at the St Fagans National Museum of History near Cardiff) before volunteering for the Royal Flying Corps in 1915. He was commissioned in August 1917 and served as a pilot and instructor. After the war ended, he remained in the Royal Air Force as an instructor and one of his pupils was the future King George VI, with whom he used to enjoy long walks in the country. At that time, he remarked later, the future king did not have a stutter.

A recruitment drive for the Royal Flying Corps was announced in the *Western Mail* on 10 August:

> Welsh Youths' Opportunity in Flying Corps.
> Colonel A.W. Elles, the officer in command of the recruiting area of Glamorgan and Monmouthshire, said on Thursday that local youths had now every chance to become officers in the Royal Flying Corps, and he expected to find South Wales strongly represented so soon as it was generally known that the way had been opened up and that no suitable candidate would be disappointed. There are developments on a big scale, and extensive arrangements have been made for the training of officers. Welsh youths should not miss the present opportunity. Applicants will be supplied at any recruiting office in South Wales with all necessary information. All applicants must be between 17 years and 8 months and 25.[51]

The same edition also carried details of the remarkable military service of Roy Makepeace, originally from Barry:

> Private Roy Makepeace, a grandson of the late Mr William
> Nash, Fleur-de-Lis, who has been home on leave and returned to

Taliesin Mordecai

London on Thursday, has had remarkable experiences in the war. He joined Botha's forces when the rebellion broke out in South Africa in September 1914, being then only fifteen years of age. He, with 600 others, was captured by the Germans, and was imprisoned for six months. Upon his release he came over to England and joined the South African Infantry, leaving shortly afterwards for France, in which country he spent two years. Whilst taking part in the Somme Battle, he was sent with a message from the headquarters to a bombing party who had captured some German trenches. He came upon a trench occupied by six Germans. With the exception of a stout stick, he had nothing to defend himself, but boldly shouted to the enemy, 'Hands up!' and they threw down their rifles. He was awarded the Military Medal, and invested on 26 July by the King, who, with the Queen and Princess Mary, warmly congratulated him upon his achievement. Since his return to Fleur-de-Lis, the local reception committee – of which Mr Henry Watts, a South African veteran, is the chairman – has presented him with a gold watch in recognition of his action.[52]

Royal Victor Nash Makepeace was born in Barry in 1899. The family then emigrated to South Africa, and when war was declared he enlisted in the South African Army. After being released he was interviewed by a reporter and described what he had endured:

Trooper Roy Makepeace, son of Mr T.G. Makepeace, who joined General Botha's forces in South Africa on the outbreak of the rebellion, and who was taken prisoner by de Wet's army, relates a graphic story of German treatment of Union prisoners and cruelty to natives. Captured by Maritz, Trooper Makepeace and other prisoners were transported from place to place in wagons, placed under guards, served with scanty rations, and forced under threats of being put in chains to do work to assist the enemy's military operations. They witnessed inhuman things which 'turned their blood cold'. Native prisoners were almost starved to death, made to work through the night making huts for the German guards. Two small Bushmen, weighing not more than 60 lb, were fastened to a tree with a donkey trek chain fixed round their necks. These Bushmen were taken in their wild state from the desert, where they used to live on herbs, and were fed like wild animals. Both died owing to such treatment. At Fransfontein many deeds of barbarism were performed by the Germans on the natives. Two, lean and starved, who were said to have stolen sheep, were brought before the prisoners and shot.[53]

He then sent a telegram to his parents saying that he was going to Europe. He fought at Delville Wood on the Somme

Royal Makepeace

in 1916 with the 1st South African Infantry Regiment and said later that he was physically and mentally exhausted after three charges against the German positions. His helmet had two holes as the result of being struck by shrapnel. He came across a wounded German who asked him for water and then attempted to wrest his rifle from him. Makepeace drove the bayonet through his chest three times.

When the King asked him how old he was, Makepeace gave an honest response and, as a result, he was dismissed from the Army two days later. He enlisted in the Royal Flying Corps and was shot down on his first mission. Surviving the war, he was promoted to lieutenant at the age of 19 and later founded the Aero Club of South Africa.

On 11 August, Lieutenant David Beynon Davies, 30, of 52 Squadron, took off at 12.40 p.m. on an artillery observation mission in an R.E.8. The son of John and Nancy Davies of Esgereinon, Cross Inn, Cardiganshire, Davies had attended university and gained a BA before enlisting. His observer, Lieutenant Ray Haliburton Sawlor, born in Nova Scotia in 1886, was a wireless engineer before enlisting in the New Brunswick Regiment of the Canadian Army and later being attached to the Royal Flying Corps.

Their aircraft was attacked at 1.15 p.m. by *Vizefeldwebel* Julius Buckler of *Jasta* 17 and shot down. Both men were killed. Davies was buried in Ramscappelle Road Military Cemetery, with Sawlor in the adjacent grave.

David Davies

Julius Buckler was born in Mainz on 28 March 1894. He won the Iron Cross Second Class as an infantryman in 1914, but was severely wounded and invalided out of the German Army. He then volunteered for flying duties and won the Iron Cross First Class in 1916, before being wounded four times in 1917 and a fifth time in May 1918. Surviving the war and registering 36 confirmed kills, he was also awarded the *Pour le Mérite*. He died in Bonn on 23 May 1960, aged 66.

Second Lieutenant Griffiths Ifor Gibson died of wounds, aged 22, on 12 August. He served with 6 Squadron, having previously served with the 11th Battalion of the West Yorkshire Regiment (Prince of Wales' Own). He was the only son of Frederic and Mary May Gibson of 22 Llantwit Road, Treforest, Glamorgan.

Born in Pontypridd, he had attended Colston School, Stapleton, Bristol before being articled as an architect to his father. Enlisting in August 1914 in the 5th Welsh Regiment, he had served at Gallipoli, where he took part in the landing at

Julius Buckler   Griffiths Gibson

Suvla Bay and eight further months of fighting before being wounded by a bullet through the chest. He was invalided home but recovered to join the recruiting staff at Pontypridd. Gibson was commissioned in January 1916 and served with the British Expeditionary Force in France and Flanders before volunteering for the Royal Flying Corps in June 1916. He underwent training at Hendon and returned to France the following month, being wounded again on 10 August 1917. He was the observer in an R.E.8 which took off at 6.15 p.m. on an artillery patrol.

His pilot, Lieutenant Pickett, survived, and sent to the parents an account of what happened:

> We had gone up to do a shoot rather a long way over the lines, and low clouds and bad visibility made the target very difficult to see. While we were busy we were suddenly attacked from above by nine Albatros scouts. Their machines were twice as fast as ours, and they simply made rings round us. I knew that it was useless to attempt to fly straight for even a second. I don't know how long the scrap lasted, but your son got off 100 rounds. I don't know how the machine managed to get home – the propeller, wings and engine were shot through, and so badly wrecked, that it had to be 'walked off'.[54]

Pickett crash-landed the aircraft at Abeele aerodrome and Gibson was evacuated for treatment at Number 3 Canadian Casualty Clearing Station, but died two days later of gunshot wounds to his chest and right leg. He was buried in Lijssenthoek Military Cemetery.

The victory over Pickett and Gibson was claimed by *Leutnant* Ernst Hess of *Jasta* 28, who was himself shot down and killed on 23 December 1917 after 17 confirmed and four unconfirmed victories. Born in Wiesbaden on 8 January 1893, he gained his pilot's licence in September 1913. He was awarded both classes of the Iron Cross and the Knight's Cross with Swords.

On the same day, 12 August, Captain Rodric Mathafarn

Ernst Hess

Williams was reported missing. He had been flying an Airco DH.5 single-seater fighter on patrol when it was brought down north of the Houthulst Forest. Born in 1894 in Liverpool to Welsh parents, he attended University College Wales, Aberystwyth, and served in the Officers' Training Corps. He enlisted as a private in the 13th Royal Welsh Fusiliers in October 1914 and was later commissioned. While serving in Egypt with the 2nd Battalion of the Royal Welsh Fusiliers, he was struck down with pyrexia and then haematuria. After a bout of severe diarrhoea he requested a transfer to the Royal Flying Corps and was invalided home in November 1916.

Four days before his death, Williams had attacked two German Albatros scouts and driven one of them down to the ground, out of control.

The circumstances surrounding his death were reported in a Liverpool newspaper:

Dr Richard Williams of Bryn Celyn, Llangoed, Anglesey, ophthalmic surgeon, formerly of Rodney Street, Liverpool, on Friday received from the War Office the following telegram: 'Regret to inform you that Captain R.M. Williams, RFC, reported missing August 12th. This does not necessarily mean that he is wounded or killed. Further news sent when received.'

On Saturday morning, Dr Williams received the following letter from Major T.A. Cairnes, commanding the squadron in which Dr Williams' son Captain R.M. Williams was engaged, dated

13 August, 1917: 'Dear Sir, I very much regret to have to inform you that your son, Captain R.M. Williams is missing. He was on patrol duty yesterday and did not return. From evidence from a ground observer, it is thought he attacked an enemy machine, and was in turn attacked by another, as one of our scouts – type unknown to the observer – was seen going down out of control in the afternoon. I very much fear that this was his machine, as no other was missing about this time, although, of course, it is not certain. As to his fate, I am afraid I can surmise nothing. He may have regained control lower down. He is a very great loss to me and my squadron. He was a thoroughly gallant fellow, and doing extremely well, and was universally liked and respected. I only hope he may be all right. Please accept all our sympathies in your great anxiety.'[55]

It was not until September 1919 that his burial at Veldhoek, north-east of Ypres, was confirmed. Unfortunately, by this time the grave marker had been lost and he is now remembered on the Arras Flying Services Memorial.

The Arras Flying Services Memorial

Williams had taken off from 32 Squadron's aerodrome at Droglandt at 4 p.m. and was last seen at 5.20 p.m. at around 5,000 feet over Houthulst. He was shot down by *Leutnant* Julius Schmidt of *Jasta* 3 – the 11th of his total of 15 victories.

On 14 September, Schmidt shot up the Welsh ace Arthur Rhys Davids' aircraft and forced it to land. Ten days later Schmidt himself was shot down and severely wounded. He recovered and survived the war, dying on 2 July 1944, having been awarded both classes of the Iron Cross, the Knight's Cross with Swords, and other decorations.

On 14 August, Flight Sub-Lieutenant Seisyllt Hugh Lloyd of the Royal Naval Air Service was killed, aged 19, while flying with 10 (Naval) Squadron. He is also commemorated on the Arras Flying Services Memorial. His parents lived in Pumpsaint, Llandeilo, Carmarthenshire. Lloyd had taken off in a Sopwith Triplane on an observation patrol. He was hit by anti-aircraft fire near Zillebeke Lake at 4 p.m. and was last seen heading west under heavy fire.

Julius Schmidt   Seisyllt Lloyd

Allan John Lanman also served with the Royal Naval Air Service. Born in Monmouthshire in October 1874, he joined the Grenadier Guards in September 1897, then transferred to the Royal Engineers shortly afterwards, joining their Balloon Section. He served in the South African War of 1899–1902 and in May 1912 he joined the newly-formed Royal Flying Corps, being posted to 1 Squadron.

In June 1914 he transferred to the Royal Naval Air Service and was a Steersman, part of the crew testing airships at Wormwood Scrubs. On one test flight in August 1914 to Farnborough, the airship developed engine trouble and it was noted:

> Unable to run over 900 revs without severe knocking. Main driving shaft distinctly out of vertical. On cutting out the aft engine, discovered the cause of trouble was in the aft universal joint: impossible to put right without stopping both engines: so stopped aft engine and ran on forward one alone. After Guildford this coupling nearly fired and water had to be poured on to keep it cool. One shot fired at us 1 mile west of Dorking at 8.30 p.m.[56]

HMA 9 airship

Lanman was described as: 'A most excellent officer and is quite invaluable. Great ability to command and a fine sense of discipline.'[57]

He gained his aeronaut certificate and his airship certificate from the Royal Aero Club and flew in the airships HMA *Beta* and HMA *Delta*. Lanman served throughout the war as a training instructor, initially with the rank of Warrant Officer, before being commissioned as Lieutenant on 1 April 1918. He was awarded the OBE in 1927 and died in Reading in 1947.

Second Lieutenant William Harold Trant Williams died of his wounds on 22 August, aged 19. Educated at Liverpool College, his family having moved to Merseyside after leaving their hometown of Corwen in Merionethshire, he then studied medicine at Liverpool University and was in his second year when he joined the Inns of Court Officers' Training Corps and then the Royal Flying Corps. He obtained his wings in June 1917 and was posted to 29 Squadron on the Western Front at the beginning of August.

On 14 August he had crashed and completely wrecked his aircraft on landing, but was unhurt himself. Two days later,

Allan Lanman   William Williams

he left his aerodrome at 6.25 a.m. in a Nieuport 17 and at 6.50 a.m. was seen in combat with two enemy aircraft south of Houthoulst Wood. He was shot down by Manfred von Richthofen and rescued from the wreckage by German troops. Taken to a nearby military hospital as a prisoner of war, he nevertheless died of his injuries six days later and was buried in Harlebeke New British Cemetery.

Second Lieutenant the Honourable Francis Walter Stafford McLaren died at home on 30 August, aged 31, and was buried in St John the Baptist Church cemetery, Busbridge. He was the son of the 1st Baron Aberconway, and had been the MP for Spalding since 1910. McLaren died of internal injuries after a flying accident a mile out at sea from Montrose Airbase, Scotland, flying an Avro with 18 Training Squadron.

A national newspaper carried his obituary:

Second Lieutenant the Hon. Francis W.S. McLaren, RFC, MP for the Spalding Division, met his death while flying at Montrose yesterday morning. He was about a mile out at sea in fine weather at a considerable height when his machine was seen to descend rapidly, almost perpendicularly, and then to right itself again, move along on the level, and circle once or twice. When about 60 ft from the water, it suddenly dived straight down into the sea. Before a rowing boat from the beach reached the spot, two motor fishing boats had arrived, and after some difficulty Mr McLaren, who was unconscious, was removed from the aeroplane. He had received severe internal injuries and was badly hurt in the face, and his death took place just before the boats landed at the harbour. Mr McLaren had been at Montrose since July. A military inquiry into the cause of the accident will be held.

Mr McLaren was the youngest son of Lord Aberconway, and was born in 1886. He was educated at Eton and Balliol, where he took honours in modern history, and afterwards became a member of the Inner Temple. When the war broke out he joined the RNVR [Royal Naval Volunteer Reserves], and went with the armoured cars first to Belgium and later to Gallipoli, where his car took part in an advance and his driver was shot by his side. He accompanied the armoured cars when they were sent to Egypt. He spent some

Francis McLaren

months there, but resigned from the RNVR when there seemed little chance of active service with the armoured cars, and came home and joined the RFC. Before his training was completed at Brooklands, he became seriously ill, and remained so for several months.

At the very time when he had been pronounced well by his doctor, Mr McLaren learned, to his amazement, from a letter from a constituent, that without his knowledge he had been invalided out of the Army. For several months he besieged the War Office until at last he secured reinstatement, and although he was beyond the age when men are usually admitted into the Royal Flying Corps, he was after some delay readmitted and was posted to a flying squadron for training at Montrose. He was nearing the end of the advanced course when his death occurred.

He had represented Spalding in the Liberal interest since January 1910, and while in the House was Parliamentary Secretary to Mr (now Lord) Harcourt when Commissioner of Works and Colonial Secretary. He was a JP for Denbighshire. Mr McLaren married in 1911 Barbara, daughter of Sir Hubert Jekyll, KCMG, and leaves two sons, aged three and two. The news of the death was received with profound regret at Spalding, and flags at the clubs and elsewhere were placed at half-mast. Mr McLaren is the 12th Member of Parliament who has died on service during the war.[58]

Second Lieutenant Thomas Thompson Pritchard died in a flying accident on 30 August and was buried in Llanyre (St Llyr) Church cemetery near Llandrindod Wells. His death was reported as follows:

Clyro Flying Officer Accidentally Killed
It is with regret that we record the death of Lieut. Thomas
Pritchard of the Royal Flying Corps, and nephew of Mrs Reynolds
of Baskerville Arms, Clyro, who was killed while flying at Salisbury
Camp, Wiltshire, on Thursday, 30 August. He was 21 years old.
Lieut. Pritchard joined the Gloucester Hussars as despatch rider
in January 1916 and was given his commission in the Royal Flying
Corps in February last. He only recently commenced flying solo.[59]

Captain Leonard Alfred Hardwick-Terry was killed while
flying on 31 August, aged 21, while serving with 24 Squadron.
He was flying a DH.5 on a practice offensive patrol when his
aircraft lost its wings in a dive and crashed. Hardwick-Terry
was buried in Aveluy Communal Cemetery Extension. Born in
Mumbles, Swansea, he was an only son.

Lieutenant George Guy Barry Downing, from Llanishen,
died on 4 September, aged 23, and was buried in St Isan
Church cemetery, Llanishen, Cardiff. In 1913 he had entered
the Slade School, University College, London, but once the
war began he enlisted in the 9th Welsh Regiment and then
volunteered for the Royal Flying Corps. On 2 September

Leonard Hardwick-Terry's Memorial

1916, he was flying over the German lines when his aircraft was seriously damaged by anti-aircraft fire, and he himself was wounded. He succeeded, however, in driving off two German machines which had also attacked him, and in landing within the French lines. He was invalided home, and while recovering from his wound had a severe attack of diphtheria, but in March 1917 he was certified fit for light duty and acted as an instructor at aerodromes in England. He was then appointed officer in a training school in Scotland, but had only been there a few days before he was killed in a flying accident.

Morgan William Slade was born in 1897. He had attended Shebbear Methodist College in Merthyr Tydfil and was a student teacher before he enlisted in the Royal Flying Corps in August 1915 as an air mechanic. He was then trained as a wireless operator, but after being admitted to hospital with shell shock in September 1917, he was not discharged to duty until April 1918. After the war ended, he became a Methodist minister, but continued to suffer from the after-effects of his shell shock until he died in March 1954.

George Downing   Morgan Slade

It was announced on 22 September that Royal Flying Corps Serjeant J.G. Morris from Dafen, Llanelli, had been awarded the Military Medal.

John Lawrence Hughes, from Swansea, had been studying dentistry before the war, but terminated his studies and joined the Royal West Kent Regiment. In August 1915, he was commissioned as a second lieutenant in the 17th Welsh Regiment and served in France from May 1916. In June 1917 he joined the Royal Flying Corps and trained as an observer, being promoted to the rank of lieutenant and joining 25 Squadron. On 1 October his aircraft, a DH.4 piloted by Second Lieutenant Charles Oliver Rayner, a Canadian, was returning from a bombing raid to Carvin when it was shot down near Burbure and both men were killed. They are buried alongside each other in Lapugnoy Military Cemetery. John Hughes was 25.

Lieutenant Sydney Sutcliffe was killed the following day, 2 October. Aged 24, he was attached to 11 Squadron. He was buried in Cabaret-Rouge British Cemetery, Souchez. Born in Bradford, his family had moved to Llandudno when his father, a well-known entertainer, opened a summer show at the town's Pier Head Pavilion. Before the war, Sydney was a Pierrot in his father's shows.

He had enlisted in the Royal Welsh Fusiliers and was awarded the Military Medal in April 1916 for his bravery during a German gas attack. He then transferred to the Royal Flying Corps and, on the day he died, he was the observer in a Bristol F.2B which took off on a distant offensive patrol at 4.45 p.m., piloted by Second Lieutenant J.M. McKenna. They were seen later in combat with several German aircraft between Douai and Cambrai and were shot down by *Vizefeldwebel* Hans Oberländer of *Jasta* 30 around 6.10 p.m. Both men were killed. They were accorded a full military funeral by the Germans, with several British prisoners of war attending. Photographs of the ceremony were taken and sent to the men's families.

A returning prisoner of war wrote later that Sutcliffe's

Sydney Sutcliffe

aircraft had been attacked by seven German aircraft, driving off four of them before ultimately falling victim to the remaining three aircrafts' machine guns. Oberländer was credited with downing six enemy aircraft in total and was wounded in September 1918 but survived the war.

Second Lieutenant Edward Pugh Lewis from Tregynon near Newtown died on 6 October 1917, aged 20. He was serving with 9 Squadron and on an artillery observation flight when his R.E.8 aircraft was hit by a British shell. It was seen to come down in a spin, lost its tail at 2,500 feet and crashed near the Yser Canal one mile south-west of Pilckem.[60] Lewis and his observer, Lieutenant Hubert Granville Holt MC, aged 23 from Manchester, were both killed. They were buried alongside each other in Mendinghem Military Cemetery.

Air Mechanic 1st Class John Stanley Clarke was born in Wrexham on 31 October 1898. Educated at Tewkesbury Grammar School, he was a clerk employed at Birmingham University. He enlisted in the Army Ordnance Corps in May 1915 as he was still under age for active service. Transferring to the Royal Flying Corps in June 1917, he was made Gunner Observer the following month. He was killed on 10 October, aged 18, when his DH.4 was shot down by *Leutnant* Bongartz of *Jasta* 36 over Westroosebeke. Clarke lies in Harlebeke New British Cemetery. His commanding officer, Major Pattinson, wrote of him: 'I am very sorry to lose him, as he was an excellent gunner, and put up a good fight recently against a number of German machines, shooting one down. He was very popular with all ranks in the squadron.'[61]

Heinrich Bongartz

Heinrich Bongartz was born on 31 January 1892 in Gelsenkirchen. A school teacher before the war, he served as an infantry officer, fighting at Verdun in 1916. He then joined the German Air Service and recorded 33 victories before the war ended. Wounded no fewer than five times, he gained both classes of the Iron Cross, the Knight's Cross with Swords, and the *Pour le Mérite*. On 29 April 1918, he was in a dogfight with aircraft from 74 Squadron when he was hit in the head by a bullet which caused the permanent loss of sight in his left eye. Post-war, he helped supervise the dismantling of the German Air Service and was seriously wounded in the leg during fighting with the Spartacists in Germany. During the Second World War he served as a supply officer on the Eastern Front and later as a night fighter commander. He died on 23 January 1946.

On 12 October, a DH.4 of 57 Squadron took off at 11.45 a.m. on a bombing reconnaissance patrol, going missing east of Roulers. The following month this newspaper report appeared:

> Mrs Pughe-Evans, widow of Mr Pughe-Evans, the Welsh composer, of Redcroft, Sketty Road, Swansea, has received a telegram through a Berne bureau stating that her only son, Second Lieutenant Hubert Pughe-Evans, Royal Flying Corps, who was reported missing on October, 10 [*sic*], is a prisoner of war at Karlsruhe, Germany, and is quite well.[62]

Born in Swansea in 1895, Hubert Pughe-Evans was the

Hubert Pughe-Evans

observer, and the pilot was Second Lieutenant G.W. Armstrong. They had been forced down by *Leutnant* Kieckhäfer of *Jasta* 29 and taken prisoner. Pughe-Evans had been commissioned into the Welsh Regiment on 6 August 1915. His father, David Pughe-Evans, had been a promising composer and singer who had died of illness at the age of 31. Hubert was repatriated on 13 December 1918. He was a civil engineer after the war and served as a pilot in the Second World War.

Fritz Kieckhäfer was born in Berlin in January 1896 and achieved eight victories before he was wounded while attacking an R.E.8 on 4 May 1918. He died of his wounds on 7 June.

On 13 October 1917, Second Lieutenant Thomas Penrose Heald died. He was 25 and the son of George and S.J. Heald, who owned a waste paper company and lived at 181 Cathedral Road in Cardiff. Born in May 1892, by 1911 Heald was in Ulverston with his brother, learning how to make paper. He was a keen motorcyclist and, in October 1914, wrote asking to enlist in the newly-formed Welsh Army Corps as a motorcyclist. The proud owner of a 3.5 h.p. Rudge, he stated that he wanted to do something useful for the war effort. He may have served as 2911 Serjeant Heald in the Royal Engineers, obtaining a commission on 12 August 1917.

He took off for an artillery observation mission in an R.E.8 of 6 Squadron at 6.20 a.m. and was claimed to have been shot down by *Leutnant* Gallwitz of *Jasta* 2 at 6.42 a.m. Heald was killed but the pilot, Flight Serjeant G.W. Halstead, survived.

Thomas Heald was buried in Ypres Reservoir Cemetery. Karl Gallwitz recorded ten victories before being injured in a crash the following year (see page 296).

Lieutenant Alister Douglas Stewart was killed in a flying accident on 13 October, aged 28. His parents lived at Plas Ladwig in Bangor, and he was educated at Colet House in Rhyl and afterwards at Cheltenham College. He then trained for a career in land agency at Cirencester Agricultural College and was employed as the land agent for Little Green and Stansted Estates in Hampshire. In 1914, he was offered a post in the War Land Department and worked there until 1917 when he joined the Royal Flying Corps. He had received great praise from his superior officers.

Whilst flying a machine earlier that year he had had a mishap:

> He will be remembered locally as the pilot of the aeroplane which, during the summer holidays, suddenly developed engine trouble during a flight over Cheltenham. He recognised the playing field of his old college as a possible place for a forced landing, and though he narrowly missed the Junior House and the pinnacles of the College Chapel, he brought it down close to the library, with no worse damage than the breakage of the propeller and the end of one wing.[63]

Stewart left a widow, Dorothy, whom he had married in 1914, and he was buried in Upavon Cemetery. His funeral was attended by his surviving brother; his second brother, Captain Norman Sinclair Stewart of the Royal Scots, having been killed at Hooge near Ypres in September 1915.

A newspaper report of 20 October 1917 carried an account of the fate of a Welsh airman:

> Anxiety is felt as to the fate of Lieutenant Charles Dalkeith Scott, only son of the late Captain Dalkeith Scott, Superintendent of Police at Llanelli. The young officer was in Canada when war broke out, but came to England with the first Canadian contingent,

in the Gordon Highlanders. In that regiment he subsequently obtained a commission, and was twice wounded in France. A few months ago he joined the RFC, and was in a flight over the enemy lines when his companion (Lieutenant Cooke) and he were attacked by ten Gothas. The two Britishers made a brave fight, but were overpowered. Lieutenant Cooke managed to reach the British lines, and, when he had returned, sent scouts out who reported they saw Lieutenant Scott's machine landed behind the German lines. It is presumed he is a prisoner.[64]

Sadly, Scott did not survive the crash. His body was unable to be identified and he is remembered on the Arras Flying Services Memorial. Born in Llanelli in 1889, he was educated at Bath College, where he played for the first rugby XV; then he emigrated to Vancouver Island where he worked as a chauffeur. He enlisted in the 16th Battalion of the Canadian Expeditionary Force and entered France early in 1915. Scott fought at the Second Battle of Ypres and, in January 1916, was commissioned. In October of that year he was wounded and sent home. He learnt to fly in September 1917 and was posted to France once more, before fighting his final battle a few weeks later.

On 21 October, Second Lieutenant Ivor Lee from Newport

shot down a German Albatros fighter between Cambrai and Bullecourt. He had enlisted in the Royal Flying Corps early in 1915 and arrived in France the following November. He flew with 11 and 18 Squadrons as an observer/gunner and received his commission in September 1916. Lee survived the war

Ivor Lee

Photograph of his drawing

and served in a Home Guard anti-aircraft battery during the Second World War.

He later made a sketch of the action.

On 12 November, Captain Idwal Owain Griffith gained his flying certificate after flying an Armstrong-Whitworth biplane at the Armament Experimental Station at Orfordness. Born at Capel Garmon, Llanrwst, Denbighshire, in September 1880, he was educated at Llandovery College and at Balliol College, Oxford, where he read Mathematics followed by Physics. After a distinguished undergraduate career, he was elected to a Fellowship at St John's College, Oxford.

During the First World War, he performed distinguished service in the Royal Flying Corps on the scientific and experimental side, and received the Air Force Cross for his work. His particular contribution was in the field of night flying. When war broke out again in 1939, he worked as Director of Studies in organising technical courses for Royal Air Force cadets.

He married in 1909 and had one son. Idwal Griffith died in Oxford in September 1941.

Second Lieutenant Herbert John Stone, of 19 Squadron, was killed on 15 November, aged 27, and was buried in Bailleul Communal Cemetery Extension. He was originally from Roath Park in Cardiff and was flying a Spad 7 when he crashed on a low level patrol. He was taken to hospital but died of his injuries. A member of the Roath Road Methodist Church, the following tribute was paid to him in the parish magazine:

> We said in a footnote in our last issue that Second Lieutenant
> Herbert John Stone was one of the most brilliant of our 'Roamers.'
> Many of those who knew him best have since confirmed our
> words. Our friend started his Army career in the early days of the
> War as a Private in the 7th (Cyclist) Battalion Welsh Regiment,
> rapidly rose to be Serjeant, then discarded his cycle and won
> his spurs in a mounted Brigade. Did some excellent work as a

Idwal Owain Griffith   Herbert Stone

Signaller, became an Instructor and finally was gazetted to a commission in the Royal Flying Corps. As he said in the latest letter we had from him dated 22 October, 'I have at last got across the water, although it has taken me three years to do it.' A fortnight at the Front, over the enemy lines, and one of the bravest and best of our boys, who had been Teacher as well as Scholar in our School (the 28th 'Roamer') paid the price of his loyalty and devotion with his life, a life that was exceptionally rich in promise.

To us it seemed his life was too soon done,
Ended, indeed, while scarcely yet begun;
God, with His clearer vision, saw that he
Was ready for a larger ministry.[65]

Second Lieutenant George James Howells, who had resided in Lydart, Monmouthshire, died on 23 November, aged 24, while serving with 8 Squadron. He was buried in Cambrai East Military Cemetery. Originally enlisting in the Royal Army Medical Corps, he left after a few months due to 'enlistment under misapprehension'.[66] He joined the Artists Rifles and then volunteered for the Royal Flying Corps.

On 23 November, he was the observer in an Armstrong Whitworth F.K.8 which was being flown by Second Lieutenant William Albert Booth. They had left Mons-en-Chaussée aerodrome at 1.15 p.m. on a bombing mission over Cambrai,

and were engaged in combat by seven German aircraft and shot down south-west of Marcoing by *Vizefeldwebel* Fritz Rumey of *Jasta* 5 – the fifth of his eventual 45 victories.

George Howells

Fritz Rumey

Fritz Rumey was born on 3 March 1891 in Königsberg. He had joined the German Army before the war began and saw service on the Eastern Front in 1914, where he won the Iron Cross Second Class. In August 1915, he volunteered for the Air Service and trained as an observer before qualifying as a pilot the following year. He was awarded the *Pour le Mérite* in July 1918. On 27 September, his Fokker D.VII was damaged during a dogfight and he jumped from the stricken machine. His parachute failed to open and he plunged to his death.

A Welsh airman had a fortunate escape which was reported that month:

> Caerphilly Airman's Adventure
> Captain Elias, son of Mr and Mrs D. Elias, Old Bank House, Caerphilly, is in hospital at Rugby, suffering from concussion. Captain Elias has had some thrilling experiences. While returning from a flight over enemy territory, his squadron was attacked, his observer was wounded, and the machine, owing to the control being shot away, turned turtle. It was, however, righted, and Captain Elias was able to return to the British lines. He was twice hit while in mid-air, and on landing was struck by shrapnel. Captain Elias, who was educated at Lewis' School Pengam, and the Cardiff Intermediate School, was, before enlisting, cashier at the London and Provincial Bank, Bargoed. He played centre forward for the Caerphilly and Bargoed Soccer teams, and is the holder of the local golf championship.[67]

Ivor Glyn Elias was born in September 1891 and had served as an officer with the Royal Welsh Fusiliers and the Royal Field Artillery before joining the Royal Flying Corps in May 1917. His aircraft crashed badly in an emplacement near the front lines. He was badly shaken but he and his wounded observer, P. Hammond, survived their ordeal. Elias died in 1970.

Second Lieutenant James Graham Glendinning died on 2 December, aged 20. He was serving as an observer with 57 Squadron. He and his pilot, Second Lieutenant John Turton Orrell, had taken off from Sainte-Marie-Cappel aerodrome at 10.10 a.m. in a DH.4 on a bombing and photographic patrol.

Born in Abergavenny on 20 March 1897, Glendinning was educated at Abergavenny Grammar School and Epsom College, where he was captain of the rugby team and a prize-winning athlete. Glendinning had joined the Oxfordshire and Buckinghamshire Light Infantry as a private, before gaining a commission in the 3rd Battalion of the Monmouthshire Regiment in April 1916. He then served with the 6th Cheshire Regiment in France for six months before transferring to the

Royal Flying Corps in 1917.

They were shot down at 11.05 a.m. north-east of Moorslede by *Leutnant* Bongartz of *Jasta* 36 (see page 133). Orrell was also killed and both men lie in Harlebeke New British Cemetery.

James Glendinning

Second Lieutenant Wilfrid Bevan from Gowerton near Swansea was killed on 3 December, aged 20, while serving with 20 Squadron. He is commemorated on the Arras Flying Services Memorial. Bevan was the pilot of a Bristol F.2B which left its aerodrome at 11.25 a.m. on a northern offensive patrol. It was last seen north of Hollebeke at 12.10 p.m. in combat with German aircraft. Neither Bevan nor his observer, Lieutenant Francis Beresford Gloster, were seen alive again.

Air Mechanic 2nd Class William Henry Roberts, 36, died the same day in a flying accident while serving with 59 Squadron as a pilot, and was buried in Grand Ravine British Cemetery, Havrincourt. His father was a minister of religion in Cardiff, and William and his late wife had resided in Aberdare.

On 12 December, Captain Richard Henry Probyn Miers of 31 Training Squadron was killed. He was buried in St Margaret and All Saints Church cemetery in Wyton, Cambridgeshire. His death was reported thus:

Clydach Airman Fatally Injured in a Flying Accident
Mr Henry N. Miers, JP, Ynyspenllwch, Clydach, received a wire on Wednesday night conveying the news that his eldest son, Capt. R.H.P. Miers, Royal Flying Corps, had met with an accident that had terminated fatally. The deceased joined up at the outbreak of war, and was sent to Egypt, where he did some excellent work, being mentioned in dispatches and being promoted from lieutenant to major, his regiment being the Glamorgan Yeomanry. He relinquished this post in order to join the RFC as captain. He fought in the South African War as a trooper. He was over military age, and prior to the war he was a civil and mining engineer and estate agent. He was also a JP for the county of Glamorgan. He leaves a widow and three children.[68]

An unusual recruit to the Royal Flying Corps was announced that month: 'Sky pilots is a term sometimes applied to clergymen and ministers. The Rev. J. Pugh Jones, curate of a

Highgate Church, is determined to earn it in a literal sense, for he has joined the Royal Flying Corps to train as a pilot.'[69] Jones survived the war to take up a post as Pastor to a Welsh church in Minnesota, USA.

Thomas Morgan Evans of Tir Gwilym Farm, Pencoed, Bridgend, had been a collier in the Heol-y-Cyw area before the war and possibly served in a mines' rescue team. He enlisted at the start of the war in the Royal Munster Fusiliers before transferring to the Royal Engineers, where he gained a commission after serving with a railway unit. He was wounded during the fighting at Mametz Wood in July 1916, and, after recovering, commanded a tunnelling company during the Battle of Messines in 1917. He joined the Royal Flying Corps later that year and was injured in a crash on Christmas Day while attached to 82 Squadron, flying an Armstrong Whitworth F.K.8. Evans survived the war only to die from tuberculosis in the 1930s.

Thomas Morgan Evans

Christmas Card drawn by Thomas Morgan Evans

WALES AND THE FIRST AIR WAR 1914–1918

At the end of the year it was reported that a Welsh airman had achieved a notable feat:

> The distinction of having been the first British airman to cross the Austro-German lines on the Italian front is claimed to belong to Lieut. W.J. Hamilton Morgan, RFC. He is the eldest son of Alderman Morgan W. Morgan, High Sheriff of Breconshire, and Mrs Morgan, of Abercrave, Swansea Valley. He has flown in Egypt and France, and was transferred to Italy a few days after the great Austro-German offensive. He has only just attained his majority. He was educated at Christ College, Brecon.[70]

Lieutenant Arthur Lewis Jenkins was killed in a flying accident at Helperby, Yorkshire, on 31 December and was laid to rest in Richmond Cemetery. His father was Sir John Lewis Jenkins from Llangadock. Jenkins was born in 1892 and was educated at Marlborough College where he gained a scholarship to study Classics at Balliol College, Oxford. His death was reported in a local newspaper:

Welsh Airman Killed
The death occurred on Sunday night, while flying in Yorkshire, of Lieut. Arthur Lewis Jenkins, brother-in-law of Mr W. Llewellyn

Williams, KC, MP. Deceased was a son of the late Sir J. Lewis Jenkins, and was only 25 years of age. He was a clever writer of verse. Whilst doing night patrol work, something went wrong with the engine, and the machine crashed to the ground, and the airman was instantaneously killed. He had seen service in India, Mesopotamia, Aden and Egypt. He was one of the best boxers and footballers at Oxford University. His

Arthur Jenkins
(Reproduced by kind permission of Marlborough College)

144

latest published verses were entitled 'The Inn of the Sword', a song of youth and war, and appeared in *Punch* some time ago.[71]

His sister Elinor was also a published poet, and died in 1920, aged 26.

At 10.30 a.m. on 31 December, the troopship *Osmanieh* struck a mine laid by German U-boat UC-34 in the entrance to Alexandria Harbour, Egypt. Her commanding officer, Lieutenant Commander David Mason, Royal Naval Reserve, along with two other officers, 21 crew, an army officer, 166 other ranks and 8 nurses were killed. Built in 1906 by Swan Hunter and Wigam Richardson of Wallsend for the Khedival Mail Steamship Company, the *Osmanieh* was taken over by the Admiralty in May 1916 and commissioned as a 'Fleet Messenger'. The ship was bringing over 1,000 personnel to Egypt.

Among those killed in the sinking were five Welsh airmen. Air Mechanics 3rd Class Richard David Browne and William Cartwright were attached to 55 Kite Balloon Section. Their bodies were never identified and they are commemorated on the Chatby Memorial in Alexandria. Browne was 33 and had lived in Dolgellau, Merionethshire, with his wife, Madge.

The *Osmanieh*

Cartwright was 31 and was a resident of Wrexham, where he lived with his wife, Edith, in Saxon Street.

The bodies of Air Mechanics 3rd Class E.W. Jackson, J. Rees and R.J. Williams were found and were buried in Hadra War Cemetery, Alexandria. Jackson, 29, had lived with his wife in the same house in Saxon Street in Wrexham as William Cartwright. Rees was 36, and his next of kin was his sister who lived in Porth, Rhondda. Williams was 26, and his parents lived in Bethel, Caernarvonshire.

CHAPTER FOUR

1918

'Below twenty, boys are too rash for flying.
Above twenty-five they are too prudent.'

W.J. Abbott

THE FINAL YEAR of the war was to see victory for the Allies and
an armistice being declared on 11 November. It was also to see
the fiercest fighting of the war, with more casualties occurring
than in any other year. In March, the Germans launched their
spring offensive, which saw them break through the Allied
lines before it was halted. The Allies later launched their own
offensive and, in 100 days, drove the Germans back and forced
them to surrender.

At the start of the final year of the war it was announced
that Charles Alexander Holcombe Longcroft had been
awarded the Distinguished Service Order. Born in Llanarth,
Cardiganshire, on 13 May 1883, he had attended Sandhurst
and been commissioned into the Welsh Regiment. He learnt
to fly in 1912, and requested a transfer to the Air Battalion
of the Royal Engineers, later the Royal Flying Corps. By 1914
Longcroft was in command of 1 Squadron and finished the
war as General Officer Commanding 3 Brigade. He retired
from the Royal Air Force in November 1929 and was knighted
in 1938. Air Vice-Marshal Sir Charles Alexander Holcombe
Longcroft died in London in 1958.

Charles Sandford Wynne-Eyton was gazetted the
Distinguished Service Order on 1 January 1918 while serving

Charles Longcroft

Charles Wynne-Eyton

with 2 Squadron. Born in 1889 in Mold, he was serving as a second lieutenant with the Royal Field Artillery when he gained his flying certificate on 9 August 1915 at Hendon.

After the war ended, he remained in the Royal Air Force and made an unsuccessful attempt to fly solo across the Atlantic in 1930.

He served as a wing commander during the Second World War, gaining the Air Force Cross in June 1944. Believed to be the oldest operating pilot in the Royal Air Force in the Second World War, he was killed on 14 November 1944 when the Liberator II he was piloting on a flight from the Middle East to Lyneham, crashed into a mountain near Autun, France, in a snowstorm.

Charles Wynne-Eyton was buried in Choloy War Cemetery, France.

The first Welsh flying casualty of the last year of the war was Flight Lieutenant William Basil Loxdale Jones of the Royal Naval Air Service, who was killed, aged 28, on 7 January. He was the son of the late Bishop of St Davids, the Right Reverend William Basil Jones, and was a graduate of Keble College, Oxford. He had volunteered for service in September 1914,

William Jones

obtained a commission in the Royal Marine Light Infantry and saw service in France. He was described as 'of very poor physique, and almost deformed, he would never have been passed for military service; he was transported and wounded on the Western Front in his own car at his own expense.'[1]

In May 1915, he became an observer in the Royal Naval Air Service, and in August he was posted to Gallipoli. Here he was mentioned in dispatches. In March 1917, he saw service in Italy and was again mentioned in dispatches. On 7 January, his aircraft came down in the sea while on a photographic patrol near Saseno Island. The aircraft's engine had failed and the machine crashed into the Adriatic. His body was not recovered and he is commemorated on the Chatham Naval Memorial.

Lieutenant Azariah Phillips, who died on 12 January aged 19, was buried in Trawsfynydd's Penycefn cemetery. His parents resided in Blaenau Ffestiniog. On 18 January an inquest was held in Salisbury into the circumstances surrounding his death.

As the result of an unusual accident near the Old Sarum Aerodrome on Friday morning, serious injuries were sustained by Second Lieutenant Azariah Phillips, from which he died in the Infirmary the next day. The circumstances were related to the City Coroner (Mr A.M. Wilson) at the inquest on Monday evening.

Mr T.G. Sturgess was chosen foreman of the jury.

Lieutenant Etienne Bruno Hamel, of the Royal Flying Corps, said that Second Lieutenant Phillips was attached to the same squadron as he was at Old Sarum Aerodrome. He was 19 years of age, and had only been with them about a week. He was learning to fly, and on Friday morning at 9.25 he went up in a machine with Lieutenant Whitcut as pilot. Witness saw them go up. They started off in the usual manner, riding to a sufficient height to clear the buildings. Then the propeller appeared to strike a pole which was about 48 feet high, and the machine turned on its back and fell to the ground. He helped to extricate Lieutenant Phillips from the wreckage. The pole was used for testing the weather and had been fixed for about a month.

Answering the Foreman, witness said the machine went straight for the pole and struck it before it had circled at all. The engine cut off the pilot's line of sight, being in front of him as he rose, and he could not see the pole.

A Juryman: Could there not be something on the pole which airmen could see?

Witness: That is not for me to say. It might be improved, I suppose.

Lieutenant D.V.D. Marshall, ASC, acting Flight Commander, attached to the RFC, said that at nine o'clock on Friday morning he flew the same machine which Mr Phillips subsequently used and found it in perfect flying order. He landed at about 9.15 and ordered Lieutenant Whitcut to take up Mr Phillips for instruction. He watched them start. They took off slightly across wind and got sufficient height to clear the buildings. Then they came into collision with the pole. This was a hollow steel tube painted red and white but it was rather difficult to see. The machine crashed to the ground, and both Mr Phillips and the instructor were badly hurt.

A Juryman: Could not the pole be shifted to another place?

Witness: I can't tell you. That is a matter for the RE [Royal Engineers] Office.

Captain A.P. Woolwright, RAMC, said he attended both officers immediately after the accident. Mr Phillips had a compound fracture of the right thigh, a simple fracture of the left thigh, and dislocation of the left shoulder. He sent him to the Infirmary.

Mr Shebsell Yahilevitz, house surgeon, said the patient was admitted at 10.15 on Friday morning. He described the injuries and said he was suffering from haemorrhage and shock. A preliminary anaesthetic was administered with a view to controlling the haemorrhage, purifying the wound and correcting the dislocation. Later, when the shock had considerably passed off, loose fragments of bone were removed. Apart from two short periods of embarrassed respiration, the patient was fairly comfortable till Saturday evening, when witness was called and found him with distressed respiration and obviously dying. He expired at 6.30 p.m. The cause of death was respiratory cardiac failure, induced by fat embolism.

The Coroner said that that was all the evidence he could call at present, but it was very necessary that the pilot should be called because he was the only one who could give a satisfactory account of what had happened. The inquest would be adjourned till Monday next at 6 p.m. at the Council Chamber, when the doctor expected Lieutenant Whitcut would be well enough to attend.

Adjourned Inquest 1918 January 25th

The adjourned inquest on Second Lieutenant Azariah Phillips, who was killed in an aviation accident at Old Sarum, was concluded on Monday evening in the Council Chamber, when a verdict of 'Accidental Death' was returned.

The pilot of the machine who was flying with the officer who was killed, Lieutenant H.M. Whitcut, of the 5th South Staffs, attached to the RFC, who was injured, gave his version of the fatality.

On Friday, January 11th, he was ordered by Lieutenant Marshall to take out Lieutenant Phillips between half past nine and ten for instruction. They took off against the wind and saw they had plenty of room to clear the buildings. He was flying along and the next thing he remembered was that he was on the ground endeavouring to get Phillips out of the machine. His conclusion was that the machine hit the tall weather pole somewhere in the under-carriage of the machine.

The Coroner: When you took off, did you see the pole?

Witness: I could not see it at all. If I had I should have known what to do. He added that in the aeroplane he would be in the back seat and could see directly to the right or left, but could not see straight ahead.

You knew where the pole was?

I knew there was a pole up, but I didn't know anything about it. It is quite a recent introduction.

How long have you been here?

I arrived there on 16 November.

You have flown since then?

I have flown about 60 or 70 hours.

The pole was about 48 feet high?

I should think it was about that.

It is a wind gauge?

I am not sure. To the best of my knowledge it is for registering the speed of the wind, but I could not say whether that is correct.

You have flown since the pole has been up?

Oh, yes.

The Foreman: Have you been advised by your superiors that there was any danger from the pole previous to your going up?

The witness replied in the negative.[2]

Second Lieutenant Albert Payne, Royal Flying Corps of Travis Street, Barry Docks, also met with a fatal accident on Sunday, 13 January, when making a trial flight from Hendon (where he was stationed) to Ipswich. After emigrating to Canada before the war, he had enlisted in the Canadian Expeditionary Force. Payne had arrived in France two years earlier, but was wounded and discharged, and stationed at the head offices of the Canadian government in London. There he saw a recruiting poster for the Royal Flying Corps and subsequently enlisted. He had a brother, Serjeant W.J. Payne, who was serving with the Army Service Corps, and two brothers-in-law serving, each of whom had been mentioned in dispatches and granted the Meritorious Service Medal.

Albert Payne (front of aircraft)

The full story of the accident was told at the

inquest in Hendon on the body of Payne and Francis Harry Varney Vise, aged 22, the pilot. A Captain Sevinbright said that Vise was an experienced pilot, although he was flying a machine that he had never flown before. He had, however, flown one which was very similar, and the slight differences were pointed out to him before the flight. Witnesses learnt that the two men reached an altitude of 1,500 ft and then descended to about around 1,000 ft. He believed that the machine stalled on the turn. The climate conditions were not against flying.

Captain Clear of the Manchester Regiment, attached to the School of Instruction, said that he saw most of the flight. The machine took off steeply and, when 100 ft up, it made a turn and flew at a height of 800 ft. It then made a left hand turn, got into a spin and fell. The petrol tank burst and caught alight through the machine striking the ground and not in the course of descent. He could not account for the accident. It was stated that the engine was examined before the machine left the ground and was perfectly satisfactory.

On 25 January, Albert Payne's funeral took place at Barry's Merthyr Dyfan Cemetery. Eight officers, about 40 men from the Lancashire Fusiliers and about 50 officers and men from the Royal Flying Corps attended. The body was conveyed on a carriage and covered by the Union Flag and a wealth of floral tributes from comrades and friends. Among the numerous wreaths was one from the officers of the School of Instruction, Hendon.

On 15 January, a newspaper carried an account of a wounded Welsh airman:

Wounded Air Mechanic T.M. Preece, wireless operator in the RFC, has been brought to the military hospital, Exeter. Previous to joining he was a medical student at the University College, Cardiff, and he had been overseas nearly eighteen months. He is the son of Mr J. Preece, Maesyrhaf, Porth.[3]

Preece recovered from his wounds and survived the war.

T.J. Keane

It was announced on 18 January that Corporal T.J. Keane of Llanbadarn in Radnorshire had been awarded the Meritorious Service Medal. Before enlisting in the Royal Flying Corps he had worked in a post office.

Second Lieutenant Robert Clifford Lovell was killed on 26 January. He was 26 and serving with 101 Squadron. His parents lived in Newport and their son was buried in Hazebrouck Communal Cemetery. He and his observer, Lieutenant Seaforth William McKenzie from New Zealand, had taken off in their F.E.2b from Clairmarais at 11.00 p.m. on 25 January on a mission to bomb German airfields, but the weather soon closed in, reducing visibility to virtually zero. When their aircraft failed to return they were listed as missing, though it was later discovered their aircraft had crashed behind the lines at Le Nieppe, killing them both.

On 1 February, Air Mechanic 2nd Class George Chappel Willicott died of natural causes and was buried in Cathays Cemetery in Cardiff. Aged 35, he served with 45 Squadron and had lived with his wife Gertrude in Roath, Cardiff.

Another air mechanic also died of natural causes a week later, aged 25. Daniel Edwin Evans was buried in Reading Cemetery. He was from Llanrhystud, Aberystwyth, Cardiganshire.

Second Lieutenant Ernest Victor Edwards, 29, died on 16 February while flying. He was buried in Ismailia War Memorial Cemetery in Egypt. Born on 2 July 1889 in Pembroke, he was educated at the High School, Middlesbrough, and the County School, Pembroke Dock. On leaving school he entered the

Seaforth McKenzie

Robert Lovell

Civil Service and was then employed by the Avon Rubber Company in London. He joined the 3rd County of London Yeomanry in April 1908, and served for five years before joining the Army Reserve. He was called up when war broke out in August 1914 and served at Gallipoli. He landed at Suvla Bay in August 1915 and, on being wounded, was invalided to Egypt. After recovering he rejoined his regiment and went with them to Salonika and then to Palestine. He transferred to the Royal Flying Corps and was gazetted second lieutenant on 10 February 1918. Edwards died in a flying accident and his Commanding Officer and Adjutant wrote of him: 'I never saw anyone with more backbone; a true Britisher and much loved.' A Cadet noted: 'To live with him was to come under the influence of an exceptional strength of character and a capacity for cheerfulness as amazing as ever present, combined with a wonderful personality.'[4]

Lieutenant Arthur Cuhelyn Morris, 23, died the following day, while serving with 18 Squadron. He was buried in Aire Communal Cemetery in France. The son of a church minister, he had enlisted in the 19th Royal Welsh Fusiliers before joining the Royal Flying Corps. He was the observer in a DH.4 piloted by Second Lieutenant F. Jones on a bombing raid on Ascq when he was shot through the head by an enemy pilot. Second Lieutenant Jones survived and returned the aircraft to base.

Lieutenant William Joseph Brown fell on 21 February, aged 29. He died in Egypt in a flying accident and was buried in Cairo War Memorial Cemetery. He was from Llanelli and had served in the 1st County of London Yeomanry.

On 15 March, Air Mechanic 2nd Class Rhys Robert Humphreys, 20, of 35 Training Squadron, died of natural causes and was buried in Nazareth Calvinist Methodist Chapel cemetery in Penrhyndeudraeth, Merionethshire. He was the son of John Evan and Elizabeth Humprheys of Isallt, Llanbedr.

Second Lieutenant Walter George Cotterill-Jones had learned to fly at Hendon in 1916. Born in Caersws in February 1879, he served as a serjeant with the Northamptonshire Yeomanry before joining the Royal Flying Corps. He set off for a local flight from Andover Aerodrome on 17 March while serving with 105 Squadron, but crashed. Pulled from the wreckage, he died at Rombridge Farm, Penton, and is buried in St Ives Public Cemetery, Huntingdonshire.

Lieutenant Edward Trevor Akrill-Jones, aged 19, was killed in a flying accident on 18 March while training with 88 Squadron, and was buried in St Mary Old Church cemetery, Bolsover. He was taking off in an S.E.5a when it swung and crashed. His father was a church minister in Porthcawl and his brother, Second Lieutenant Robert

Walter Cotterill-Jones

Rowland, was killed while serving with the 9th King's Own Yorkshire Light Infantry on 9 April 1917. A tribute to Edward appeared in his old school magazine:

EDWARD TREVOR AKRILL-JONES: School House, 1910–15; second son of the Rev. D. Akrill-Jones (O.B.), of Bolsover Vicarage, near Derby, Lieut. (Notts and Derby) Sherwood Foresters, attached RFC. He was wounded near Thiepval in 1916 and since his recovery had been training with the RFC. Quite recently he had received his pilot's 'wings', and on Monday, March 18th, met his death from an accident while flying in Norfolk. So the war takes toll of our best and most beloved. It was one bright spring term, less than ten years ago, he came to Brecon, a very small boy with a big head and large wondering eyes. He was christened 'The Babe' and continued to be called so long after the title had become obviously inappropriate. A singularly good looking, happy, sturdy, charming boy he grew up; sound in all his ways, thoughtful and painstaking in School, a keen member of all three teams, above all a loyal friend. His close friendships were indeed proverbial and they endured to the end. In the middle of 1914 he was contemplating taking up Modern History with a view to trying his luck at a 'Varsity Scholarship'; but the war changed all that. He was only sixteen, but nothing would keep him quiet at School. He couldn't bear to think that he was out of it, while two of his dearest friends had just joined up. He was determined also to be in it as a volunteer and not as a conscript. So barely seventeen, he left in the summer of 1915, chucking up in the middle a promising cricket season in which he was likely to make many runs, and joining the Inns of Court. He found his way out to France in time to take part in the latter stages of the Somme Push and was wounded in one of the unsuccessful attacks on Thiepval. He was still so young that he was not sent out again on his recovery, and so turned his attention to flying, and in acquiring this art he spent the rest of his all too short life. 'Akrill,' surnamed 'The Babe,' remained a child at heart always. Death has but conferred on him an immortality of youth.[5]

Also on 18 March, the announcement was made of a gallantry award to a Welsh officer:

A special supplement to the *London Gazette* issued on Saturday announced that among other honours the King has approved, the award of a bar to the Distinguished Service Order to Squadron-Commander Edwin Rowland Moon, DSO, RNAS for 'resource and gallantry' displayed by him in the following circumstances: 'On January 6, 1917, whilst on a reconnaissance flight over the Rufiji Delta [nowadays Tanzania], with Commander the Hon. Richard O.B. Bridgeman, DSO, R.N., as observer, he was obliged by engine trouble to descend in one of the creeks, where it became necessary to destroy the seaplane to avoid the possibility of its being captured. For three whole days the two officers wandered about the delta in their efforts to avoid capture and to rejoin their ship. During this time they had little or nothing to eat, and were continually obliged to swim across the creeks, the bush on the banks being impenetrable. On the morning of January 7 they constructed a raft of three spars and some latticed window-frames. Alter paddling and drifting on this for the whole of January 7 and 8, they were finally carried out to sea on the morning of the 9th, when Commander Bridgeman, who was not a strong swimmer, died of exhaustion and exposure. In the late afternoon Flight-Commander Moon managed to reach the shore, and was taken prison by the Germans. He was released from captivity on November 21, 1917. He displayed the greatest gallantry in attempting to save the life of his companion.'

Squadron-Commander Moon, whose splendid deed is thus singularly recognised, is well-known in South Wales business circles as secretary and a director of the Southern Equitable Advance Company (Limited), of 1 Edward's Terrace, Cardiff, and 11 Charles Street, Newport. He has only recently arrived back in this country after his series of remarkable adventures in German East Africa, having been released from the captivity of the German forces by our victorious troops towards the latter part last year.

The Royal Humane Society have awarded the commander their silver medal for his gallant, but ineffectual, effort to save the life of his observer, who was the second son of the fourth Earl of Bradford, whose elder brother, Viscount Newport, married a daughter of Lord Aberdare.[6]

Born in Southampton in June 1886, his family owned a boat-building business. Moon designed, built and flew the first aircraft to take off from Southampton Airport. He survived the war but was killed on 29 April 1920 while piloting a flying boat. An inquest was subsequently held:

The Felixstowe Coroner on Saturday held an Inquiry into the deaths of Major Edwin Roland Moon, aged 34, married, a Squadron Leader in the RAF and Lieut. Albert John Fyfield, aged 24, a Flying Officer, who were found dead under the wreckage of the flying boat which crashed into the water off Felixstowe on Thursday. The machine was out for practice purposes when the accident occurred and four of the crew of six were drowned. Medical evidence as to the cause of death having been given, Lieutenant Packenham Walsh, one of the saved, gave an account of the flight from leaving the slipway.

'After about an hour' he said 'and at two thousand feet up Major Moon took control from me, as he wished to do a glide. When about fifteen hundred feet up the machine received a bump on the tail.'

The Coroner – 'What caused that?'

Witness – 'I do not know. Such things do happen in the air. It threw the machine out of control and developed into a spin. Major Moon then did all he could to right the machine but the distance from the water was not sufficient to allow of a complete recovery. The machine stuck the water on a fairly natural keel.'

Lieut. Walsh expressed the opinion that if they had another hundred or two hundred feet Major Moon would have got out of the difficulty alright.

The Coroner – 'Do you have any recollection of what happened when she did strike the water?'

Witness said 'the machine absolutely collapsed. It was impossible to do anything as the boat was upside-down.' The witness went under and when he came up he did not see anybody else at that time.

The Coroner remarked that there appeared to be nothing wrong with either the machine or the piloting and he recorded a verdict of 'Death from injuries received through the sudden accidental fall of a flying boat.'[7]

Edwin Moon
(Courtesy of the estate of Peter T. New)

Moon had first been awarded the Distinguished Service Order in June 1917. The citation read: 'Since April 1916, has carried out constant flights over the enemy's coast, including reconnaissances, bomb-dropping and spotting for gun fire in all weathers. Has shown great coolness and resource on all occasions.'[8]

He was buried in Southampton Old Cemetery with a wooden marker which is apparently part of the propeller of the aircraft in which he died.

Cadet Glynne Thomas Jones died on 19 March while serving with the 1st Cadet Wing. He was buried in Abercynon Cemetery in his home town. His death was reported thus:

Cadet Glynne Jones, RAF, son of Mr and Mrs J.T. Jones, Lynwood, Abercynon, late of Mountain Ash, has died in hospital and was buried during the week-end at Abercynon. He was a Llandovery College boy, where he spent several years. He played for the first Rugby team for two seasons, and when sixteen years of age took first in the high jump. He joined the No.1 RFC as soon as he was eighteen, and had finished his training for a commission when he collapsed and died after a double operation at St John's Military Hospital, Hastings last week. Since last August, until he joined up, he had been on the staff of Dr Walford, medical officer of health for Cardiff. Last January he passed the London matriculation examination.[9]

On 20 March, Able Seaman G.H.G. Walker of the Royal Naval Air Service died, aged 19. He was attached to HMS *Daedalus*, a shore airfield. His mother lived in Pontnewydd and he was buried in Holy Trinity Church cemetery in the town.

Second Lieutenant Charles Jenkins died on 21 March, aged 21, and was buried in Haverfordwest's St Mary's Church cemetery. He was a native of the town and educated at Haverfordwest Grammar School and then at the London Wireless College. He is also remembered in a small stained glass window in the church's porch.

After serving for some time with the Royal Engineers on the Western Front, in early 1917 Jenkins joined the Royal Flying Corps and trained at Winchester and Oxford. In November 1917, he gained his commission, and his 'wings' were awarded in early 1918. He was killed at Upavon whilst practising aerobatics in his Sopwith Camel. He dived steeply at about 880 feet, but never came out of the dive. His Squadron Leader wrote: 'Had your son lived he would have made an extraordinary successful service pilot.'[10]

Serjeant James Ryan was killed on 23 March, aged 29, while flying a D.H.4 on a bombing raid on Mannheim. He was serving with 55 Squadron and was buried in Charmes Military Cemetery, Essegney, France. He left a widow, Jennie, in Canton, Cardiff.

Airco DH.4

Captain Alyn Reginald James of Gresford in Denbighshire, aged 23, of 62 Squadron was the pilot of a Bristol F.2B which took off at 4.20 p.m. on 24 March on a trench strafing mission from Péronne to Ham. He and his observer, Lieutenant John Mathews Hay, never returned. Both men are commemorated on the Arras Flying Services Memorial. James and Hay had previously downed two German aircraft.

James trained as a pilot in Gloucestershire in 1917 and flew to France in January, but during the crossing his engine failed and he was forced to land in the English Channel. He was rescued and continued his journey to the Western Front. On 13 March, he took off with Hay in a F.2B for an offensive patrol in the Cambrai sector. He left this account of what happened:

Whilst on offensive patrol, we joined in an attack on a large formation of enemy aircraft (30 or 40 machines) and in the fighting that followed two enemy aircraft got in a position underneath our tail. I was instructed by my observer to turn to the left and he was able to get a burst of twenty rounds into one of the machines. The machine was observed to turn on its back and dive vertically and, although it was kept in sight for several thousand

feet, I did not see it right itself, and it appeared to me and my observer to be quite out of control.[11]

His second victory occurred two days later:

Whilst on offensive patrol between Cambrai and Le Catelet, we attacked a formation of seven enemy aircraft 6,000 feet below us. In the course of the fighting,

Alyn James

I followed a machine round in a circle in such a position that my observer was able to fire a burst of about 30 rounds into it. The machine went down in a vertical nosedive and disappeared in the clouds below. This machine was also seen to go down out of control by Second Lieutenant Staton and Lieutenant Gordon. Afterwards, I dived on another machine, firing a burst of about 50 rounds, and the enemy aircraft went down in a spin.[12]

Also commemorated on the same memorial and who also died on 24 March was Second Lieutenant William Knox, aged 25, of 54 Squadron. Knox was born in Glenbuck, a mining village in Ayrshire, in 1893. The family moved to Wales when his father became the first principal of the South Wales and Monmouthshire School of Mines. William enrolled as a student, and the family lived in Radyr. He was the president of the rugby team of the School of Mines. In 1917, he trained as a pilot and was posted to 54 Squadron in France in early 1918. On 24 March, he took off at 5 p.m. on an observation patrol in a Sopwith Camel and was last seen two miles south-west of Péronne at 1,500 feet.

On 27 March, Lieutenant Edmund Sydney Howells, 19, died. He was buried in Milford Haven Cemetery. His father was the Canon of Milford Haven. Howells was acting as a flying instructor and was killed in an accident in an Armstrong Whitworth F.K.3 of 120 Squadron piloted by Second Lieutenant J. Armstrong which fell from 700 feet and crashed. Educated at the King's School, Worcester, Howells was on his way to study at Oxford when the war broke out. He was commissioned into the Welsh Regiment and served in France, being wounded in 1916. On recovering, he returned to his regiment and was transferred to the Royal Flying Corps. He served for some time in Egypt before being recalled to act as an instructor at home in 1917.

Lieutenant Sidney Collier was killed on 28 March, aged 22. His father was a minster of religion in Llandudno Junction. He was buried in La Chaudière Military Cemetery, Vimy.

Sidney Collier

Formerly with the 6th Manchester Regiment, he had been awarded the Military Cross in February 1916. Serving with 5 Squadron, he was the observer in an R.E.8 which was being flown by Second Lieutenant R. Parkhouse which left their aerodrome at 9.40 a.m. on an aerial patrol. They were flying over Méricourt when they were attacked by five German aircraft. Canadian troops of the 43rd Battalion fired on the enemy, bringing one to the ground. They also witnessed the R.E.8 being shot down. Both crewmen were killed.

*

The Royal Air Force came into being on 1 April 1918 with the amalgamation of the Royal Flying Corps and the Royal Naval Air Service. In addition, the Women's Royal Air Force was created on the same day. Volunteers over 18 years of age from the Women's Auxiliary Army Corps, Women's Royal Naval Service, Voluntary Aid Detachment and the Women's Legion were invited to join the new service, subject to a medical examination and a satisfactory reference.

There were to be two classes of member: mobile or immobile. The mobiles lived in quarters on or near the base and were subject to postings. Immobiles lived at home and worked at their nearest base. Work was divided into four categories: clerks and typists; household duties (cooks, waitresses and domestic work); technical, such as tinsmiths, photographers, wireless

Women of the WRAF

operators and carpenters; and non-technical (tailoring work, shoemakers and motor cyclists).

The recruiting information stated:

> At this moment the call for the new Service must go out to women with special appeal. The Royal Air Force, on which so much that is vital depends, offers new spheres of labour to women, and those who direct it look to the women for immediate, ungrudging cooperation and support.[13]

The service was to be known as 'The Penguins', because women were not to be trained as pilots. Their role was to release men from ground-based duties to train as pilots and observers. In 1920 the service was disbanded.

The Honourable Violet Douglas-Pennant, whose father played a prominent role in the Welsh slate industry as the owner of Penrhyn Quarry in north Wales, was appointed as the Commandant of the Women's Royal Air Force. Born in January 1869, she worked in social reform and management before being appointed to the Women's Royal Air Force. She quickly found that for 14,000 Women's Royal Air Force personnel, there were merely 70 officers. There were equipment shortages,

Recruiting Poster

including uniforms and medical supplies, and poor quality accommodation. Her own office and working conditions were basic, and she was so unhappy at the 'rife immorality'[14] within the 500 Women's Royal Air Force camps that she tried several times to resign her position before eventually being dismissed on 28 August 1918. A Select Committee was set up to investigate her claims and it found no evidence to support her accusations. She was later sued for libel by two senior Women's Royal Air Force officers for comments she had made, and she was never again employed by the government, spending the remainder of her life fighting to clear her name until her death in October 1945.

Annie Maria Whyte, from Mill Road, Ely, Cardiff, enlisted in the Women's Army Auxiliary Corps on 7 December 1917, aged 24, while living at Eaton Terrace, Knightsbridge, London. She worked as a waitress at a hostel in Uxbridge until 17 January 1918 when she transferred to the Armament School of the Royal Flying Corps. On 1 April she joined the Women's Royal Air Force and worked as a forewoman waitress until the end of the war.

Violet Douglas-Pennant   Annie Whyte

It was not long before the first Welsh airman of the new service met his end. Lieutenant Evan Davies Jones was killed in action on 2 April, aged 25, while attached to 10 Squadron. He was the youngest son of Sir Evan Jones of Pentower, Fishguard, Pembrokeshire, and was educated at Haileybury before graduating from Trinity College, Cambridge, in 1915. He gained his MA in January 1918. He was commissioned into the Royal Fusiliers in August 1914 and then transferred to the Royal Flying Corps, gaining his pilot's certificate in September 1917. He was the pilot of an Armstrong Whitworth F.K.8 which was shot down by enemy ground machine-gun fire. The observer, Second Lieutenant W. Smith, was also killed. The two men were buried alongside each other in Lijssenthoek Military Cemetery.

In a letter to his father, Major Keith Murray, O.C. No. 10 Squadron provided details of Jones' death:

I am very sorry to have to tell you of the death of your son Evan Davies Jones on April 2nd. He and his Observer left the ground at 12.30 p.m. on Counter-Attack Patrol, and from all evidence we can

gather he had dived down on some target in the enemy lines. At any rate, he was flying very low, and was heavily fired at by enemy machine-guns. He was seen to turn back, partly shut off his engine, and glide back into our own lines. When so low that their heads could be seen, the pilot seemed to disappear, as tho' he had fainted and fallen forward, and the machine at once dived straight into the ground. A party of Infantry were within a few yards, and a Medical Officer also, but they found the machine totally

Evan Jones

wrecked and both occupants dead – undoubtedly killed at once. They were buried yesterday at the Cemetery at Rémy, about one-mile south of Poperinghe. Jones had many friends in this Squadron whom he knew before he came here – they all wish me to offer their sincerest sympathy.[15]

Lieutenant Jack Greville Moore was killed in a flying accident on the same day while training. Aged 19, he was born in Burma, though his parents later settled in Tenby. He had enlisted as a private in the 28th London Regiment in October 1915 before transferring to the Royal Flying Corps a year later. Commissioned in February 1917, he was posted as a pilot to 81 Squadron. Whilst flying an Avro 504, he stalled the machine at a height of about 100 feet and it nosedived into the ground. He survived and, after recuperation and more training, he rejoined 81 Squadron at Scampton where he was killed while flying a Sopwith Camel which failed to come out of a spin and crashed. Moore was buried in Newport Cemetery, Lincoln.

Lieutenant Ernest David Jones from Llanfaes, Brecon, is commemorated on the Arras Flying Services Memorial. Aged 19, on 2 April he was the pilot of an R.E.8 of 52 Squadron which took off at 12 p.m. on a bombing patrol. His aircraft was the 75th victim of Baron Manfred von Richthofen, being shot down north-east of Moreuil at 12.35 p.m. His observer, Second

Lieutenant R.F. Newton, was also killed. Jones had enlisted in the Army Reserve on 24 January 1916, as he was too young to serve. In September 1917, he was commissioned as a second lieutenant in the Royal Flying Corps. After training he was sent to France to join 52 Squadron

Ernest Jones

in February 1918. He and Newton were von Richthofen's first Royal Air Force victims.

Von Richthofen's combat report stated:

> Around 12.30 I attacked, above the wood of Moreuil, an English RE at an altitude of 800 metres, directly under the clouds. As the adversary only saw me very late, I managed to approach him to within 50 metres. From ten metres range I shot him until he began to burn. When the flames shot out, I was only five metres away from him. I could see how the observer and pilot were leaning out of their plane to escape the fire. The machine did not explode in the air but gradually burnt down. It fell uncontrolled to the ground where it exploded, and burnt to ashes.[16]

A Welsh newspaper in April 1918 carried an account of a close encounter with von Richthofen:

> A young Welsh airman has called at this office to tell me the thrilling story of an encounter which he, with several other British airmen, had with Baron von Richthofen's 'circus'. He gave me the account on condition that his name was not disclosed, and the only clue I can give is that he comes from the Llanelli district. 'We were at a great altitude,' he said, 'when we saw the Baron's much-dreaded circus making for us – all fast scout machines coming at a terrific pace. Although we were outnumbered, the seven British machines put up a stiff fight until one of ours went down in flames and another was being forced down as well. My own machine was suddenly attacked from both sides, and our only way to escape was to nosedive. We dived 5,000 feet, but the enemy was down with us, the light in his favour. We nosedived again. So did he. It was touch-and-go, but we just managed to land a few yards on the right side of the line. On that occasion the Baron had twenty scout machines with him, but sometimes his squadrons are much larger than that. He is much advertised by the Germans, and though reported dead last autumn, is still flourishing.'[17]

The fortunate Welsh airman was Second Lieutenant Albert Vernon Gallie from Llanelli who had enlisted in the 4th Welsh

Regiment shortly after the outbreak of war, aged 17, and had transferred to the Royal Flying Corps in 1917. At 10.10 a.m. on 7 April 1918, he took off in a Sopwith Camel of 73 Squadron on an observation patrol. He was later seen in combat with enemy aircraft west of Villers-Bretonneux. His aircraft crashed, but he was uninjured. His attacker was the Red Baron himself. Gallie went on to down four Fokker D.VIIs before the war ended – just missing the title of 'ace'. The first was shot down on 6 June east of Montdidier, another north-west of Conchy on 11 June, a third on 16 July above Château-Thierry, and his final victory came on 25 July east of Launoy. Albert Gallie survived the war and worked as a surveyor, marrying Agnes Mary Glover in 1928 in Wolverhampton.

Captain Frank Emlyn Williams of 57 Squadron died in Egypt on 7 April, aged 23, and was buried in Ismailia War Memorial Cemetery. He left a widow, Elizabeth, in Caerwys Rectory, Flintshire. Born in Merthyr Tydfil, his family then moved to Mountain Ash where Frank was employed as a surveyor at Nixon Colliery. In October 1913, he began a course of study at the South Wales and Monmouthshire School of Mines. He was commissioned as an officer in the 5th Welsh Regiment and served at Gallipoli where he was wounded twice. A Lieutenant Tremellen from Aberdare reported: 'I saw Captain F.E.

Williams, Mountain Ash, go out with ten men to locate snipers. He returned shot through the cheek. He made light of his wound and refused to be carried on a stretcher.'[18]

In 1916, Williams volunteered for the Royal Flying Corps and was awarded the Military Cross

Frank Williams

for his part in the fall of Jerusalem in December 1917. He died of injuries sustained in a training accident and his death was reported in a local newspaper:

> On Tuesday, the sad news came from the War Office to Mr Tom Williams, M.E., Troedyrhiw House, Mountain Ash, that his elder son, Capt. Frank Williams, attached to the Royal Flying Corps, had died in a military Hospital in France. This gallant officer was formerly a Lieutenant in the 5th Welsh Territorials, and saw service in the Gallipoli Campaign, in which he was wounded. By bravery and devotion to duty, he earned his Captaincy, and was then transferred to the Flying Service. He married just a few months ago Sybil, only surviving daughter of Rev. J. Sinnett-Jones, MA, Rector of Caerwys, Flintshire, and formerly Vicar of Mountain Ash, whose two officer sons have made the supreme sacrifice in this war. The deceased officer, when on his wedding leave, was the recipient of a handsome presentation from the officials of Messrs Nixon's Navigation Colliery, at the hands of Councillor William Millar, the senior official. The bereaved parent is the agent for Messrs Nixon's Co., and has another son in the Army.[19]

Lieutenant Noel Parry Davies died on 8 April, aged 18, and was buried in his home town of Swansea in Bethel Welsh Congregational Chapel cemetery, Sketty. Educated at Swansea Grammar School, he was later employed in a bank in London. He was a prominent member of the YMCA, both in Swansea and London, and was also a member of the Swansea Sea Scouts. Davies had joined the Royal Naval Air Service some 18 months previously and was killed while flying over Edinburgh when his aircraft developed an engine problem and crashed.

Air Mechanic 3rd Class Augustus Albert Winter died of natural causes on 12 April while serving with the Royal Air Force School of Photography. He was buried in Aldershot Military Cemetery, leaving a widow, Leah, in Cardiff.

Ivor Idris Pearce was also an Air Mechanic 3rd Class. He was 27 when he died of illness in Aldershot on 17 April. He was buried in his home town of Penarth, leaving a widow, Olive,

Augustus Winter   Ivor Pearce

in Newport. Before enlisting he was employed as a cabinet-maker.

On 19 April 1918 it was reported that a Barry airman had been decorated for his service:

> Serjeant-Major T.J. Huxter, of the Royal Air Forces in Palestine, who was mentioned in General Murray's dispatches, has been awarded the Meritorious Service Medal. When an apprentice at the Barry Railway Locomotive Works, he joined the Royal Field Artillery at the commencement of the war, when only eighteen years of age. He was subsequently transferred to the Royal Flying Corps, and sent to Egypt in 1915, being last year promoted to the charge of one of the aeroplane depots in Cairo, as technical serjeant-major. He is the son of Mr and Mrs R. Huxter, 17 Guthrie-street, Barry Docks, and has been mentioned in the honours list by the King.[20]

Lieutenant Evan Idris Howell was killed in a flying accident at the Beverley Aerodrome in Yorkshire on 21 April while serving with 72 Training Squadron. A native of Pontypridd and prior to the war a school teacher, he had enlisted in the Northamptonshire Regiment and was sent to France in August 1916, probably with the Dorsetshire Regiment.

T.J. Huxter

Evan Howell

He was buried in Glyntaff Cemetery in Pontypridd and left a widow, Annie. A Yorkshire newspaper reported on the subsequent inquest:

Triple Air Tragedy in Yorkshire
Inquests were held on Tuesday on three members of the Royal Air Force who were killed in a flying accident in East Yorkshire on Sunday. Their names were: Lieutenant Harry Estcourt Robinson, 19, whose home address is 49 Colebrook Avenue, West Ealing, London W., Second Lieutenant John Alfred Clayton, 26, Prospect House, Horsehay, Shropshire, and Lieutenant Evan Idris Howell, 27, 17 Ebenezer Terrace, Rhydyfelin, Pontypridd, Glamorgan. The evidence showed that Robinson (instructor) and Clayton (pupil) were in one machine, and Howell, who was on the verge of graduating, in another. The officer commanding said that he saw the machines falling and at once flew across to them. He found the machines on the ground absolutely wrecked, and the three men were dead in the wreckage. Another officer said that he saw the machines collide in the air at a height rather under 2,000 feet, but he did not see what they were doing immediately before the collision. A farm servant, who saw what happened, said the collision was due to one machine turning while near to the other, striking the latter's wings. One machine fell into a field and the

other on the roadside. Medical evidence showed the men's injuries to be extensive. Verdict: Accidental Death.[21]

On 26 April, Lieutenant Lewis Laugharne Morgan was killed in a flying accident. A native of Swansea, where his father ran a parcels and delivery business, W. Laugharne Morgan and Company, when the war started he was working as a clerk at the Shoreditch branch of the Capital and Counties Bank in London. He had joined the 6th Welsh Regiment before volunteering for the Royal Flying Corps. Awarded the Military Cross, his citation read: 'He crossed the lines at a height of under 100 feet, and destroyed a hostile kite balloon. Previously he destroyed a hostile scout at close range and brought it down in flames. He has shown great gallantry in many combats.'[21]

Three weeks after this action, he sustained a fracture of his leg when his aircraft was hit by enemy ground fire. He managed to return his machine to its aerodrome but the injuries were so severe that the leg had to be amputated. After recovering, he returned to his duties and was known as the 'air hog' because he participated in numerous missions. As a flying instructor with 50 Squadron, he was killed in Kent, aged 21, when his S.E.5a aircraft experienced problems during take off. It was seen to

suddenly side-slip to the right and dive vertically to the ground from a considerable height, crashing into a railway embankment. He was buried in Canterbury Cemetery with full military honours. He is also commemorated on the Rood Screen memorial inside All Saints Church, Mumbles, and on the memorial in the Parade Gardens, Swansea.

Lewis Morgan

Lieutenant Victor William Valette Lowrie died on 27 April, aged 18, and was buried in St John the Baptist Church cemetery, Radyr, Cardiff. He was educated at Llandaff Cathedral School in Cardiff and afterwards at Clifton College, Bristol, where he held the school racquets championship. He joined the Royal Flying Corps and obtained his 'wings' in record time, becoming an instructor. He was flying a Sopwith Pup when it hit an air pocket and spun at low altitude. He died later of shock and injuries at Chester War Hospital.

Captain William Humphrey Williams died on 3 May, aged 26, and was buried in Ramleh War Cemetery in Palestine. He was a resident of Caernarfon and was educated at Magdalen College School, Oxford. After leaving school at 17, he worked in a slate quarry business and then in Rochdale for the Turner Brothers Asbestos Company. When the war began, he volunteered for the Army and was commissioned as a second lieutenant in September 1914 with the Lancashire Fusiliers. He landed in Gallipoli on 22 July 1915 and served until his battalion was evacuated on 27 December.

Williams joined the Royal Flying Corps in October 1916 and became engaged to be married. He gained his 'wings' and was

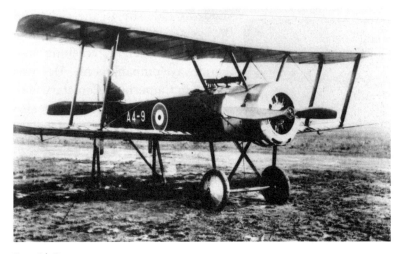

Sopwith Pup

promoted to captain. He then served as a pilot instructor in Egypt until, in the spring of 1918, he joined 142 Squadron in Palestine. He was killed in an accident flying a Martinsyde G.100 when returning from a bombing raid on the Turkish positions. He crashed on landing and a remaining bomb exploded and the aircraft caught fire. Air Mechanic 1st Class William Hewitt Fell rushed to help him but was mortally wounded when a second bomb exploded.

On 5 May, Second Lieutenant Ralph Llewelyn John Davies of 89 Squadron was killed in a flying accident at Netheravon. He was 18 and was buried in St Bride's Church cemetery, Llansantffraid Cwmdauddwr. He was from Rhayader in Radnorshire.

Second Lieutenant Owen Hugh Percy Lloyd of the South Wales Borderers gained his Royal Aero Club Aviator's Certificate on 18 May 1918. Born in Llangefni, Anglesey, in September 1897, he was employed by the City and Midland Bank Limited at St Asaph in north Wales before joining the Army. He survived the war.

William Fell's original grave   Owen Lloyd

On 25 May, the announcement of a gallantry award to a Welsh airman was made:

> Flight Commander F.W. Mathias, RAF, son of Councillor J.H. Mathias, JP, The Hollies, has been awarded the Military Cross for conspicuous bravery and gallant conduct on the Italian front. Flight Commander Mathias joined the forces in 1916, leaving Clifton College for the purpose, although only 17 and a half years of age, and became attached to the Flying Corps. He soon obtained his certificate and wings, and then went to France. He was afterwards transferred to Italy.[23]

Second Lieutenant Frederick William Mathias was born in Nelson in August 1898. He gained his flying certificate on 5 January 1917 and his Military Cross citation read: 'For conspicuous gallantry and devotion to duty. He carried out several successful shoots, doing considerable damage; he took a large number of successful photographs, and completed several long reconnaisances, obtaining valuable information.'[24]

Frederick Mathias survived the war, and after being demobilised in February 1919, joined the Welsh Regiment, relinquishing this commission in February 1920. He  subsequently studied at Caius College, Cambridge, and was then employed as a stockbroker and worked at Cardiff Docks while at the same time playing cricket for Glamorgan. Making his first-class debut against Nottinghamshire in the 1922 County Championship, he made 27 further appearances for the county, the last of which was in 1930. He also played for

Frederick Mathias

Wales against Ireland in 1926, making 65 runs and taking two wickets. Frederick Mathias died at Radyr in April 1955.

In late May, reports began to appear in the press of a mysterious illness that was eventually to claim vast numbers of lives, including many Welsh airmen and women:

> Some days ago a form of disease, of epidemic character, the origin of which is unknown, made its appearance in Madrid. The symptoms are high fever, vomiting, pains in the chest and diarrhoea. The epidemic is of a mild nature, no deaths have been reported. All classes of the population, including workmen, clerks in offices, and staff in places of amusement, have been affected. Among the garrison, 300 men of one regiment alone are suffering from the malady. The troops who relieved the guards at the Royal Palace yesterday were obliged to borrow a band from another regiment, their own band not being available owing to the number of cases of illness among its members. The doctors say there is no reason for alarm, as a complete cure is certain in four or five days. They recommend abstention from all kinds of vegetables.[25]

Second Lieutenant Vincent Clarke Lashford of Richmond Road, Cardiff, was killed on 30 May and buried in Cathays Cemetery, Cardiff. He was 24 and was flying an R.E.8 when it nosedived and crashed. His obituary appeared in a Canadian newspaper:

> The many Toronto friends of Lieut. Vincent Lashford will regret to learn of his death in the north of England which resulted from an accident while making his last flight at a finishing camp prior to going to France. Lieut. Lashford trained with the C.O.T.C. in Toronto last summer, and transferred in October to the Flying Corps at Fort Worth, Texas. He went to England at Easter. His parents reside at

Vincent Lashford

22 Richmond Road, Cardiff, South Wales. Lieut. Lashford was 24 years of age and had been in Canada five years.[26]

Also on 30 May, Lieutenant William James Kelsey of 5th Training Squadron was killed in a flying accident, aged 19. Kelsey was the son of Mrs E. Kelsey, 3 Bristol Road, Weston-Super-Mare, formerly of Pontypridd. He was buried in Glyntaff Cemetery in his home town of Pontypridd.

Second Lieutenant Desmond Maurice Macartney-Filgate was killed in a flying accident on 31 May while training with 42 Training Squadron. He was 18 and was buried in St Gregory & St Martin Church cemetery, Wye, Kent. He had attended Christ College, Brecon, and his father was formerly the manager of the *Brecon County Times*.

A newspaper reported on the subsequent inquest:

News has been received that Second Lieutenant Desmond Macartney-Filgate was killed while flying in Kent during the week-end. He was eighteen and half years of age and the son of Mrs Macartney-Filgate, Elidr. He entered an RFC cadet school last autumn and was gazetted at Easter time. The funeral took place at Wye, Kent, on Tuesday. Early in 1914 he enlisted in the Inniskilling Fusiliers as a private, but was discharged as too young. His brother, Terrence, who was at that time second lieutenant in the same regiment, is now serving in Palestine, and another brother who has been twice discharged is working on munitions in Coventry. At the inquest Second Lieutenant Robert Bramwell stated that deceased started flying some few months ago and had no previous experience. He was a pupil under instruction and commenced flying on April 8th. He had used the same machine practically all the time. About 2.30 p.m. on Thursday, he went up in ideal weather conditions and, when a little way up, the engines commenced to choke. Later the choking became acute and the engines gradually dwindled, with the result that the machine nosedived to the ground. He was then up about 100 feet, and came down in a sort of spinning nosedive to the field. Witness rushed to his assistance and found him badly injured and unconscious. He was at once removed to hospital. Witness said that if the deceased, when he found he had engine trouble, had kept straight ahead instead of turning he would not have crashed so badly. Dr F. Coke stated that death was due to shock, following fracture of the skull and other injuries. If deceased had worn some protective head covering his injuries would have been considerably lessened. A verdict of 'Death from misadventure' was returned and the jury endorsed Dr Coke's suggestion.[27]

Another home casualty was Second Lieutenant Norman Owen, aged 24, who died in a flying accident in Kent on 3 June while training with the 63rd Training Squadron. He was buried in St Tudno Cemetery, Llandudno. He had served in East Africa and in France.

Cadet Clarence Richard Hamar was killed the following day while training at the School of Aerial Gunnery in Canada and was buried in Mount Osborne Cemetery, Beamsville, Ontario. He was from Hill Crest in Radnorshire. The circumstances surrounding his death were reported in a local newspaper:

We very much regret to announce that, on June 5th, Mr and Mrs Hamar, of Hill Crest, Knighton, Radnorshire, received the sad news, that their youngest son, Clarence Richard Hamar (who emigrated to Canada in March 1913), formerly connected with the Detroit Office of Bonbright and Co., investment bankers, died on June 4th at the Canadian Aviation Training Camp, Beamsville, Ontario, of injuries sustained in an aeroplane accident. It appears that he and his pilot went on a practice flight, Cadet Hamar being engaged on gunnery practice. While they were doing 'stunts', it seems the machine nosedived and crashed to the ground, and Cadet Hamar sustained serious injuries, which rendered him unconscious. He died the following morning at 10 a.m. – never having regained consciousness. His pilot was also seriously injured, but it is hoped he may live.

A letter has been received from the Captain of the School of Aerial Gunnery (where Cadet Hamar was stationed) to the following effect: 'I regret to inform you that your son, Cadet C.R. Hamar, died on June 4th, as the result of injuries sustained in an aeroplane accident on June 3rd. His loss is keenly regretted, not only by his fellow-pupils, but by the officers of the school. Had this unfortunate accident not occurred, he would by this time have been commissioned, and would have commenced a very promising career as an officer. He had, a few days before, been selected as a promising pilot of a type which we wished to obtain for instructors. Had he lived, he would not only have been a successful pilot, but an efficient and reliable officer. Please accept this expression of sympathy from myself and the entire staff of the school.'

A letter has been received from Mr Vaughan-Clarke, Mr Hamar's great friend, an extract from which reads as follows: 'The funeral was a full military one, and was very beautiful and impressive. The Church of England service was conducted in St Alban's Church, Beamsville, Ontario, at 3.30 p.m. on Thursday, June 6th. The Rev. Randolph F. Nie officiated. The music, consisting of full choir and organ, was very beautiful. The church services were attended by a firing squad of 20 men, a band of 26 pieces, 10 pall bearers, about 50 cadets and officers, and a number of friends from Toronto, Grimsby and Beamsville. The little church was almost packed. After the service, the funeral procession marched to Mt. Osborne Cemetery, in which the Government has a plot, the line of march being about a mile-and-a-half.

'The procession was as follows: The firing squad of 20 men with officers, a band of 26 pieces, a Government car with minister officiating, a car with 10 pall bearers drawing trailer with casket,

draped with the Canadian flag and flowers, followed by the officer in charge and myself on foot. Following us were about 50 cadets and officers in march formation, followed by Mr Hamar's numerous friends in cars. Nearly a thousand people attended the service at the Cemetery. As the casket was lowered, the minister read the service and the firing squad fired three volleys over the grave,

Clarence Hamar

completing the ceremony. A marble headstone has been erected with the following inscription: "Cadet Clarence Richard Hamar, Hill Crest, Knighton, Radnorshire, Wales, killed June 4th, 1918, on active service, Royal Air Force.'"

Numerous wreaths and flowers were sent by friends of the deceased, a very large and beautiful one being in the shape of an aeroplane, made by loving hands of some dear friends. The parents of deceased have been recipients of various letters from Cadet Hamar's friends in Canada, expressing that he was highly esteemed and beloved by all his friends, and that the loss of this young life is greatly regretted by all who knew him. Mr and Mrs William Hamar wish to thank all kind friends who have sent expressions of sympathy in this their sad bereavement. Another son, Lieut. A.J. Hamar, RFC, aged 26, was killed on active service in France on April 8th, 1917.[28] (see page 70)

Serjeant W.E.A. Brooks of Roath, Cardiff, was killed in action on 16 June, aged 19. He was the observer in a DH.4 flown by Lieutenant Charles Henry Gannaway, also aged 19, which left its aerodrome at 8.55 a.m. on a bombing mission. It was later seen in combat with enemy aircraft two miles west of Roye and was shot down in flames. Both men were killed and lie in Hangard Communal Cemetery Extension in France.

Two German pilots laid claim to the victory: *Leutnant* Olivier Freiherr von Beaulieu-Marconnay and *Vizefeldwebel* Johannes Klein, both of *Jasta* 15.

Von Beaulieu-Marconnay enrolled in the German Army at 17 and was soon a *Leutnant* and Iron Cross First Class holder. He transferred to the Air Service and achieved his first kill at 19 and was later to command *Jasta* 19. On 16 October 1918 he was

Olivier von Beaulieu-Marconnay

shot in the thigh in an air battle, probably by another German pilot. He managed to fly home and was hospitalised. When it was realised that he would not survive, he was awarded the *Pour le Mérite* for his 25 victories. He died ten days later and was buried in Berlin.

Johannes Klein achieved 16 victories and survived the war, dying in 1926. He was awarded the Knight's Cross with Swords and the Iron Cross First Class.

Lieutenant John Meirion Hughes of 103 Squadron was also killed on 16 June and is remembered on the Arras Flying Services Memorial. He was 21 and from Porthmadog, Caernarvonshire. The observer in a DH.9 piloted by Second Lieutenant Sidney Hirst, his aircraft took off at 10 a.m. on a bombing operation but received a direct hit from anti-aircraft fire over Crape-au-Mesil. The pilot was also killed.

Mary Ann Hancox of Kimberley Road, Roath, Cardiff, was 48 when she enlisted in the Women's Royal Air Force on 21 June 1918. Employed as a tailoress before the war, she died in 1954.

On 22 June, it was announced that Hugh Pughe Lloyd, whose father was from Merioneth and whose mother was born in Llanegryn, Merionethshire, had been awarded the Military Cross:

For conspicuous gallantry and devotion to duty. During an offensive patrol he dropped bombs on motor transport, one lorry being completely destroyed and others damaged. Enemy troops advancing to the attack were then engaged with machine-gun fire, which inflicted numerous casualties on

Mary Hancox

them. Later, he bombed an enemy battery coming into action, the horses of which bolted, a great number of the gun detachments being killed. He has on all occasions shown the greatest pluck and determination in carrying out any tasks allotted him.[29]

The following year Lloyd was awarded the Distinguished Flying Cross. His citation read:

This officer has rendered signal service on many occasions, notably on 1 November 1918, when, noticing four hostile batteries harassing our advancing infantry, he, by sending calls to our artillery, succeeded in silencing them. During this flight he was continuously attacked by hostile formations, which he succeeded in driving off; despite this opposition, he carried out a low reconnaissance, obtaining most valuable information as to the position of our advanced troops.[30]

Lloyd was born in 1894 and attended King's School, Worcester, and Peterhouse College, Cambridge. He enlisted in the Royal Engineers in 1915 and served as a despatch driver in France, where he was wounded. After recovering he joined the Royal Flying Corps, qualified as a pilot and was posted to

52 Squadron. He flew over 150 patrols in R.E.8s. After the war ended, he remained in the Royal Air Force and served throughout the Second World War before retiring in 1953 with the rank of Air Chief Marshal; he died in July 1981.

Lieutenant F. Williams of 62 Squadron was killed on 24 June. From Builth Wells in Breconshire, he was buried in

Hugh Lloyd during the Second World War

Cabaret-Rouge British Cemetery, Souchez, after his Bristol F.2B was shot down. He had taken off at 6.15 a.m. on an observation patrol, but was attacked by four to five enemy aircraft over Lille. His observer, Second Lieutenant E. Dumville, was also killed and the victory was claimed by *Leutnant* Paul Billik of *Jasta* 52.

On 10 August, Billik was shot down and captured after being credited with 31 victories. He was to die in a landing accident in Berlin in March 1926 while piloting one of the world's first passenger aircraft.

Second Lieutenant Henry Hill Stephens, of Llanfrechfa, Monmouthshire, died aged 19 on 28 June and was buried in Aire Communal Cemetery. Flying with 42 Squadron, he was an observer in an R.E.8 and was hit by machine-gun fire from the ground. The pilot survived. His death was reported thus:

> Mr G.A. Stephens, School House, Llanfrechfa Lower, the death
> of whose younger son, Sec.-Lieut. H.H. Stephens, RAF, has been
> reported has received a letter which speaks in glowing terms of
> the young fellow's gallantry and devotion to duty from Major
> H.J.F. Hunter: 'Capt. Puckle, your son's pilot, and your son had
> only been out about half an hour when a machine-gun bullet
> fired from the ground hit your son and went through his lungs.

> Puckle at once came home as fast as he could, and medical aid was on the spot, but nothing could be done. He was one of our very best observers, and wonderfully keen.'[31]

On 1 July, Air Mechanic 2nd Class Charles Davies, 22, attached to 9 Squadron, died

Henry Stephens

of wounds and was buried in Aubigny Communal Cemetery Extension. He was from Llandudno Junction.

Second Lieutenant David Bracegirdle Jones was 23 when he died of his wounds on 3 July while serving with 84 Squadron. He was buried in Crouy British Cemetery, Crouy-sur-Somme. From Rhostryfan, Caernarvonshire, he had emigrated to Canada before the war and was working as a plumber when he enlisted in 6th Battalion of the Canadian Expeditionary Force in October 1914. He was awarded the Distinguished Conduct Medal in 1916 for his work with the Canadian Signal Troop. His citation read: 'For conspicuous gallantry when repairing telephone wires under fire, and for general good work.'[32]

On 27 June, he had set off on a morning observation patrol, flying an S.E.5a. He was hit by anti-aircraft fire over Petit Blangy and attacked by enemy aircraft and forced to land.

Air Mechanic 2nd Class Arthur Charles Cokeley was killed in action aged 18 on 4 July and was buried in Cathays Cemetery in Cardiff. His parents lived in Roath in Cardiff. Cokeley had enlisted in October 1917 and worked

The aircraft David Jones learnt to fly on

as a tinsmith and sheet metal worker. He was serving at Felixstowe Air Station.

On 4 July 1918, three 'Large America' (Felixstowe F.2A flying boats), N4513, N4297 and N4540, were patrolling off Zeebrugge when they were attacked 20 miles south-east of the North Hinder lightship by four German Hansa-Brandenburg W.29 fighter floatplanes. *Oberleutnant zur See* Friedrich Christiansen claimed N4297 and N4540, although these both made it back to England and were repaired.

N4513 was piloted by Lieutenant Sydney Anderson, who was wounded early on in the fight but, despite serious injury, he managed to shoot down a W.29. However, N4513 was then forced down too. Of the crew, Cokeley was killed but Lieutenant Anderson, Lieutenant Kenneth Lawson Williams and Boy Mechanic Albert Edward Victor Hilton, who were all wounded, survived the landing in the sea and were rescued. N4513 was later placed under tow but sank on the way back to port.

The two Felixstowe F.2As that Friedrich Christiansen forced down were his eighth and ninth victories. He was awarded both classes of Iron Cross, the Knight's Cross and

the *Pour le Mérite*. He ended the war with 13 victories in total, including a submarine and an airship, and was recalled for duty during the Second World War. He died at Innien in Aukrug in December 1972.

Lieutenant Arthur Eldred Barker Sutton died on 4 July, aged 24 and was buried in Bebington Cemetery, Wirral.

Friedrich Christiansen

Born at Rock Ferry, his parents were living at Menai Bridge,
Anglesey. Educated at Bromsgrove School, he had enlisted in
the King's Liverpool Regiment. An inquest was held into his
death and reported:

> A Westminster Coroner's jury this afternoon returned a verdict of
> Suicide During Temporary Insanity in the case of Lieutenant Alfred
> Eldred Barker Sutton, 24, 6th Kings Liverpool Regiment attached to
> the RAF, who shot himself at Millbank Military Hospital yesterday
> morning. Lieutenant Sutton was well off financially, and had no
> love affair. There was no motive for his suicide, but he had recently
> suffered from influenza, and the doctors stated that this may have
> caused him to become mentally depressed. It appeared from the
> evidence that Sutton had been to France, and returned to England to
> join the RAF. He had seventeen days' leave and was to have a slight
> operation to his nose. Sister Gallaway said Sutton had his operation
> on June 20 and recovered from it, but on the 24th he was seized with
> influenza and was in bed till the 30th, when he was quite normal.
> She did not know he had a revolver, which was against the rules.
>
> Serjeant-Major Barker said that soon after 9.20 yesterday
> morning he was standing at the entrance to the hospital when he
> heard a sharp noise behind him, but he did not associate it with
> firearms. A second or two later there was a confused noise, and
> witness discovered that Lieut. Sutton had fallen from the top floor
> into the basement.
>
> The Coroner said that in a letter written to the officer by a lady
> friend was the remark: 'Surely you won't be turned down. That
> would be damnable.' Of course the man might have had some idea
> at the back of his mind that he was going to fail in his examination
> for the RAF.[33]

Private 2nd Class John Owen Jones, 34, of the Number 2
Fighting School (Marske), died of illness on 7 July and was
buried in Betws Garmon Cemetery. He was born at Waunfawr,
Caernarvon.

Second Lieutenant Robert Stanley Edwards was serving with
47 Training Squadron when he was killed in a flying accident
on 7 July. He was buried in Cathays Cemetery in Cardiff.

John Otto Boole was born in Rainford, Lancashire, in 1892 but, by 1911, he was an engineering apprentice living in Plymouth Road, Penarth, with his widowed mother. He enlisted in the Royal Engineers and was promoted to serjeant. Boole was serving as a second lieutenant in the Royal Air Force when he was killed in a flying accident on 9 July 1918. The S.E.5a he was piloting was involved in a mid-air collision over the Brecon Beacons with an S.E.5a flown by Second Lieutenant Richard Carter Pellow from Cornwall. Both men were killed. Boole was buried in Penarth Cemetery.

Serjeant Percival Henry Williams was flying a Sopwith Camel with 54 Squadron when he set off on an observation patrol on 15 July. He was shot down near Dormans by *Leutnant* Erich Löwenhardt of *Jasta* 10. Born in Cardiff, Williams was buried in La Ville-aux-Bois British Cemetery, aged 24.

Erich Löwenhardt was born the son of a doctor in Silesia on 7 April 1897. He saw service on the Eastern Front where he was wounded. After being commissioned in October 1914, he was wounded once more and awarded the Iron Cross Second Class.

John Boole

Erich Löwenhardt

Early in 1915, he received the Iron Cross First Class for saving the lives of five wounded men in the Carpathian Mountains. He volunteered for the German Air Service and qualified as a pilot in 1916. In 1918, he was awarded the Knight's Cross with Swords and the *Pour le Mérite*. After being credited with 54 victories, Löwenhardt's aircraft collided with that of another German pilot. He bailed out, but his parachute failed to open and he was killed, aged 21, on 10 August 1918. He was the third-ranking German ace of the Great War.

Second Lieutenant Trevor Emlyn Ockwell Hawkins of Werfa Place, Aberdare, was serving with 103 Squadron on 20 July. He was the observer in a DH.9 which was on a bombing mission when it was attacked by aircraft from *Jasta* 52. It was seen to be out of control in a slow spin over Armentières. The wing crumpled and the aircraft crashed, killing Hawkins and the pilot, Second Lieutenant S.E. Carson. It was claimed by *Leutnant* Paul Billik (see page 186). Hawkins was buried in Strand Military Cemetery, south of Ypres.

Lieutenant Henry James Ball was serving with the 22nd Training Squadron in Egypt when he died, aged 31, of his injuries on 24 July. He was buried in Hadra War Memorial Cemetery, Alexandria. His parents lived in Tutshill, Chepstow.

Lieutenant Richard Francis Lewis, 20, was killed on 25 July. He is commemorated on the Arras Flying Services Memorial. Before enlisting, he was studying medicine at Cardiff Medical School. He was an only son. His father was a medical examiner in Cwmparc in the Rhondda Valley and his mother was a schoolteacher. Serving with 73 Squadron, he took off at 6 p.m. in a Sopwith Camel on an observation patrol but came into contact with hostile aircraft near Fismes and was shot down.

Also on 25 July, Air Mechanic 3rd Class Gordon Thomas of 20 Training Wing, who was originally from Cardiff, died and was buried at Hadra in Egypt.

Captain Owen Vincent Thomas was killed in a night-time flying accident on 29 July 1918, aged 24, while piloting a Bristol F.2B and instructing another pilot in night observation. His

IN LOVING MEMORY OF
CAPTAIN OWEN VINCENT THOMAS
ROYAL AIR FORCE,
WHO DIED OF BURNS RECEIVED IN A
FLYING ACCIDENT
29TH JULY 1918,
AGED 24.

"A GOOD PILOT, A GALLANT
OFFICER, A MOST DELIGHTFUL
COMPANION, AND A POPULAR
AND UNASSUMING GENTLEMAN."

This small tribute is erected by
one of his comrades of the battle
of the Somme of 1916.

Owen Thomas   The church memorial

aircraft caught fire when a parachute flare became stuck in its tube. Two of his brothers, Captain Robert Newton Thomas and Second Lieutenant Trevor Thomas, had been killed, in 1917 and 1916 respectively. A graduate of Jesus College, Cambridge, he had been commissioned into the 13th Royal Welsh Fusiliers in November 1914. He now lies in St Alban the Martyr Church cemetery, Coopersale, Essex.

Air Mechanic 2nd Class David Jones died on 1 August. He was serving with the No. 2 Air Ammunition Column and was buried in Glyntaff Cemetery, Pontypridd. As the circumstances of his death were unusual, an inquest was ordered and reported on shortly afterwards:

> A remarkable revelation was made at an inquest held by Mr Ernest Roberts, the deputy-coroner, on Saturday at Treforest on David Jones, second air mechanic, of 12 Stow Hill, Treforest.
> Mary Jones, the widow, said her husband was 23 years of

age. He came home from France on July 16, and applied for an
extension of time to get married on July 31. It was refused. They,
however, got married before the Pontypridd Registrar, and her
husband died the same day. He complained of feeling unwell in the
stomach, and asked for a drink. They gave him water and rubbed
him with embrocation. Between ten and twelve that night he
started groaning and died.

Charles Alfred Pearce, a colliery haulier, brother-in-law, said
the man was taken to the registrar's office in a taxicab, and
on returning to the home he was obliged to go to bed. They
sent for the doctor who said he would come the next morning.
About twelve o'clock, Jones became delirious and talked about
aeroplanes.

Dr Pegler said he saw David Jones between twelve and one
o'clock on Thursday. There were no marks of violence and the body
seemed well nourished. He had some acute illness of gastritis and
influenza, followed by heart failure.

The Deputy-coroner said Jones appeared to be well until a
few hours before his death. He suggested the jury should return
a verdict in accordance with the medical evidence. This the jury
did.[34]

Lieutenant Charles Vincent Todman of 16 Squadron
was killed on 3 August, aged 26. Born in Laugharne in
Carmarthenshire, he had gained a BA before enlisting in
the 9th London Regiment, when he gave his occupation
as that of a teacher. He was later commissioned into the
10th Battalion and was gassed in September 1917 at the
Third Battle of Ypres. In May 1918, he joined the Royal Air
Force. Todman was the observer in an R.E.8 which was on
an artillery observation sortie when it was driven down by
three enemy aircraft east of Vimy. It crashed to the ground
at 6.55 p.m., killing him and the pilot, Lieutenant Percy
Charles West. It was claimed by *Leutnant* Paul Billik of *Jasta*
52 (see page 186). Todman was buried in Aubigny Communal
Cemetery Extension.

Second Lieutenant Herbert C. Faulks died of wounds on
8 August, aged 20. He was serving with 8 Squadron and was

from Cathays in Cardiff. He was the observer in an Armstrong Whitworth F.K.8 piloted by Lieutenant J.R.M.G. MacCallum which was hit by ground machine-gun fire while carrying out co-operation duties with the advancing British tanks. They were laying smoke screens between the tanks and the German anti-tank guns. The F.K.8 was forced to land and MacCallum survived. Faulks was buried in Fouilloy Communal Cemetery, Somme.

Air Mechanic 2nd Class Edwin Hodges died of illness on 11 August, aged 47. Born in Aberdare, he was buried in Llantwit Cemetery in Neath.

Lieutenant Roy William Angus, eldest son of Mr and Mrs F.W.J. Angus, manager of the Labour Exchange, Newport, and nephew of the late Colonel J.R. Angus, South Wales Borderers, were all formerly of Barry. Roy Angus had lived at 74 Princes Street in Barry and was killed, aged 23, on 13 August whilst flying an F.E.2b with 148 Squadron when it failed to pull out of a test spin and crashed. The observer, Air Mechanic 1st Class G.W. King, was also killed. Angus was buried in Pernes British Cemetery in France.

Serjeant Sidney Edward Lewis, 19, was killed in action on the same day while serving with 55 Squadron and was buried

in Charmes Military Cemetery, Essegney. His parents lived in Pontrhydyfen in Glamorgan. He was an observer and had participated in 12 raids over the German lines. A report on his fate stated:

Roy Angus

Prior to the day on which he lost his life, he had brought down two enemy machines, and had been mentioned in dispatches. On the fatal day he was attacked by six German machines over German territory. Without hesitation, he decided to tackle his opponents, and by splendid manoeuvring succeeded in sending one of the machines crashing to earth. In such an unequal contest, however, Serjeant Lewis stood no chance, and he received a bullet which killed him instantly. His pilot was also seriously wounded, but succeeded in breaking away from his enemies and piloting his machine to safety in France.[35]

Second Lieutenant Herrick Peter Gladstone Leyden was also killed on 13 August, aged 20. He was attached to 104 Squadron and was born in Pontardawe. He was buried in Perreuse Chateau Franco British National Cemetery. Leyden was the pilot of a DH.9 which was on a bombing raid on Ehrange Railway Junction. Another DH.9 of the squadron was hit by anti-aircraft fire, broke up and fell onto Leyden's aircraft, killing him and his observer, Serjeant A.L. Windridge.

One Welsh newspaper told of a mishap that had occurred to a Welsh airman:

A Swansea airman, Flight Lieutenant I. Ronald Watkins, son of Mr Walter I. Watkins, Swansea, is in hospital in England after an exciting adventure in the air in which he was shot in the arm and leg whilst flying over the German lines. His machine, subsequent to his serious injuries, crashed to earth, but he was rescued and brought into the British lines.[36]

The same edition also stated that: 'Lieut. Arthur Williams of the RAF, son of Mr W.S. Williams, architect to the Tredegar Iron and Coal Company, has been wounded whilst flying on the Western Front. It is believed that the wounds are not of a serious nature.'

Private 1st Class Austin William Hicks, aged 20, was killed in an accident on 16 August while serving at the 'N' Airship

Station. He was buried in Cefn Coed y Cymmer Cemetery, Merthyr Tydfil, his home town.

Second Lieutenant William Fitton of 6 Squadron was 23 when he was killed in a flying accident on 19 August. He had previously been awarded the Military Medal. Flying an R.E.8, he was practising landings when his aircraft crashed and caught fire. He was buried in Wavans British Cemetery. His wife Amy lived in Deganwy, Caernarvonshire. Fitton had served with the Lancashire Fusiliers at Gallipoli and wrote home in 1915 while recuperating from a slight bayonet injury and bronchitis. He told a harrowing tale as one of three snipers who fired into bushes and killed a Turkish woman. As they looked more closely at her they found her to be camouflaged in green and with 43 British Army identification discs around her neck – trophies of soldiers she had probably killed.[37]

Lieutenant John Edgelow Wase was killed while flying on the same day, aged 23, while serving with 218 Squadron. He and his observer, Second Lieutenant J.C. Cavanagh, were in a DH.9 which was returning to its aerodrome when it went into a spinning nosedive and crashed, killing both men. A native of Prestatyn in Flintshire, Wase was buried in Les Baraques Military Cemetery, Sangatte. Educated at the King's School in Chester, he had been commissioned into the King's Regiment (Liverpool) before transferring to the Royal Flying Corps.

Also on 19 August, Second Lieutenant John Haydn Davies, a former student of the School of Mines at Treforest, Pontypridd, was killed in action. Serving with 98 Squadron, he was the observer in a DH.9 piloted by Lieutenant C.H. Roberts from Sheffield which took off at 6.40 a.m. on a bombing mission. They were seen in combat with a Fokker D.VII over Roiselle before being shot down in flames. Both men are commemorated on the Pertrain Military Cemetery Memorial at Pargny, France. Davies had previously been involved in an accident as the pilot of a DH.9 on a test flight on 11 July 1918 which caught a wheel in a rut when landing and crashed.

Despite the carnage of the Great War, sporting activities still took place. On 26 August, it was reported that:

> Before a large crown at Bargoed on Saturday, Air Mechanic George Hatto (Cardiff) met Billy Jones (Ynysddu) in a fifteen-round contest. It was a good bout, but Hatto showed himself much superior than Jones, who in the sixth round dropped to the board and claimed a foul. This was overruled, and before the end of the round his seconds threw in the towel. Hatto being the winner.[38]

George Hatto fought eight professional bouts between 1914 and 1920, winning three of them. He died in 1974.

Second Lieutenant Kenneth Percival Window was from Cornerswell Road, Penarth. He was killed in a flying accident on 28 August, aged 19, while serving with the 43rd Training Depot Station, and was buried in Penarth Cemetery. His brother Lionel had been killed in action on the Somme on 13 November 1916, also aged 19. Kenneth Window was employed by the London and Provincial Bank in Cardiff before he enlisted in July 1917. After achieving high marks in his training tests, he was ordered to serve at home as a flying instructor. He was badly wounded when his machine crashed, suffering fractures of both legs and severe internal injuries. He died at 7.15 the same evening at a Red Cross Hospital where his mother was working as a Voluntary Aid Detachment nurse.

On 29 August, Lieutenant William Lewis was reported missing:

> Young Cardiff Airman Missing
> Mr George Lewis of 22 Alma Road, Cardiff, who is a partner in the firm of Morgan and Co., boot manufacturers, Charles Street, Cardiff, received a telegram from the Secretary to the Air Ministry on Monday stating that his youngest son, Lieut. William Thomas Samuel Lewis, an observer in the Royal Air Force, has been reported missing since August 29. Lieut. Lewis, who is only 18 and a half years of age, was educated at the Cardiff High School, and, leaving school at seventeen years and nine months, joined the

RAF as a cadet. He had only been over on the western front about a fortnight. It was his first journey over the Hun lines. The other members of the squadron did not see him fall during the fight which took place, and no information is yet obtainable as to his fate. The hope is held that he may have landed safely somewhere, as in his last letter home Lewis hinted to his father that he had been experiencing pretty bad weather for flying. Two brothers also in the Army have been invalided.[39]

Lewis was the observer in a DH.4 of 57 Squadron which was on a bombing raid when he and his pilot, Serjeant T.H.C. Davies, were attacked and driven down near Douai by *Oberleutnant* H-H von Boddien of *Jasta* 59. Davies managed to land the aircraft safely and both men were captured and spent the remaining months of 1918 as prisoners of war.

Hans-Helmut von Boddien was born in Mecklenburg and served in a regiment of cuirassiers from 1912. Wounded in a cavalry skirmish, he joined the Air Service in December 1915, initially as an observer. After training as a pilot, he joined *Jasta* 11 in May 1917 and was appointed commanding officer of *Jasta* 59 in January 1918. He shot down five enemy aircraft before

William Lewis post-war   Hans-Helmut von Boddien

being wounded in the leg and spent three months in hospital recovering. When the war was over, he went to Lithuania to fight the Russian Red Army and disappeared on a flight in November 1919.

A national Welsh newspaper provided some helpful clarification for the home readership on the role of the Royal Air Force:

Our Anonymous Pilots. One or two interesting explanations are made with regard to the work of the Royal Air Force. One relates to the question often asked as to why the names of pilots who bring down enemy machines are not published. It should be borne in mind that other airmen are engaged in perilous work, such as 'spotting' for the artillery, without any possibility of bringing down a German machine. The others belong to a fighting squadron – and enjoy it – and soon earn the name of 'ace.' Moreover, if an airman does good work of any type he is rewarded, and his name appears in the *London Gazette*, and publicity is shared fairly. The other question refers to machines which are brought down. It is understood that we do not include in our list of aircraft lost those machines which are damaged on our side of the line but do include those which are missing. The Germans only include those machines damaged beyond salvage. Most of the fighting is over their lines, and any machine brought down is, therefore, not missing.[40]

Some sense of the excitement created by air flight is conveyed in a press article that appeared at the end of August:

Garw Airman's Unexpected Flying Visit Over The Valley
During the last weekend an aeroplane came suddenly and unexpectedly over the Garw Valley. This being the first time for a 'plane to make its appearance in the district, the sensation was very great, and as it was after the people had left work, the streets were crowded as the visitor passed over the Braichycymmer Mountain, the inhabitants thus having the unique experience of seeing a young hero soaring high and low, performing wonderful feats in the air. The 'plane was noticed to descend, and finally

landed on the Football Field on the Braichycymmer Mountain. In a few minutes crowds, or rather, thousands of people were seen were seen wending their way up the mountain, and the intense excitement gave place to wild enthusiasm when it became known that the 'man in the machine' was none other than our gallant young friend Flight Lieutenant Stanley Thomas of the Royal Flying Corps (son of Mr David Thomas, colliery contractor, Waun Bant, Pontycymmer). Needless to say, the Garw folk are 'mighty proud' of our young airman, and the way he has 'made good' in his Majesty's Forces on land and in the air. Ever since then the Football Field has been visited by a constant stream of spectators, and it may be truly said that every man, woman, and child has seen the aeroplane. The young hero joined the Army a few years before the out-break of the war, and fought at Mons with the 'old contemptibles' and was then a non-commissioned officer. He has been wounded three times, and is an expert flyer.[41]

Captain Iorwerth Gwilym Davies died on 2 September 1918 while flying as an instructor with 54 Training Depot Station, near Fairlop, Ilford, Essex. From Aberangell, Merionethshire, he was performing aerobatics in an Avro 504k when the biplane nosedived into the ground. He was retrieved from the wreckage but died shortly afterwards, aged 25. He was buried at Cemmaes Calvinistic Methodist Chapel cemetery in Montgomeryshire.

Thursday, 12 September, saw the announcement of a gallantry award to a Welsh airman:

First Class Air Mechanic T.H. Cronin of 8 Park Street, Swansea, now stationed in Devon, has been presented by Major Morris, RAF, with the bronze medal and certificate of the Royal Humane Society in recognition of his gallantry in rescuing Aircraftsman Stead from drowning in the Plymouth Cattewater on January 18th last. Stead was washed overboard from the Cattewater breakwater during a heavy gale, which was so violent as to wash away a large crane. Day was just dawning and snow was falling when Cronin heard the cries of a comrade in distress. Without the least hesitation, he plunged into the icy cold and boisterous waters and, after some 20 minutes' strenuous exertions, succeeded in getting Stead ashore in a very exhausted condition. The presentation took place on the deck of a warship.[42]

Flight Cadet William Rice Jones was also killed in a flying accident on 13 September. From Tregaron, he was buried in Bwlchgwynt Calvinistic Methodist Chapel cemetery, Tregaron. His death was reported thus:

Mr and Mrs Jones, Ochr Farm, received the sad news on Friday of the death of their eldest son (Flight Cadet W.R. Jones) who was 29 years of age. Cadet Jones was a member of the Cadet Corps in an English county. On Friday he was told with five others to take machines to an aerodrome. When within a mile of his destination his machine got out of control and nosedived to earth, a drop of 500 feet. Death was instantaneous. Mr D.D. Wlliams, Gwynva, and Mr Johnnie Jones, Ochr, proceeded to the place on Saturday and made arrangements for bringing the body to Tregaron. The coffin, draped in the Union Jack, was escorted to the station by eight cadets from the local aerodrome. The time of department from Paddington was announced on Sunday evening at Jewin C.M. Chapel where deceased was an active worker, and the platform was crowded with Welshmen from all parts of London. The body was received at Tregaron on Tuesday by a large number of sympathisers. The service at Bwlchgwynt was conducted by the Revs. M. Evans and Dan Jones. Veterinary Lieut. T.R. Jones, a brother, is on his way to Mesopotamia, and three weeks ago was home on leave with his deceased brother. Cadet Jones, before joining the Army, was in the drapery business in London and Birmingham. He served two years at Harrods and then he held a lucrative post at a big establishment in Croydon. Early in 1915, just before the Derby scheme came into operation, he joined the Army as a private and was soon drafted to France where he took part in the severe fighting in the Arras and Somme regions. He was quickly promoted to the rank of corporal and, in 1917, was recommended for a commission and gained admission in the RAF.[43]

On the same day, Second Lieutenant Eric Bramall Smailes died as a prisoner of war in Germany. He was 18 and had served with 104 Squadron. His parents lived in Monkton House, Marine Parade, Penarth, and he was buried in Niederzwehren Cemetery, Kassel. Smailes had been commissioned on 14 August 1918 as an observer, and was flying in a DH.9 piloted by Second Lieutenant J.E. Kemp on a bombing raid to Mannheim on 7 September when they were attacked by *Leutnant* Kurt Seit of *Jasta* 80 and forced to land. Both men were taken as prisoners of war, Smailes dying later of his wounds. Before enlisting he had been employed as a clerk.

Kurt Seit was born on 30 July 1894. An engineer, he enlisted with the infantry and was awarded the Iron Cross Second Class on 3 November 1914. He then transferred to the Air Service and received the Iron Cross First Class after his first victory on 22 July 1918. Wounded four times during the course of the war, he achieved five victories.

Major Thomas Llewelyn Davies was 25 when he died on 25 September. He was buried in Cwmgelli Cemetery, Swansea. His parents lived in Dillwyn House, Brynhyfryd, Swansea. A former student of the University College of North Wales, Bangor, Davies was killed in a flying accident, as was the pilot, at Worthy Down Camp, Winchester.

While serving with the Royal Field Artillery, Davies was awarded the Military Cross. His citation read:

> For conspicuous gallantry and devotion to duty in reorganising a battery which had lost all its officers, N.C.O.s, and gunners. Two days afterwards he not only commanded the battery in an attack, but personally laid the guns, and it was due to his splendid example that the battery was able to change its position and come into action again with the rest of the brigade. He displayed throughout the operation a complete disregard of hostile fire.[44]

The pilot of the aircraft was Captain William Ernest Dawson, aged 24, from Llantarnam Hall, Newport. He was buried in St Mary Church cemetery, Malpas. His obituary appeared in a local newspaper:

We greatly regret to learn of the death, which occurred at
Winchester, on Monday, of Lieut. Ernest Dawson, second son of
Mr and Mrs W.F. Dawson, Llantarnam Hall, Newport. No details
as to how the young officer met his death have been received. He
was a member of the Royal Air Force, and had done a good deal
of flying over the British and German lines on the Western Front.
Lieut. Dawson, who was about 24 years of age, joined the 4th
Welsh Regiment upon the outbreak of war, and was subsequently
transferred to the Royal Air Force. He was educated at Malvern
and Charterhouse. Much sympathy will be felt with the parents,
whose other two surviving sons are serving in the 4th Welsh
abroad.[45]

Clerk 1st Class William Emrys Foster died of illness on the
same day, aged 45. He was working at 'X' Aircraft Park in Egypt
and was buried in Hadra War Memorial Cemetery, Alexandria.
His parents lived in Dinas in the Rhondda Valley. Foster was a
married man with five children who lived at 96 Queen Street,
Treforest, Glamorgan.

Second Lieutenant Leslie Bernard Simmonds of 57
Squadron was shot down on 16 September, aged 21. From
Newport, he is commemorated on the Arras Flying Services
Memorial. His obituary was carried in a local newspaper:

With reference to the report of Saturday evening concerning Sec.-
Lieut. L.B. Simmonds, the only information his parents, Councillor
C.P. Simmonds and Mrs Simmonds have received, apart from a
wire reporting him as 'missing', is a letter from his Commanding
Officer, who writes: 'The squadron set out on Monday last, and
when over enemy territory they met a number of hostile machines
and became engaged. His machine was seen to fall badly out of
control, and the report given of him left but a minimum of hope
that he and his pilot would escape with their lives.' He stated they
would cause inquiries to be dropped over enemy lines to German
airmen – asking for news of them, and would immediately report.
Meanwhile, all possible inquiries are being made, and his parents
and their many friends still hope they may hear he is alive though
a prisoner of war.[46]

Leslie Simmonds

Leslie Simmonds' father was the mayor of Newport in 1912–13 and ran a chain of provision merchants with shops on Chepstow Road, Caerleon Road, Shaftesbury Street, Stow Hill and Caerleon. Simmonds had emigrated to Argentina before the war to work on the railways. His pilot, Second Lieutenant Julian Ferreira, 18, a South African, took off in their DH.4 at 10.30 p.m. on a bombing mission. They were attacked by Fokker D.VIIs and were shot down in flames one mile east of Marcoing.

Second Lieutenant William Kellow died on 17 September, aged 25, and was buried in Naves Communal Cemetery Extension in France. A graduate of Cambridge University, he was from Penrhyndeudraeth, Merionethshire. He was the pilot of a Bristol F.2B of 22 Squadron that took off at 2.30 p.m. that day on an observation patrol. He and his observer were observed in combat with enemy aircraft east of Cambrai, and were seen to be falling out of control. The observer, Second Lieutenant H.A. Felton from Tottenham, was also killed.

Second Lieutenant Thomas Martin Phillips was killed on 18 September. From Manselton in Swansea, he was buried in Rue-Petillon Military Cemetery in Fleurbaix. He had attended King's College, London, and was a pilot with 103 Squadron. His DH.9 had taken off at 9.50 a.m. on a bombing raid and was hit by anti-aircraft fire at 11.40 a.m. The aircraft went into a spin north-west of Lille at 15,000 feet. The observer, Second

Lieutenant R.E. Owen, was also killed and is buried in the same cemetery. Flight Cadet Albert Daniel Morgan of 47 Training Depot Station was training to be a pilot. He was killed while flying on 18 September and was buried in Cardiff, his home city. His death was reported in a newspaper:

At an inquest to-day on Flight Cadet Albert Daniel Morgan (28), Royal Air Force, a verdict of 'Accidental Death' was returned. He was flying in Yorkshire the previous day, when his machine went into a vertical nosedive and crashed to the ground, deceased being instantly killed. He was stated to be perfectly qualified to fly solo, and the machine was in perfect order. The deceased belonged to Cardiff, and his wife resided in Lowther Road, Doncaster.[47]

It was also reported that another flying accident had occurred in Wales:

Aeroplane Fatality in Caernarvonshire
An inquest was held on Thursday touching the death of Air Mechanic Ely Walker Shaw (18) 31 Abbey Walk, Halifax, who died after an accident in an aerodrome. Evidence was given by Chief Mechanic F.F. Garnett that the deceased joined the RAF five months ago. Witness noticed the accident. The machine was in charge of Capt. Tuck, a very experienced pilot, and the deceased was a passenger. The machine started all right but when it was about 25 feet in the air it fell to the earth. Deceased was lying among the wreckage, the machine being damaged beyond repair. Deceased was taken to a hospital in a neighbouring town, but he lived only three quarters of an hour after the accident. The machine was going on a trial trip and the engine had been thoroughly examined in the morning. After the accident all the controls were tested and were found all right. No one was allowed to touch the machine which had fallen until it was thoroughly examined.
    Lieut. James A. Barnes, a pilot in the RAF, who also witnessed the accident, said that Capt. Tuck took the air perfectly, and after rising about 30 feet he was apparently trying to turn into the small wind then blowing, when the machine

losing the necessary speed turned on its side and finally cashed to earth, nose first. The pilot did exactly what was right. There might have been a pocket of air which the machine got into. Witness was certain there was no error of judgment on the part of the pilot. The accident was due to the unknown state of the atmosphere. It was stated that Capt. Tuck, who is in a military hospital, did not remember anything about the accident. In answer to the Coroner, a witness said that if the machine had been at a higher altitude, the accident would not have happened, as it would have righted itself. A verdict of 'Accidental Death' was returned.[48]

Air Mechanic 2nd Class Alfred Henry Warden died of natural causes on 25 September, aged 19. From Roath Park in Cardiff, he was buried in Cathays Cemetery in the city.

Second Lieutenant Arthur Saunders Jones, of 108 Squadron, was killed in action on 27 September, aged 18, and buried in Sanctuary Wood Cemetery in Belgium. His parents lived in Prestatyn, Flintshire. He was the pilot of a DH.9 which took off from its aerodrome at 10.30 a.m. on a bombing mission.

Alfred Warden

Theodore Smith

The aircraft was hit by anti-aircraft fire and was soon out of control between Kortemark and Torhout.

Two days later, Lieutenant John Ledger Bromley, from Rhyl, was shot down and killed, aged 21, while flying with 11 Squadron. He is remembered on the Arras Flying Services Memorial. Educated at Rossall School in Fleetwood, he enlisted in the Army Service Corps in July 1916. Bromley was awarded his 'wings' in September 1918, 12 days before he was killed. He was the observer in a Bristol F.2B flown by Second Lieutenant Theodore Thomas Smith, a Canadian, which took off at 7.20 a.m. on an offensive patrol over Cambrai. It was shot down over the German lines, possibly by *Offizierstellvertreter* Josef Mai of *Jasta* 5, and both men were killed. Smith's father was a Methodist minister.

Josef Mai was born on 3 March 1887 and was educated in Berlin. He joined the German Air Service in May 1915 and was made a pilot in July the following year. He was awarded the Iron Cross First and Second Classes. Mai had 30 confirmed victories and 15 unconfirmed by the end of the war. In the Second World War he served as a flying instructor; he died in Germany in January 1982, aged 94.

Josef Mai

Second Lieutenant Hugh Spencer Thomas from Carmarthen was 19 when he was killed on 29 September while serving with 27 Squadron. He was the pilot of a DH.9 which was on a bombing raid. It was shot down over Busigny by *Unteroffizier* Karl Treiber of *Jasta* 5. Both pilot and observer were killed and were buried in Escaufourt Communal Cemetery in France

Karl Treiber was born in 1895 and had only joined the *Jasta* that month. He claimed seven victories before the war ended. He flew Messerschmitt fighters during the Battle of Britain in 1940 and was shot down and captured. He was repatriated later in the war owing to his age.

On 1 October, Serjeant Dafelyn Tawelog Austin Jones, from Ebbw Vale, died on the day he was due to be gazetted for a commission, aged 21. He was buried in his home town. Jones died in Coventry Hospital of injuries caused when his S.E.5a crashed at 10.30 a.m. that day.

Also on 1 October, Second Lieutenant Frank Owen was killed, aged 30. He was serving with 108 Squadron and had previously been awarded the Distinguished Conduct Medal. Born in Rhymney in Monmouthshire, he was buried in Harlebeke New British Cemetery in Belgium. Owen had enlisted with the 151st Field Company of the Royal Engineers and landed in France in December 1915. The citation for his Distinguished Conduct Medal appeared in April 1916. It read: 'For conspicuous gallantry and initiative. When acting as guide, Serjeant Owen observed a bomb fall near a trench full of men. He instantly ran forward and threw the bomb over the parapet. In all probability he saved many lives.'[49]

In a letter written to his sister Sarah on 15 January 1918, Owen wrote:

> No doubt you will be pleased to learn that I have been accepted for the Royal Flying Corps and hope to proceed to one of their depots in a day or two ... I've got such a great presentiment that now and again makes me feel a bit down. I start to think that this next time I go to France will be the last ... The Kaiser will be astounded when he learns that Frank Owen have [*sic*] joined the Royal Flying Corps. I guess he'll tell the German airman to be careful and keep his eyes skinned or Frank will be there first.[50]

He was the observer in a DH.9 which was on a bombing raid on Ingelmunster when it was shot down by *Vizeflugmeister* Hans Goerth of Marine-Feld *Jasta* 3. The pilot, Lieutenant George Alfred Featherstone, was also killed.

The official report stated:

At 1715, whilst flying east towards Thielt between Isseghem and Mautebelle, a large number of enemy aircraft – afterwards 33 were counted – were seen to be climbing west, apparently with the intention of cutting the formation off from the line. The formation turned west and dropped its bombs on Ingelmunster Station at 1725. Immediately the bombs were dropped, the enemy aircraft attacked from above and in front, coming out of the sun, then continued to attack from behind, both above and below. The combat continued for about 10 minutes over Roulers. Very close formation was kept throughout the combat by our machines. Three enemy aircraft were shot down in flames. One enemy aircraft broke up. Two enemy aircraft fell out of control, one of which was seen to crash, near the railway line between Ingelmunster and Roulers. The enemy formation was afterwards seen to be attacked by British aircraft. One enemy aircraft was seen to be shot down out of control at about 1745. Three of our

Hans Goerth

machines failed to return. One was shot down, but managed to reach our lines.[51]

Hans Goerth achieved seven victories from June to October 1918 and was awarded the Iron Cross First Class.

Second Lieutenant Alan Thompson Watt Boswell, of 108 Squadron, was killed on 2 October, aged 28. From Canton in Cardiff, he attended Cardiff High School and obtained a degree at University College, Cardiff. He represented Wales in hockey and football (three caps) as an amateur, and appeared for Cardiff City Football Club's reserve side as an amateur. He also played for Glamorgan Cricket Club in 1914 against Weston-super-Mare, scoring seven runs as Glamorgan won by an innings and 64 runs.

Boswell was the pilot of a DH.9 which was on a bombing raid on Menin. The aircraft was last seen at 3,000 feet west of Menin before it went missing. Neither Boswell nor his observer, Second Lieutenant Robert Percy Gundhill were seen alive again. Both men are commemorated on the Arras Flying Services Memorial.

Leutnant Josef Carl Peter Jacobs of *Jasta* 7 claimed the

victory. Born in the Rhineland on 15 May 1894, he enlisted in the German Air Service at the beginning of the war. Boswell's DH.9 was his 35th victory; his final total was 48. He was awarded both classes of the Iron Cross, the Knight's Cross with Swords and the *Pour le Mérite*. He survived the war and continued to work in aviation, though he did not serve in the Luftwaffe during

Josef Jacobs

the Second World War. He died in Munich on 29 July 1978, aged 84.

Ethel Maud Lilian Richards was serving with the Royal Air Force when she died on 2 October, aged 26. From Cwmbran in Monmouthshire, she had enlisted in Cardiff in January 1918 in the Women's Auxiliary Army Corps and stated she was prepared to work anywhere that was required. She was posted in February to the Artillery and Infantry Co-operative School in Winchester as a waitress. When the Women's Royal Air Force was formed on 1 April, she transferred across, probably carrying out similar duties. She was buried in Shorncliffe Military Cemetery.

Second Lieutenant Donald Robert Phillips served with 11 Squadron and was killed on 4 October, aged 19. From Colwyn Bay, he was buried in Grévillers Military Cemetery. He had been on the reporting staff of the *North Wales Weekly News*, who subsequently printed extracts of his last letter home, written the day before he died:

I have been doing the job of adjutant during the past few days and consequently have not done much flying, but today I am down for another 'show', so expect to be flying again tomorrow. Today I managed to get the task of fetching the Colonel's machine from one place of Northern France to another and thus had the opportunity for seeing part of our back areas including some of those towns which were nearly taken by the Germans in the March push. I am beginning to get to know Northern France now and hope that after the war I may be able to revisit it and renew old acquaintances. I continue this letter after a most upsetting incident, which for once has had a satisfactory ending. This morning two of our machines collided at 10,000 feet and naturally everybody has been a bit upset all day. This evening, when the 'show' returned, I found my friend Taylor – a really nice boy with whom I share my hut and whom I knew last year at Stamford – had not returned. I was rather upset, but news has just come through that he was shot up but landed safely on our side of the lines. Hurrah! I feel so relieved, and when he returns I shall be very glad.[52]

The irony of part of this letter is that Phillips' machine collided with another British aircraft the following day, killing all four men.

Buried close by in the same row is Lieutenant Benjamin Stewart Buckingham Thomas MC, a pilot with 11 Squadron, who was killed on the same day, aged 24. Originally from Pembroke Dock, he was killed in the same accident while returning from a patrol. His Bristol F.2B aircraft was seen to collide with a similar machine being piloted by Donald Phillips. He had been awarded his Military Cross on 29 January 1917 during his service with the 9th Welsh Regiment for gallantry in holding an exposed flank and organising and leading a counter-attack. Thomas had joined the Royal Flying Corps in September 1917 and arrived in France on Easter Monday 1918. As noted, the two other crew members of the two aircraft were also killed and all four men lie next to each other in Grévillers Cemetery – a sad reminder of an accident of war.

A letter he wrote home, while serving as an infantry officer, was published in a local newspaper:

We got about 50 yards from the trenches and were set on draining work so that the water could flow from the trenches back to the rear. The men were only too glad to get down in the mud, though up to their middles in icy water, yet preferred that to walking in the open. I can tell you it was no joke pottering about above your knees in beastly smelling water, with bullets flying about all over the place. However, nothing happened, and after five hours' work, we returned to billets. We were having breakfast when a swagger staff-colonel came in and asked the adjutant about our night's work. He was accompanied by a young-looking lieutenant with rather a lot of ribbon which seemed strange to us. When he had gone the adjutant burst the news on us that the young officer was the Prince of Wales [the future Edward VIII]. Rather funny wasn't it![53]

Second Lieutenant F.S. Towler, aged 18, died while flying in an Airco DH.9A on 5 October. He was from Cathays in Cardiff and was serving with 110 Squadron as an observer. He was buried in Niederzwehren Cemetery, Kassel, in Germany.

Private 2nd Class Thomas Hanford, of Maesteg, died of pneumonia on 10 October while serving with 48 Squadron. He was buried at La Kreule Military Cemetery, Hazebrouck, Belgium.

Helen Gwynne-Vaughan had been appointed Commandant of the Women's Royal Air Force in September 1918. Formerly Chief Controller of Queen Mary's Army Auxiliary Corps Overseas, she had family connections with Llandovery. An update on her work was provided for newspaper readers:

> Mrs Gwynne-Vaughan, C.B.E., as the new commandant of the Woman's Royal Air Force, is, says the *Globe*, proving an extremely popular personality, especially so with the working members of the ranks who are impressed by her kindly and sympathetic charm of manner. The organising work of the force is most important, for it lies afar as well as near at hand. For example, a women workers' camp, the first in Egypt under canvas, is being worked by the detachment of the force. It is an interesting coincidence that the administrators of the two principal women's services of the forces, Mrs Burleigh Leach, of Tenby, and Mrs Gwynne-Vaughan, the wife of a Carmarthenshire professor, both hail from South Wales. Miss Elsie Towyn Jones is also holding a very important administrative post in the WRAF.[54]

Educated at Cheltenham Ladies' College and King's College, London, in 1909 she was appointed head of the Botany Department at Birkbeck College, London. She married in 1911 and put her career on hold as she nursed her sick husband, who died in 1915. She was invited to form the Women's Army Auxiliary Corps in 1917 and was stationed in France. After her appointment to the Women's Royal Air Force, she overhauled the administrative system, introduced a new blue uniform, set up Berridge House in Hampstead for the training of women officers, and introduced proper military protocol. She was instrumental in changing attitudes towards service women.

Gwynne-Vaughan received the CBE in 1918 and in 1919 she was made a Dame of the British Empire. Leaving the Women's Royal Air Force in 1919, she became a professor at Birkbeck College. During the Second World War, Gwynne-Vaughan served as Director of the Auxiliary Territorial Service until she retired from military service in 1941, whereupon she returned to Birkbeck College and retired as professor emeritus in 1944. She died in 1967.

Elsie Towyn Jones was the elder of two daughters of the Reverend Josiah Towyn Jones, the MP for East Carmarthen. She became an official in the Women's Army Auxiliary Corps in October 1917 and, after a period as transport officer responsible for the travel arrangements of the WAACs, she was promoted to Quartermistress of the WAAC in France in March 1918, being responsible for all uniform supplies. In June of that year she survived a bombing raid. In a letter to her father she wrote: 'We have top-hole dug-outs and they are absolutely bombproof.'[55] In August, after recovering from a fever, she was recalled to

Helen Gwynne-Vaughan   Elsie Towyn Jones

London to use her 'invaluable technical knowledge'[56] to advise
Sir Douglas Haig.

Second Lieutenant Frederick Cawley, aged 20, was killed
while flying on 13 October at the 35th Training Depot Station. He
was buried in St Mary's Church, Marshfield, Monmouthshire.
His death was reported in a local newspaper:

> An inquest was held at Colchester on Tuesday on 2nd Lieutenant
> Frederick Cawley, 20, of the RAF, whose home is at St Mellons,
> near Cardiff. Deceased obtained his commission in December
> 1917, and was an accredited flying officer, and a very steady pilot.
> While flying, his machine 'stalled' on a turn and nosedived to the
> ground from a height of about 200 feet. Deceased was removed
> on an ambulance to the Military Hospital at Colchester, where he
> died from a fracture of the base of the skull. The Coroner found a
> verdict in accordance with the medical evidence.[57]

On 15 October, Arthur Wellesley Rees Evans was shot down.
Born in June 1898, also in St Mellons, he had been working
for ship-owner D.P. Barnett at the Baltic Buildings, Cardiff
Docks. In December 1916, he was rejected for an Officer
Training Course, as he had tuberculosis in both lungs. He was
finally passed fit for the Royal Flying Corps on 22 August 1917.
He underwent flying training at Old Sarum Training Base,
Salisbury, and passed on 5 April 1918. He joined up with 110
Squadron on 15 October and took off as the pilot of a DH.9A on
his first mission on 21 October, a bombing raid on Frankfurt.

Heavy clouds meant that the formation broke up on its
way to Cologne and only five of the 13 bombers reached
Frankfurt. The DH.9As were attacked by enemy aircraft and
five were brought down. Evans' parents received information
that their son was missing. His father sent letters and
telegrams to the Air Ministry and the International Prisoners
Agency in Geneva, asking for word of their son, and they
finally heard that he was alive and well as a prisoner of war
in Germany. Both he and his observer, Lieutenant Thompson,
had survived the attack and on 3 December he left Germany

for Wales. Evans was demobilised on 7 February 1919 and on 14 February resumed his civilian occupation. His father died just a few months after his son returned home. Arthur Evans died in 1965, aged 66.

Second Lieutenant Reginald Hopkin Hill Griffiths, aged 20, was killed on 17 October. He had been awarded the Military Cross and was from Aberavon. He was buried in Harlebeke New British Cemetery. Griffiths was the observer in an aircraft flown by Lieutenant George William Edendale Whitehead, who played cricket for Kent in 1914. The mayor of Lauwe in Belgium wrote a letter to Whitehead's father, describing what happened:

> On Thursday, October 17th, at nine o'clock in the morning, an English aeroplane appeared flying very low and carrying two persons, Lieutenant Whitehead and Lieutenant Griffiths. Your son raised himself in the machine, and with a flag in his hand, amid the cheers of the population, proclaimed our happy deliverance. The aeroplane flew over the town repeatedly, always saluted by the inhabitants, until when flying near the Railway Station, which is twenty-five minutes walk from the centre of the town, it was fired at by German machine-guns. Flying at a low height, it was hit by bullets which, alas, wounded your son and his observer. The machine made a steep dive and the lifeless bodies of your brave men were borne into a room in our hospital. They were buried the next day in the Military Cemetery by a party of English soldiers.[58]

Reginald Griffiths

Cadet Frederick Donald Frost died on 18 October, aged 29. Attached to the Cadets Distributing Depot, he was buried in St Woolos Cemetery, Newport. He was born in Newport but met his future wife, Kathleen, in Durban, South Africa.

His obituary read:

The death took place at Shorncliffe Hospital from pneumonia of Cadet Frederick Donald Frost, RAF, of Durban, youngest son of Mr Edward Frost, Malpas. He was an old Newport Intermediate boy. Acquiring a knowledge of architecture and drawing, he passed into the office of the late Mr C.J. Fox and later that of Mr Maples Linton, architects. Going to South Africa, he was appointed architect to the Corporation of Durban, where his brother, Mr Arthur Stanley Frost, has been Assistant Engineer for some years, and he carried out some important undertakings. He married, in 1913, Kitty Unigeni, daughter of Mr C.R. Bishop, Durban. He left as soon as the Durban Corporation could release him to join the RAF at home. In consequence of many delays and disappointments in securing a place in drafts, he decided to come over at his own expense, and after persevering efforts, and with the support of the High Commissioner of South Africa, he was accepted as a cadet in the Naval section of the RAF. He joined at a distribution depot in North London, where he was three days, and then contracted influenza. Apparently he recovered, and was sent to Shorncliffe, but was unfortunately attacked with double pneumonia, passing away on Friday. The body was brought to Newport, and the funeral took place on Thursday.[59]

It was during this time that the influenza pandemic began to claim an increasing number of lives. Private 2nd Class Hugh John Wyldbore Smith-Marriott, of the Recruits Depot, died of illness on 19 October, aged 20, and was buried in St Michael Churchyard Extension, Heavitree, Exeter, near to where his parents were residing. He was born in Boverton, near Llantwit Major.

Private 2nd Class William George Dawson Taylor also died of natural causes, on 21 October, aged 18. He was serving at the Blandford Recruits Depot and was from Swansea. He was buried in Caversham Cemetery.

Private 2nd Class John Evans Edwards, whose wife Gertrude lived in Haverfordwest in Pembrokeshire, died of illness on 22 October, aged 35, while serving at an armaments school. He was buried in Milford Haven Cemetery.

On 23 October, an article appeared which shows the uncertainty associated with airmen who went 'missing' and the anxiety caused to their families, not knowing if these men were dead or alive: 'Flight Lieutenant Frank Owen, RAF, residing at Havard's Row, Rhymney, is reported missing. Quite recently he was the recipient of a gold watch from the Rhymney Welcome Home Fund as a token of his being awarded the D.C.M.'[60] In reality, Owen, as noted earlier in this chapter, had been killed on 1 October over the German lines. Hence it took longer for news of his death to be passed to his family.

The article continued:

> Second Lieutenant Percy Phillips, RAF of Swansea, is reported missing. In a letter from his major, it is stated that when engaged on a bombing expedition some Hun scouts attacked the formation, and it is believed Second Lieutenant Phillips' machine must have been hit in the engine. He was last seen going down in a spiral, apparently under full control, so there are great hopes he got safely down.[61]

Phillips was more fortunate; he survived the incident.

Air Mechanic 2nd Class John William Daniels, 32, died of illness on 23 October in Italy while attached to the 171 Battery of the Royal Garrison Artillery. He was buried in Giavera British Cemetery, Arcade. His parents ran the post office in Llanbrynmair, Montgomeryshire.

Private John Thomas Boddy from Llangattock died of natural causes on 24 October, aged 43, while serving with the Recruits Training Wing at Blandford. He was buried in his home town churchyard, leaving a widow. He had joined

John Boddy

the Royal Air Force only a few months previously, and had been a gardener at Penmyarth House on the Glanusk Estate.

Clerk 2nd Class Thomas Nathaniel Evans died on 25 October, aged 33, also of natural causes. His widow Beatrice lived in Manselton, Swansea. He was buried in St John the Baptist Church cemetery in Clydach, Swansea. He had worked at the 2 Aircraft Repair Depot in Calais.

Private 1st Class Henry Jones died of illness on the same day, aged 32, while serving at the 8th Aircraft Acceptance Park at Lympne. A native of Gaerwen on Anglesey, he was buried in Gaerwen Calvinistic Methodist Chapel cemetery.

Private Harry Dugdale Lloyd Jones died of meningitis on the same day, aged 19. His home was Bronheulog, St David's Road, Caernarvon and he was buried in St Peblig's Church cemetery in Llanbeblig. Jones was serving with 209 Training Depot Station at Lee-on-Solent.

Air Mechanic 2nd Class Hezekiah Morgan died on 29 October, aged 21. He was attached to 500 Siege Battery of the Royal Garrison Artillery and was killed in action. From Tonyrefail, he was buried in Romeries Communal Cemetery Extension.

Second Lieutenant William Vernon Jackson, 19, of 206 Squadron, from Clydach in Swansea was killed on 30 October. He was buried in Y Farm Military Cemetery, Bois-Grenier. He was the observer in a DH.9 which was attacked while on a bombing mission. The pilot survived.

Second Lieutenant John Edward Prosser, aged 18, of 98 Squadron was killed on the same day. Born in Aberdare, his parents had moved to Swansea. He was buried in Quiévrain Communal Cemetery in Belgium. Prosser was the observer in a DH.9 which was on a mission to bomb Mons Railway Station. On its way back to base, it was attacked by enemy aircraft and was claimed by *Leutnant* Helmut Lange of *Jasta* 26. The pilot, Lieutenant D.W. Holmes, was also killed.

It was Lange's eighth victory and he survived the war, though it is not known what happened to him subsequently. He was awarded the Iron Cross First Class.

Also on 30 October, Lieutenant Jabez Gilbert Pagdin, 20, who was born in Shotton in Flintshire, died of pneumonia in the 4th Northern General Hospital in Lincoln. Before enlisting he had been studying engineering at Liverpool University. He now lies in St Deiniol's Church cemetery, Hawarden. Pagdin had joined the Royal Flying Corps as a second lieutenant in the Kite Balloon Service before being promoted to lieutenant and serving in Salonika and Egypt.

Air Mechanic 2nd Class William Harold Gillett died of natural causes on 31 October, aged 35. He was attached to the Recruits Training Wing, Blandford, and was buried in Saints Eleri and Mary Church cemetery in Llanrhos, near Llandudno.

Private 2nd Class George Jones died of natural causes on the same day, aged 21. He was serving with 14 Squadron in Egypt. From Llandinam in Montgomeryshire, he was buried in Kantara War Memorial Cemetery.

Private 2nd Class D. Roberts of the 14th Balloon Company also died on the same day of natural causes. His widow lived in Llithfaen near Pwlhelli. He was buried in Busigny Communal Cemetery Extension in France.

Lieutenant Simon Davies Evans died of influenza on 1 November, aged 22, while serving with 12 Squadron. From Beulah near Newcastle Emlyn, he was buried in Rocquigny-Equancourt Road British Cemetery, Manancourt.

Private Albert Wallace Frayling died of natural causes on

the same day, aged 33, at the 4th Northern General Hospital, Lincoln, while serving with the 435th Training Squadron. He was buried in Cathays Cemetery in Cardiff. His widow lived near the cemetery, and before the war he had been a furniture dealer.

Serjeant Thomas Hindle from Nelson was buried in his local cemetery after also dying of illness on 1 November at Southall Hospital. He was 24 and was serving at the Armaments School in Uxbridge.

Air Mechanic 1st Class Stanley Short was 25 when he died of natural causes on 3 November. Born in Abertillery, he and his wife Esther and daughter Violet lived in Carmarthen. He was buried in Carmarthen Cemetery and had served with 119 Squadron.

Lieutenant Francis Sumsion of 62 Squadron was killed on 4 November, aged 25. He and his wife Sarah lived in Pontyclun, Glamorgan. He was buried in Blaugies Communal Cemetery in Belgium. He had formerly served with the 3rd Welsh Regiment and was flying a Bristol F.2B, with his observer being Captain William Geoffrey Walford, when it was attacked. The aircraft was last seen going down at 10.15 a.m. with a broken wing south-west of Mons. They were the ninth and final victims of *Leutnant* Helmut Lange of *Jasta* 26 (see page 220).

On 4 November, the announcement was made of the award of Distinguished Flying Cross to Captain Arthur Watts Williams of Bryn Glas, Newport. Born on 12 May 1895, he was educated at Repton School, Derbyshire. He served with the Army Service Corps before being commissioned into the 4th Dragoon Guards in December 1914. He gained his Royal Aero Club licence in a Caudron biplane at Hendon on 8 April 1916 and joined the Royal Naval Air Service twelve days later. The citation for his Distinguished Flying Cross read:

Captain Williams, with 2nd Lt. Watters as Observer, took part in a night raid on a railway junction. Getting well over the objective, they descended to 500 feet and released four bombs on a moving train. They then, in face of heavy and accurate fire, flew up and down the junction and railway track, at altitudes varying between 250 ft. to 90 ft., bombing the railway and sweeping the station and sidings with machine-gun fire. Captain Williams has carried out fifteen night bomb raids with great success, proving himself an able and courageous pilot. In these raids he has been ably assisted by his Observer, 2nd Lt. Watters. This officer possesses qualities invaluable in an Observer – quickness in detecting hostile movements as well as first-rate marksmanship.[62]

Married in 1916, Williams divorced his first wife in 1924 and emigrated to Kenya with his second wife where he worked as a farmer and company director. He became a magistrate in Nairobi in 1937 and served in the Royal Air Force Volunteer Reserve during the Second World War, being mentioned in dispatches. He died in Kenya in June 1955.

Air Mechanic 3rd Class Thomas John Evans, 27, died of influenza on 5 November. He was serving with 115 Squadron

A photograph of Arthur Williams and a painting of him by Sidney Watts White

and was buried in Charmes Military Cemetery, Essegney. His parents lived in Pentre, Rhondda.

On 6 November, DH.9s from 99 Squadron took off on a bombing mission. Lieutenant Thomas Llewellyn from Roath Park, Cardiff, was an observer in one of the aircraft and they were attacked by a number of Pfalz D.III scouts. The combat report read:

> About 20 enemy aircraft attacked rear of formation over Buhl and 3 enemy aircraft attacked the tail of above machine (Llewellyn) just after dropping the bombs. The Observer (Llewellyn) fired a drum into the nearest machine and saw him go down in a steep sideslip with smoke issuing from machine for about 4,000 feet. He could not follow him down further owing to the other two machines attacking (his) tail.[63]

Air Mechanic 2nd Class Ivor Morgan was 20 when he died of pneumonia at a casualty clearing station on 7 November. He was serving as a wireless operator with 10 Squadron and was from Marlas Farm, Pyle, Bridgend. He was buried in Kezelberg

Military Cemetery, east of Ypres.

Air Mechanic 3rd Class Walter John Sheppard died of illness on the same day and was buried in St Mary's Church cemetery, Coity, Bridgend.

Lieutenant Evan Lindsay Pritchard Evans died at Hillington Hall, King's Lynn on 7 November. He was 23 and was buried in St Mary's Church cemetery, Hillington, Norfolk. Formerly of Mountain Ash, he had lived at Northlands, Maindy, Cardiff, and had been a student at the School of Mines in Treforest. He died

Thomas Llewellyn

of illness at Hillington Hall which was being used as a hospital at the time.

Captain Bentfield Charles Hucks died of influenza on 7 November. Born in Stanstead, Essex, in October 1884, a report on him was printed in August 1915:

The London Gazette on Friday announced that Second-lieutenant (now Lieutenant) Bentfield C. Hucks, Special Reserve, has been appointed a flight officer in the military wing of the Royal Flying Corps. Lieutenant B.C. Hucks is well known at Cardiff as a motorist and an intrepid airman. Formerly employed at the Docks, he subsequently devoted himself to motoring and, for some time before the war broke out, had turned his attention to aviation. His exhibitions from the Ely Racecourse and his flight across the Bristol Channel are well remembered by local residents. He was one of the first British airmen to 'loop the loop'. His appointment in the military wing of the Royal Flying Corps will cause great satisfaction to a wide circle of friends in the city.[64]

An article appeared shortly after his death:

By the death of Capt. Benfield Charles Hucks, which has occurred from pneumonia following influenza, there passes from our midst one of the earliest and greatest pilots in the history of British aviation, and it seems doubly tragic to think that he died on the very eve of the glorious triumph of the Allied forces, towards which he had contributed so splendid a share.

Hucks was born in 1884 at Stanstead, Essex, and was the youngest son of a consulting engineer. He was a first-class motorist, and it was only natural that to one of his temperament the new science of flight should have appealed strongly from the very first. He took his Royal Aero Club certificate in May 1911 on a Blackburn monoplane at Filey, but he had been actively associated with flying since 1910, for he was assisting Grahame White at the Blackpool meeting, and also accompanied him on the famous visit to the United States. In the autumn of 1911, he gave a most successful series of exhibitions in the West of England, and from that date down to the outbreak of war, he rendered magnificent service to British aviation by the remarkable demonstrations of the progress of this science which he gave in almost every part of the country. It is probably no exaggeration to say his name will be remembered by hundreds of thousands of people who, through him, saw flying for the first time in their lives, and thus realised it had become an accomplished fact and not a mere dangerous experiment.

The educational work has perhaps never been fully appreciated as it deserves. To record all the many fine flights he made during his career would be difficult, but it is worth mentioning that he was certainly one of the first to recognise the commercial possibilities of the aeroplane and to demonstrate them by carrying goods from one town to another – long ago, be it remembered. On the eve of the General Election, it is also interesting to know that he put an aeroplane to political uses for the first time at the Midlothian election in 1911 by distributing from the air in various parts of that constituency the literature of one of the candidates.

At the outbreak of war, he at once volunteered for active service, and did excellent work in France for a time until pleurisy unfitted him for the strenuous conditions of aerial fighting. After his recovery he took up the testing of new machines being attached to the RFC and to the Aircraft Manufacturing Company for this purpose. The unique experience he had gained during his pre-war flying, his skill in looping and other evolutions, and his knowledge of active service, stood him in good stead, and when it is possible to relate in full the valuable work he has done for the Air Services, as one may devoutly hope may be done at no distant date by Mr Holt Thomas, or someone equally in a position to appraise his merits, Hucks will hold a prominent place in the list of brave men who have done so much for their country and for the good of the world in general.

He was essentially a brave pilot, for none knew better than he the risks of research work in the air. His technical knowledge was such, however, that he could study a machine, however new its design or startling its features, on the ground before taking any undue risks. In other words, he could with confidence rely on his brains to reduce to the lowest possible point the dangers of his work, and the fact that he has now succumbed to an ordinary kind of illness, after flying in the aggregate probably more than any living pilot, shows the brilliance of his work. He was always spoken of by those who knew him well as a really steady pilot. Everyone had confidence in him.

Hucks had a delightful personality when one knew him. He was by nature serious and somewhat retiring, and not given to making friends rapidly, but had an exceptionally keen sense of humour. I shall always treasure the memory of a week in Paris with him a year ago, and the adventures of our flight back to England, interrupted in the middle by a thrilling night of air raids in Calais. Sheltering together under a heavy bombardment for many hours, one gets a more intimate insight into the character of a friend than might be possible under other circumstances, and the friendship of Hucks meant far more to me from that night forward.

I would like to suggest that some permanent and visible memorial be erected in due course in the neighbourhood of Hendon, where he accomplished so much of his life's work. Meanwhile, the deepest sympathy will be undoubtedly offered by his countless friends, to his relatives, and to his colleagues at the Aircraft Manufacturing Company, whose loss is severe. There will never be another Hucks. May he rest in peace.[65]

Hucks was the sales manager of the Automobile Company in Charles Street, Cardiff, when he was caught speeding in his motor car and banned from driving for three years. He then learned to fly, gaining his certificate in 1911, and bought an aeroplane. On 1 September 1911, he became the first man to fly across the Bristol Channel, and ten days later became the courier of the first letter to arrive in Cardiff by air. He was buried in Highgate Cemetery, London.

Sadly, the number of casualties continued to rise even after the Armistice was signed on 11 November – many as the result of the influenza pandemic. The toll soon exceeded the number of combat deaths during the war.

Annie Roberts had joined the Women's Royal Air Force on 14 May 1918. From Holywell, she was serving as a member with the 4th Training Depot Squadron when she contracted pneumonia and died on 12 November. She was buried in Maeshyfryd Burial Board cemetery in her home town.

Driver Frances Mary Dulcie Llewellyn-Jones enlisted

LOOPING
THE LOOP
BY
B. C. HUCKS.

This is a reproduction of the striking
16-sheet Poster, in six colours, produced by The B. C. Hucks Company
to advertise their demonstrations.

Demonstrations of
Looping the Loop by

Mr. B. C. Hucks is the first British
Airman to Loop the Loop and fly
upside down, and is always a
powerful attraction wherever he is
announced to give his looping
demonstrations.

B·C·HUCKS

The B. C. HUCKS Company

Expert Organisers of Aviation Meetings

166, PICCADILLY, LONDON, W

The B. C. Hucks Company invite inquiries from those
who wish to promote a Demonstration of Flying in any
part of the Country. Their experience in the organisation
of successful Flying Meetings is unique, and they will
willingly give advice and detailed information on request.
Address your inquiry to The B. C. Hucks Co., 166, Piccadilly,
London, W. 'Phone Regent 2942.

Bentfield Hucks	Poster advertising his air show

on 23 August 1918, aged 22, and was posted for duty at the end of September. She died on 13 November in the Military Hospital, Mexborough, in Yorkshire and is buried in Newport's Christchurch Cemetery. She was daughter of the Reverend David Ernest Llewellyn-Jones and Frances Eliza Sophia of Maindee Vicarage, Newport.

Second Lieutenant E.B. Haynes of Number 1 (S) Aircraft Repair Depot died on 14 November, aged 45. His widow Florence lived in Newport and he was buried in St Mary Magdalene Church cemetery in Usk.

A strange coincidence was reported on 15 November:

Capt. Simon Jones, DFC, RAF was a student at the Aberayron County School. Writing to Miss Nesta Howell, Portland House, an old fellow student, from France dated November 8th, he states: 'A strange coincidence occurred whilst I was returning from my leave. I flew across the Channel when returning to France. I landed at the Base Depot. From there I wanted to get to the Advanced Depot so I asked for another machine. They gave me a type I had not used before, but I decided to take it. Imagine my surprise when

I got near it to find "Aberayron" as large as life on its side.

Although the type of the "bus" was new to me, I thoroughly enjoyed the trip to the Advanced Depot. The name on the "bus" had something to do with my enjoyment. This machine, of course, must be the result of the Aberayron Weapons week. It is remarkable that an old Aberayron School fellow has had the privilege of flying Aberayron's own "bus!"' Captain Jones has often piloted Lord Weir, the controller of the RAF, across the Channel.[66]

Captain Henry Thornbury Fox Russell died on 18 November, aged 21. He was buried in St Seiriol Church cemetery in his home town of Holyhead. Educated at Churcher's College in Hampshire, he was commissioned as a second lieutenant in August 1914 and served with the 6th Royal Welsh Fusiliers. He served at Gallipoli and in Egypt and Palestine and was made Captain in June 1916.

In March 1917, he joined the Royal Flying Corps and was awarded the Military Cross for bravery in the air and for rescuing a downed pilot who was seriously wounded. Lieutenant Boddy had been shot down by Manfred von Richthofen.

The citation for his Military Cross reads:

For conspicuous gallantry and devotion to duty. He formed one of a patrol which silenced an enemy battery. He dropped bombs on two of the guns, silenced others with his machine gun and then engaged transport on the road. This operation was carried out under heavy fire and very difficult weather conditions. On another occasion he dropped bombs and fired 300 rounds on enemy trenches from a height of 100 feet. His machine was then hit by a shell and crashed in front of our advanced position. He reached the front line, and while there saw another of our machines brought down. He went to the assistance of the pilot, who was badly wounded, extricated him under heavy fire and brought him to safety. He showed splendid courage and initiative.[67]

In February 1918, he was promoted to Flight Commander and survived the war. On 18 November, he was flying a Sopwith Camel and had climbed to 900 feet when the aircraft went into a spin and crashed. His brother John was awarded the Victoria Cross and the Military Cross as a medical officer with the Royal Welsh Fusiliers.

On 20 November, Petty Officer David Howell of the Royal Naval Air Service died, aged 29. He had served as a mechanic with the Russian Armoured Car Division in the Lebanese Republic. Taken prisoner by the Turks, he died of illness while on his way home after being released, and was buried in Beirut War Cemetery. Howell had also served in Russia and Romania. His parents owned a shop in Peterston-super-Ely, Cardiff.

Private W. Jones was 44 when he died on 21 November. Born at Ystalyfera in Swansea, he was buried in Mikra British Cemetery, Kalamaria, Greece. He left a widow, Maggie.

Acting Corporal David Jones died at the Priory Hospital in Cheltenham on 23 November. He was buried in Tonyrefail Calvinistic Methodist Chapel cemetery in Llantrisant, leaving a widow, Hannah.

Flight Cadet John Hughes was 18 when he died of natural causes on 25 November while serving with 1 Squadron. He was buried in Amlwch Cemetery in his home town.

Serjeant Archibald Cyril Moore from Newport, aged 27, died on 28 November and was buried in St Woolos Cemetery.

Henry Fox Russell

David Howell

WALES AND THE FIRST AIR WAR 1914–1918

He was working at the Number 2 Stores Disability Park in Newcastle. Educated at Newport Intermediate School for Boys, he died at the First Northern General Hospital in Newcastle of injuries received as the result of a motor accident.

Leading Aircraftman John Walsh, 20, died of illness on 29 November while serving with 112 Squadron. He was buried in Aberfan Cemetery.

Air Mechanic 2nd Class John Albert Davies was 27 when he died on 1 December while serving with 66 Wing in Italy. Born in Llanelli, he was buried in Taranto Town Cemetery Extension, Puglia.

Flight Serjeant John Parry was 29 when he died on 4 December while serving with 214 Squadron. He was the son of Richard and Jane Parry of Cecil Street, Holyhead, and was buried in Lille Southern Cemetery.

Cadet John Davies, 19, was killed on 8 December. He was buried in St Caron Churchyard Extension in his home town of Tregaron.

Private 1st Class H. Jones died on 11 December, and was buried in Christ Church cemetery in Welshpool.

The following day, Air Mechanic 3rd Class Arthur Charles Williams died, aged 49. Born in Carmarthen, he had lived in London with his wife, Minnie. He was buried in Hendon Cemetery. His death was reported thus:

It was with much regret that the news of the death of Air Mechanic Arthur Charles Williams, RAF, eldest son of the late Mr Henry J. Williams, watchmaker, and of Mrs Williams, Nott-square, Carmarthen, was received in the town. His death took place with tragic suddenness at Hendon Aerodrome, London, on Thursday, the 12th inst. Deceased was 49 years of age, and was a watchmaker by trade. He joined the Royal Air Force as a mechanic about a year ago, and after serving for a short time at Farnborough and Newcastle-on-Tyne, was transferred to Hendon, where he was engaged on important work in the gun-setting department. He was billeted at his home in Shepherd's Bush, and on Thursday morning he left home apparently in normal health. He performed his duties as usual in the morning, and shortly after mid-day was observed to suddenly collapse and fall to the ground. An N.C.O. and comrades who ran to his assistance found him unconscious, and he was immediately conveyed to the City of Westminster Infirmary. He was attended by three doctors, but died a few hours later without regaining consciousness. It was found that death was due to cerebral haemorrhage, caused by overstrain whilst performing his duties.

The sudden death came as a great shock to the widow and relatives, with whom deep sympathy is felt. Prior to his enlistment, the late A.C. Williams was employed in the watchmaking department of Messrs. Selfridge, Oxford Street, London. He had won the high esteem of his employers and fellow-workmen, and by a sad coincidence he had with him at the time of his death a letter asking him to apply for his release in order to resume civil employment at their establishment. The funeral took place on Wednesday at Hendon Park with full military honours. The coffin, which was borne by a party of deceased's comrades, was wrapped in the Union Jack, and the burial service was impressively conducted by the chaplain.[68]

Quarter Mistress Janet Jones was 28 when she died on 21 December. From Llanrwst, she was buried in Seion Calvinistic Methodist Chapel cemetery in Llanrwst.

CHAPTER FIVE

1919 to 1921

'Fight on and fly on to the last drop of blood
and the last drop of fuel, to the last beat of the heart.'
Baron Manfred von Richthofen

THE CASUALTIES OF 1919 to 1921 are often overlooked, but although Germany surrendered on 11 November 1918, the Treaty of Versailles, which formally ended the war, was not signed until 28 June 1919. Each one has a Commonwealth War Graves Commission headstone, as each is treated as a casualty of active service, and the qualifying period for a headstone was death up until 31 August 1921. Many of them died of influenza or other natural causes, some perished in flying accidents, after serving during the years of fighting on the various fronts and British forces continued to fight the Bolsheviks in Russia after the treaty was signed.

Lieutenant Trevor Lewis Williams died in a flying accident on 1 January 1919. He was 21 and from Pontarddulais in Swansea. He was serving in Iraq with 72 Squadron and was buried in North Gate War Cemetery in Baghdad.

Private 2nd Class Thomas Kelly was 34 when he died on 12 January. He was buried in Abercynon Cemetery.

Aircraftman 1st Class John Lewis died on 7 February, aged 37, while serving at the 1st Aircraft Depot in France. His widow, Mary, lived in Uplands, Swansea. He was buried in Longuenesse Souvenir Cemetery, St Omer.

On 8 February, it was announced that Lieutenant Parcell

Rees Bowen from Carmarthen had been awarded the Distinguished Flying Cross, along with Second Lieutenant Robert Fawcett, for their service in Egypt:

> These officers have displayed marked courage and determination on many occasions. On 22 September, they carried out an excellent reconnaissance under difficult conditions, the clouds being very low over the hills, bringing back most valuable information.[1]

Born in 1893 and educated at St David's College, Lampeter, Bowen had enlisted as a private in the Army Service Corps and spent the winter of 1914/15 on the Western Front. In February 1915, he was sent home with badly frostbitten feet and, on recovering, joined the 5th Welsh Regiment as a second lieutenant. He served at Gallipoli and fought in Palestine where he was transferred to the Machine Gun Corps. On 16 August 1917, the announcement of his Military Cross appeared: 'For conspicuous gallantry and devotion to duty. He displayed great gallantry and skill in handling his guns under very trying conditions, and behaving with great resource and initiative in outflanking a house used as divisional headquarters and compelling the inmates to surrender.'[2]

In November 1917, he volunteered for the Royal Flying Corps and in January 1918 took up a posting as an observer, flying in an R.E.8 with 14 Squadron. In January 1919, he was hospitalised with venereal disease, caught in Palestine. He was ill for three months before being placed on the unemployed list in April.

On 3 July 1919, he embarked for Russia and served with 3 Squadron, Slavo-British Aviation Corps as an observer. At Archangelsk he met his old Carmarthen friend, Ira Jones, the Welsh 'ace' (see page 298). In August, Bowen won a bar to his Distinguished Flying Cross. The citation read:

> On August 24, 1919, whilst observer on reconnaissance over the enemy aerodrome (Toima), he was fired upon at long distance

range from an enemy machine, both himself and the pilot being wounded. The pilot having collapsed from his wound on to the controls, Observer-Officer Bowen managed to guide the machine from the back seat and flew homeward for a distance of 100 miles, by which time the pilot had slightly recovered and took control of the landing, which was safely made on the Bereznik Aerodrome. This officer's action was highly meritorious, and the guiding of the machine over a long distance was especially noteworthy in view of the wound which he had sustained in the right elbow.[3]

After being repatriated to Britain and recovering, Bowen served in Lithuania until, in July 1920, he accepted a secret British Government post in Ireland as a spy. On the night of 26/27 October 1920, he was shot dead on a Dublin street. Some accounts claim that Sinn Féin were responsible, but other sources state that he was shot by the British for failing to carry out an assassination order. He was buried with full military honours in Abergwili parish church cemetery, Carmarthenshire.

The announcement of the Distinguished Flying Cross to Lieutenant William Eustace Palk was also made on the same day as Bowen's, 8 February 1919. It read:

On 4th November, after bombing enemy troops and transport, this officer attacked, from a very low altitude, two companies of enemy infantry, turning their orderly retirement into a rout. On numerous occasions, the damaged state of his machine has borne testimony to his boldness in pressing home his attacks on various ground targets.[4]

Palk's father had been the governor of Brecon Prison, and William Palk had joined the Brecknock Territorials and served in Aden with them from October 1914, then subsequently in India. Commissioned whilst in India, in May 1916 he transferred to the Royal Engineers and served in Mesopotamia until 1917. He then joined the Royal Flying Corps in Egypt, and in 1918 was posted to France. Palk was killed in a motorcycle

Parcell Bowen

The Distinguished Flying Cross

accident on 27 August 1921, aged 26, and was buried in St David's Church cemetery in Brecon.

On 9 February, Corporal Fred Hine, aged 41, of the 1st Aircraft Depot, died of natural causes. His widow, Harriet, lived in Canton, Cardiff. He was buried in Longuenesse Souvenir Cemetery, St Omer.

Aircraftman 2nd Class John Reynold Griffiths died on 10 February, aged 23. He was buried in Holy Trinity Church cemetery in Godre'r Graig. His death was reported thus:

> It is with regret that we record the death of Private John Reynold Griffiths of the RAF, eldest son of Mr and Mrs William Griffiths (butcher), Wern Road, formerly of the staff of the Panteg Schools, Ystalyfera. A sad feature of the case is that deceased, who was only 23 years of age, had come through the heavy fighting at Armentières, and Ypres with the Royal Welsh Fusiliers, but had recently contracted influenza, and died on Saturday last at the 2nd London General Hospital, Chelsea. His remains were accorded the military honours to Paddington Station on Tuesday night, and the body reached Ystalyfera on Wednesday morning.[5]

The flu pandemic which caused more than 50 million deaths between January 1918 and December 1920 continued to exact a terrible toll on servicemen and women in 1919.

Private 2nd Class Thomas Herbert Pryce died on 13 February, aged 30. He was buried in Cathays Cemetery in Cardiff. His parents lived in Roath in Cardiff.

Air Mechanic 1st Class Edward John Collard was 32 when he died on 18 February while serving at the 1st Aircraft Depot in France. His widow, Lily, lived in Whitchurch, Cardiff. He was buried in Longuenesse Souvenir Cemetery, St Omer.

Aircraftman 1st Class Wallace Gilbert Humphreys died on 20 February, aged 30. He was serving with 8 Squadron in Belgium and was buried in Charleroi Communal Cemetery. His widow, Tryphena, lived in Newtown, Montgomeryshire.

Serjeant Francis Edward Cope of 29 Squadron was 26 when he died on 28 February. He too was buried in Charleroi Communal Cemetery. His parents lived in Caerphilly.

Corporal T.H. Gregory died on the same day, aged 26, while serving with 8 Squadron. He was buried at Étaples Military Cemetery. He was born in Pontypridd.

Flight Serjeant Lionel Randolph James, from Cardiff, also

Francis Cope (front, middle)

died on 28 February, aged 33, while serving with the 3rd Aircraft Repair Depot. He was buried in Cathays Cemetery in Cardiff.

Serjeant Ivor John Jackson died on 2 March. He was 23 and was buried in Abergavenny New Cemetery in his home town.

Private Gwilym Saunders Jones died on 7 March, aged 28. From Aberdare, he was buried in Aberdare Cemetery.

Corporal John Jones, 25, died on 10 March while serving with Number 1 Wireless School. He was buried in St Michael's Church cemetery, Llanfihangel-y-traethau, Merionethshire.

Air Mechanic 3rd Class Richard Emrys Williams died on 18 March, aged 21, serving with 99 Squadron. From Aberystwyth, he was buried in St Roch Communal Cemetery in Valenciennes, France.

On 7 April, Air Mechanic 2nd Class R. Evans, 35, of Number 2 Aircraft Depot died. From Dolgellau, he was buried in Duisans British Cemetery, Étrun in France.

Air Mechanic 1st Class E.E. Dyke from Trefonen died on 12 April, aged 33, and was buried in his local cemetery.

Flight Serjeant Reginald Tom Parry, 25, died on 3 May. He had been awarded the Air Force Medal and served at the 15th Aircraft Acceptance Park. He was buried in St Mary's Church cemetery, Welsh Newton, Herefordshire. Parry was flying a DH.9 when it spun and caught fire near Alexandra Park, Manchester.

Serjeant Arthur Baden Page was 19 when he died on 14 May while serving with 206 Squadron in Germany. He was the observer in a DH.9 flown by Second Lieutenant S.H. Gibbs which crashed and killed both men. Originally from Cardiff, Page was buried in Cologne Southern Cemetery. His brother Hector had been killed on 17 July 1918 serving with the North Staffordshire Regiment.

Lieutenant Cyril Victor Clarence Wright died of his injuries on 24 May while serving with Number 1 Marine Observers' School. He was buried in the Church of St Peter and St Paul cemetery, Aldeburgh, Suffolk, leaving a widow, Laura, in Cardiff.

He had been the observer in a DH.6 which collided in mid-air at 300 feet with another aircraft. The pilot, Lieutenant Edward Jacobi, was also killed. The two aircraft were to be flown to Hendon for storage. They were being air tested prior to their delivery flights, but the wing of the second aircraft hit the tail of Wright's and the two aircraft plunged to the ground. Wright survived the crash and was taken alive to Ranelagh Road Hospital in Ipswich, where he died, a day before his wedding anniversary.

Flight Serjeant William James Prichard was 32 when he died on 27 May. From Chepstow, he was buried in St Arvans Church cemetery, Chepstow.

Aircraftman 2nd Class J.E. Jones died on 10 July, aged 37, in Germany, while serving with 207 Squadron. He was buried in Cologne Southern Cemetery, leaving behind a widow, Sarah, living in Holywell.

On 15 July, it was announced that Private 1st Class Edgar Nancekievill of 2nd Brigade had been awarded the *Décoration Militaire avec Croix de Guerre*. Born on 9 July 1896 in Newport,

Cyril Wright

Edgar Nancekievill
(Reproduced by kind permission of Andrew Gunn)

Monmouthshire, he joined the Army Service Corps, horse transport section, aged 19, on 10 December 1915, giving his occupation as that of a saddler. He was discharged on 12 January 1916 for not being likely to become an efficient soldier. He then enlisted in the Royal Flying Corps and served until the end of the war. Edgar Nancekievill married in August 1920 in Newport and died on 17 May 1976 at the age of 79.

Air Mechanic 2nd Class C. Grove, 25, died on 30 September. He was buried in St Mary's Church cemetery, Nolton, Bridgend in his home town.

Air Mechanic 1st Class R.J. Chambers died on 22 January 1920, aged 24, and was buried in Cardiff's Cathays Cemetery. His widow Sarah lived in the city.

Also buried in the same cemetery was Air Mechanic 2nd Class A.R. Tanner, who died aged 23 on 7 April. His parents lived in Canton in Cardiff.

Private 2nd Class R.T. Jones died on 19 April, aged 29. He was buried in Saints Eleri and Mary Church cemetery in Llanrhos. His widowed mother lived in Llandudno.

Private John Peron Jones died on 27 April, aged 20. From

Cyril Wright's funeral

Brynteg in Broughton, he was buried in St Paul's Church cemetery, Broughton.

Air Mechanic 2nd Class Bertie D. Thomas died on 6 July, aged 34. His widow, Agnes, lived in Newport and he was buried in St Woolos Church cemetery, Newport.

Aircraftman 1st Class W.W. Morrow died on 5 September, aged 43. He was buried in Wrexham Cemetery, leaving behind a widow, Eva.

Private 1st Class Ivor Cyril Bines died on 3 October, aged 21. He was serving at the Royal Air Force School of Training and was buried in Cathays Cemetery, Cardiff. His parents lived in Roath.

Flight Serjeant William John Davies died on 22 October, aged 33. He was serving at the Equipment and Personnel Depot in Chingford. Born in Llanbydder, he was buried in Holy Trinity Church cemetery in Ystrad Mynach, the town in which his widow, Margaret, lived.

Leading Aircraftman D.J. Jeffreys was 22 when he died on Christmas Day. He was serving at the Aeroplane Supply Depot and was buried in St Agatha Church cemetery, Llanymynech, Montgomeryshire, near to where his parents lived.

Flight Serjeant Morgan Walters died on 30 December, aged 27. Serving with 'E' Reserve, he was buried in Carmel Congregational Burial Ground in Gwaun-Cae-Gurwen, his home village.

Aircraftman 2nd Class Tom Conway was buried in Holy Trinity Church cemetery, Ystrad Mynach, after he died on 13 June 1921, aged 40. Born at Coleford, he and his wife Maud had lived at 42 Coedpenmaen Road, Pontypridd.

Private Andrew Jones was 29 when he died on 1 July while serving at Halton Camp in Buckinghamshire. He was buried in Rhyl Church Cemetery. His parents lived in Mill Bank Road, Rhyl.

Aircraftman 2nd Class David George Roberts died on 13 July 1921 while serving at the Motor Transport Repair Depot.

He was buried in Cathays Cemetery in Cardiff, the last Welsh airman or woman to be assigned a Commonwealth War Graves Commission headstone for death in service during the Great War.

CHAPTER SIX

The Welsh Flying Aces

'Man must rise above the Earth – to the top of the atmosphere and beyond – for only thus will he fully understand the world in which he lives.'

Socrates

THE DEFINITION OF an 'ace' is generally accepted to be that of an airman who has shot down five or more enemy aircraft. Wales was able to provide the Royal Flying Corps, the Royal Naval Air Service, and later the Royal Air Force, with a number of these deadly airmen.

Lieutenant Llewellyn Crighton Davies was credited with five victories as an observer/gunner. Born in Penarth on 9 January 1889, his father was the editor of the Cardiff *Figaro* magazine. Davies was a chartered accountant at the outbreak of the war and a pre-war Territorial with the Scottish Rifles. In March 1915, he was commissioned Second Lieutenant and was awarded the Military Cross in August 1915. His citation read: 'For conspicuous gallantry in action. He handled his trench-mortars with great skill, and knocked out an enemy machine-gun that was holding up the advance. He also took charge of various parties that had lost their officers, and brought in single-handed a wounded man under heavy fire.'[1]

In February 1917, he joined the Royal Flying Corps and

was posted to 22 Squadron as an observer/gunner, flying in F.E.2bs. He registered his first victory on 6 April 1917 when he destroyed an Albatros D.III over Saint-Quentin. Two days later he repeated the act above Régny. On 5 June, he destroyed an Albatros D.V north-west of Lesdins and minutes later shot down another. His last victory came on 29 July when he destroyed in flames an unidentified two-seater over Tortequesne.

In November 1917, he was assigned to 105 Squadron and was appointed as a flying officer in February 1918. He obtained his 'wings' in March 1918 but, a few days afterwards on 13 March, he crashed his Airco DH.4 and died three days later at the 3rd Southern General Hospital in Oxford, aged 29. He was buried in Holy Trinity Church cemetery, Penton Mewsey, Hampshire.

Captain Edward Barfoot Drake also achieved five victories. He was born in 1898 in Weymouth, but the family moved to Goodwick in Pembrokeshire shortly after he was born. After joining the Royal Naval Air Service, he served on Home Defence duties, during which time he destroyed a Gotha G.IV bomber off Dover on 22 August 1917 while flying a Sopwith Camel. He was then posted to 9 (Naval) Squadron in France and, when

this became 209 Squadron with the formation of the Royal Air Force in April 1918, he scored four more victories.

On 2 May he shot down an Albatros D.V over Cayeux, and on 3 June a Fokker Dr.I north-west of Montdidier. On 27 June, he destroyed in flames a Pfalz D.III above Warfusée, and on 8 August achieved 'ace' status by destroying a Fokker D.VII north-west of Rosières.

Edward Drake

His victory on 27 June is a notable one in that the German pilot, *Leutnant* Helmut Steinbrecher, was the first pilot in history to successfully parachute from the stricken machine.

Drake was reported missing on 29 September 1918 when his aircraft did not return from a patrol. It was assumed to have been shot down by ground fire. He is commemorated on the Arras Flying Services Memorial.

Captain David James Hughes gained five victories. He was born in Wales on 16 April 1899. Initially an instructor, he joined 3 Squadron in 1918 and, flying a Sopwith Camel, shot his first victim down in flames on 8 August, an Albatros two-seater north of Chaulnes. Two days later he shot down a Fokker D.VII and, on 26 August, he destroyed an Albatros two-seater south-west of Bapaume. He gained his fourth success on 4 September when he captured a Fokker D.VII and, on 23 October, achieved 'ace' status when he downed an unidentified two-seater.

He was awarded the Distinguished Flying Cross at the end of the year. His citation read:

Fokker D.VII

A gallant and skilful officer. On 4th September his patrol was attacked by eight Fokker biplanes. Proceeding to the assistance of one of our machines that was in difficulties, Lieut. Hughes was himself attacked by two enemy aeroplanes and driven down to 4,000 feet, his petrol and oil tanks being shot through. By skilful manoeuvring, he regained our lines, pursued by one of the enemy, which, at 2,000 feet, he engaged, bringing it down in our lines.[2]

Captain Eric Yorath Hughes also achieved five victories. Born in Bridgend on 6 July 1894, the elder son of Sir Thomas and Lady Hughes, he had served with the Royal Field Artillery from November 1914 in France and Egypt before volunteering for the Royal Flying Corps in August 1916. He joined 46 Squadron in June 1917.

On 4 September 1917, he shot down an Albatros two-seater south of the River Scarpe. A week later, again south of the Scarpe, he shot down an unidentified two-seater and repeated the feat on 21 September. On 1 December, he destroyed an Albatros D.III over Cambrai. All these victories were gained flying a Sopwith Pup. He then switched to a Sopwith Camel with 3 Squadron and, on 12 December, achieved his fifth

and final victory when he shot down an Albatros D.V, also over Cambrai. He was then withdrawn from front-line service.

Hughes survived the war and was a wing commander during the Second World War before retiring from the Royal Air Force in 1947. He married Dulcie Maine-Tucker of Penarth on 17 December 1919 in London, and died in Hove, Sussex, in September 1979.

Eric Hughes

Captain Thomas Vicars Hunter was credited with five victories. He was born on 2 April 1897 in London. His father was Henry Charles Vicars Hunter JP, and his mother the Honorable Florence Edith Louise (nee Dormer), daughter of the 12th Baron Dormer of Wyng. Henry Hunter was the principal landowner in Kilburn, Derbyshire, and lived at Abermarlais Park, Llangadog, Carmarthenshire.

Educated at Ladycross School in Seaford, East Sussex, and Eton College, Thomas Hunter left Eton in August 1914 and attended the Royal Military College, Sandhurst, as a cadet. He was commissioned Second Lieutenant in the Rifle Brigade on 23 December 1914, but in January 1915 he was involved in a motor cycling accident and was hospitalised. He developed sepsis, and in July had to have a leg amputated above the knee. He was fitted with an artificial leg and was placed on half-pay. Hunter rejoined his regiment on 30 September 1916 and was promoted to lieutenant. He volunteered for the Royal Flying Corps in February 1917 and received his Royal Aero Club Aviator's Certificate on 18 April. Appointed a flying officer on 9 May, he was posted to 66 Squadron in France.

Flying a Sopwith Pup, he achieved his first victory on 12 July 1917, sending an Albatros D.III to the ground northeast of Ypres. On 27 and 28 July he shot down two more D.IIIs over Ardoye and east of Roulers. Promoted to the rank of captain on 31 July, on 3 September he shot down another German aircraft, an Albatros D.V north-east of Menin. On 30 September, he

Thomas Hunter

was appointed Flight Commander and, on 8 November 1917, achieved his final victory by downing another Albatros D.V, this time flying in a Sopwith Camel.

Shortly afterwards, 66 Squadron was posted to the Italian Front. On 5 December 1917, Hunter took off with 'C' Flight on their first combat patrol. While flying at 10,000 feet, he made a left turn. His wingman, Richard W. Ryan, later wrote an account of what happened next:

> I immediately throttled my engine fully back in order to hold my position in the turn. However, the turn had been too sharp and I lost sight of him as he turned under me. In a Camel you cannot see objects directly below you. My aircraft was in an almost stalled position and I expected to see him coming out of the turn to the left of my aircraft. In that moment our two aircraft collided.[3]

The two aircraft were now locked together and fell in a slow spin. They finally separated at around 5,000 feet. Ryan was able to make an emergency landing and suffered minor injuries and shock, but Hunter crashed into the ground and was killed, aged 20. He is buried in Carmignano di Brenta, Padua.

Second Lieutenant Percy Griffith Jones achieved five victories as an observer/gunner. Born in Mold in Flintshire, in 1913 he was working in the drawing office of an engineering company in Liverpool. He then emigrated to America where he worked for the Burlington Distilling Company in New Jersey. By 1914 he was in Philadelphia, and wrote to the Royal Engineers asking to join. He attested on 5 March 1915, aged 23, and was awarded punishments for being absent from roll-call and for having a dirty rifle. On 21 July 1916, he was wounded and was admitted to the 99th Field Ambulance with shell shock. He was repatriated to the 3rd Northern General Hospital, Sheffield.

Jones transferred to the Royal Flying Corps in 1917. On 15

Albatros D.V

May 1918, he shot down two Albatros D.Vs over Wervicq. On 29 May he did the same to a Fokker Dr.I west of Armentières, and on 30 June repeated the act to a Fokker D.VII north of Comines. He achieved his ace status on 2 July when he destroyed, in flames, a Pfalz D.III south-east of Gheluvelt. Shortly afterwards, Jones called out a warning to his pilot, Lieutenant Thomas Cathcart Traill, who ducked, narrowly avoiding a bullet which went through the cockpit and out through the windscreen. Jones was not so lucky and was killed, aged 26; he was buried at Longuenesse Souvenir Cemetery, St Omer. Cathcart Traill later commanded 83 Group during the Second World War.

Captain Leslie Morton Mansbridge also achieved five victories. He was born on 13 June 1897 in Queensborough Terrace, London, and joined the Royal Flying Corps in February 1917.

On 1 May 1917, flying a Nieuport, as he did for all his first four successes, he destroyed an Albatros two-seater over Ploegsteert. On 24 May he shot down an Albatros D.III above Zandvoorde and four days later another one over Wervicq. On 2 June, again over Wervicq, he downed an Albatros D.III. His own aircraft was forced to land and he was wounded on 3 June 1917; it had been driven down by *Flugmeistern* Kunstler of *Marinefeldjasta* 1.

Leslie Mansbridge

Mansbridge recovered and joined 23 Squadron. His fifth and final victory came flying a Sopwith Dolphin east of Warfussée to Abancourt, when he shot down a Fokker Dr.I on 22 April 1918. He died in October 1992 in Pwlhelli.

Second Lieutenant William Arthur Owens achieved five victories as an observer/gunner. Born at Llandegfan, Menai Bridge, Anglesey, on 8 January 1899, he was an undergraduate student at University College of North Wales, Bangor, from October 1915 to January 1917. He joined the School of Aerial Gunnery as a second lieutenant in March 1918, and served with 211 Squadron from April to June 1918. Owens then transferred to 49 Squadron, with whom he claimed his five victories, and was posted to Home Establishment on 14 March 1919. He was transferred to the unemployed list on 16 April 1919.

He was awarded the Distinguished Flying Cross in 1919. His citation read: 'A gallant and determined officer, who is conspicuous for his skill in aerial combats. He has accounted for five enemy machines.'[4]

Lieutenant Wallace Alexander Smart had five confirmed victories. He was born in Aberdeen on 7 January 1898, but thereafter the family moved to Cardiff when he was a small boy. He served with the Royal Engineers before being commissioned into the Royal Flying Corps in September 1917.

Wallace Smart left a diary of his flying experiences. One entry outlined his fighting technique:

To be a successful scout pilot it is necessary to be a good fighting pilot; this simply means to be able to fly thoroughly and to use a certain amount of common sense. Before attacking an opponent, decide exactly what you are going to do under all circumstances, from the time you see him don't take your eyes off him until he is shot down. If you do, you will simply be shot down in his place, because you can't find him again. I have deliberately looked away from a machine whilst fighting it, and only in one case did I get sight of my opponent before he was on my tail. In that case it was a very dud pilot. Never lose height in a fight, and don't strain the engine, it will only cut out.

Another important practice is to get close to your opponent when on 'camera gun' fighting, get so close to him that his machine fills the complete films. You cannot hit a Hun from two hundred yards range, it is hard enough to hit him at fifty yards, opening fire at long range simply wastes ammunition, at the same time the guns will probably jam; result, you can't get Huns, but you will probably get shot up.

I think these are all my impressions of England, but in England there is an excessive amount of 'hot air'; consequently the sooner you get overseas, the better off you are.[5]

In another entry, he gave a description of one of his victories:

When on an O.P. [offensive patrol] we attacked a large formation of Albatross scouts. We employed the dive and zoom tactics. On my second dive I could not get my engine, consequently I had to go clean through their formation. I fully expected to get shot down, so I decided to sell my life dearly. One Hun tried to turn above and in front of me. I pulled up at him and fired a drum of Lewis into him. I hit his aileron clean off and I must have hit his engine also, because he went down in a side slip and at about 45 degrees laterally. I did not see it crash, but it must have been just S.E. of A— as the scrap took place at P— wood at 14,000. I managed to pick my engine up immediately after shooting this Hun down. I was officially credited with that Hun as out of control.

Nothing particularly startling happened while on that sector except that on one patrol I got badly shot up from the ground

Wallace Smart with his sister

when chasing a Hun two-seater at a height of 1,000 feet. I got seven bullets just behind my seat, two through the 'office' just in front of me, and several through the fuselage and wings. Besides this I officially shared, I think, it is four Huns; all crashed.[6]

Flying an S.E.5a with 1 Squadron, he shot down an Albatros D.V over Dranoutre on 31 May 1918 for his first success, and the following day downed a Pfalz D.III over Armentières. On 1 July, he shot down a Halberstadt two-seater over Messines. On 1 October, he shot down a Fokker D.VII north-east of Saint-Quentin, and on 29 October he destroyed a Fokker D.VII over Landrecies. He survived the war and died in Radyr, Cardiff, on 23 December 1943.

Lieutenant Edward George Herbert Caradoc Williams had five confirmed victories. Born in Flint in 1895, he served as a lieutenant with 48 Squadron, where he flew Bristol fighters. He shot down an Albatros D.III on 9 September 1917 over Middelkerke and two days later another one over Ostend. On 15 September, he accounted for an Albatros D.V north-east of Dixmude and on 29 October he destroyed a Pfalz D.III north-east of Dixmude. He achieved the status of an 'ace' by destroying an Albatros D.III north-east of Ostend on 13 November.

Captain John Jordan Lloyd Williams also achieved five victories. Born in 1894 in Denbighshire, he served with the Denbighshire Yeomanry and was commissioned on 26 July 1913. After joining the Royal Flying Corps, he served as an observer/gunner in Egypt and the Middle East before training as a pilot in 1918.

His first victory came on 8 October 1917 when he captured an Albatros D.III. A week later he destroyed another one over Shellah-Sharia in Palestine. On 30 October, he captured a two-seater north-west of Khalusa. On 6 November, he destroyed a Rumpler two-seater above Um Dabkel and two days later he destroyed in flames an Albatros D.III over Muleikat.

He was awarded the Military Cross: 'For conspicuous gallantry and devotion to duty in aerial fighting. He shot down three hostile aeroplanes in a very short period, showing great initiative and fearlessness on all occasions.'[7]

Captain Alwyne Travers 'Button' Loyd achieved six victories. He served with the 5th Battalion of the Buffs (East Kent Regiment) before joining the Royal Flying Corps. Born in Hawkhurst in Kent in 1894 of Welsh parents, he was educated at Eton. He was commissioned second lieutenant in the East Kent Regiment on 23 August 1914, and was granted a commission as Temporary Second Lieutenant Flying Officer on 19 June 1916. Between 7 September 1916 and 20 September

Rumpler C.IV

Alwyne Loyd

1917, Loyd claimed six 'victories' (three shared), including four during the Third Battle of Ypres. During this period he served with 25, 22 and 32 Squadrons. He often entertained his fellow officers with his excellent voice for burlesquing operatic arias – male and female.

His first victory occurred on 7 September 1916 when he downed a Fokker E monoplane above Pont-à-Vendin while flying a F.E.2b. On 4 December, he shot down an unidentified enemy aircraft over Beaulencourt.

His next victory did not occur until 13 August 1917, by which time he was flying a DH.5 with 32 Squadron. Late that evening, he destroyed an Albatros D.V north-east of Polygon Wood. On 22 August, he downed out of control an unidentified two-seater over Bellewaarde Lake. A month later, on 20 September, he claimed two enemy aircraft in a single day. His fifth victim was an Albatros D.V south of Becelaere, and a few hours later he shot down an unidentified two-seater over Becelaere for his sixth and final victory.

On 28 September 1917, Loyd took off on patrol at 1 p.m. His aircraft was hit either by a shell from an anti-aircraft gun or by fire from an aircraft flown by *Oberleutnant* Rudolf Berthold of *Jasta* 18. He was buried in Lijssenthoek Military Cemetery, aged 23.

Nicknamed the Iron Knight, Oskar Gustav Rudolf Berthold was born in Ditterswind in March 1891. He joined the German Imperial Army in 1909 and paid for his own flying lessons, qualifying as a pilot in September 1913. He won the Iron Cross

253

Oskar Berthold

for flying reconnaissance missions during 1914 and, over the next two years, scored five victories before crashing his aircraft and suffering severe injuries which led to him being hospitalised for four months. After recovering, he returned to front-line duties, being wounded in April 1917. By this time his score was 12 victories and for this he was awarded the *Pour le Mérite*.

Berthold was credited with 16 more victories before he was shot in the arm on 10 October 1917. Hospitalised again until February 1918, he returned to duty, although he could only fly using one arm and was still on medication. By 8 August he has dispatched 14 more enemy aircraft. On 10 August, he shot down two more victims before he himself was downed. He again returned to combat until the Kaiser ordered him to return to medical care. Berthold survived the war, only to be killed by Communists in political street fighting in Hamburg on 15 March 1920, aged 28.

Flight Lieutenant William Geoffrey Meggitt had six confirmed victories. Born in Newport, Monmouthshire, in 1894, he attended Peterhouse College, Cambridge, before enlisting. He was commissioned as a second lieutenant in the 3rd Welsh Regiment in March 1915 and landed in France in August 1915. Meggitt was appointed to the Royal Flying Corps in October 1916 and posted to 25 Squadron as an observer in F.E.2bs. He gained his first victory on 22 October 1916 when he destroyed two German fighters: the first south-west of

Seclin and the second north-west of Lille. On 17 November he destroyed in flames an unidentified aircraft over Vitry and, on 15 February 1917, drove down an unidentified two-seater over Avion.

The announcement of his Military Cross came on 17 April 1917: 'For conspicuous gallantry and devotion to duty whilst one of a patrol engaging five hostile machines. He drove down one enemy machine and then attacked another, which was seen to go down vertically. He has previously brought down three hostile machines.'[8]

After gaining his pilot's certificate, he was appointed as a flying officer on 8 June 1917. The following month he was promoted to lieutenant and posted to 22 Squadron. He gained his fifth victory on 10 October, flying a Bristol fighter when he destroyed an Albatros D.V over Moorslede. The following day he drove down another Albatros D.V.

Meggitt was shot down on 8 November, but survived and spent the next 12 months as a prisoner of war. He remained in the Royal Air Force after the war ended and, in January 1922, was promoted from flying officer to flight lieutenant. He was killed on 28 January 1927 when his Armstrong Whitworth Siskin fighter crashed at Norbury, London, just three weeks after his father had passed away.

The report of the subsequent inquest into his death stated:

'Even a gale in the British Isles is not sufficient to stop a machine that is capable of flying 140 miles an hour,' said Squadron Leader Sowrey at a Croydon inquest today, on Flight-Lieut. William Geoffrey Meggitt who was killed on January 28, when his aeroplane crashed into a Norbury garden during a gale. Witness said Meggitt was flying from Northolt to Croydon. If he considered the weather conditions unsuitable, he should have ordered Meggitt not to go. He was told there was a gale at Norbury, but at Northolt it was not an exceptionally windy morning.

Eye-witnesses of the crash told how they saw Meggitt's machine battling with the wind. Once it wobbled, but suddenly the pilot appeared to right himself. 'I clapped my hands because

I thought how smartly the pilot managed it,' said Sydney Robinson, a milk roundsman. 'The machine proceeded for a short distance, but another wind seemed to catch it and it dived and dropped like a stone.' The machine fell into the garden of a house and witness helped to lift the pilot from the machine. A terrible wind had been blowing all the morning. Major Cooper, Inspect of Accidents, said he came to the conclusion the accident was due to the pilot losing control of the machine while flying at a low altitude in squally weather. A verdict of death by misadventure was returned.[9]

Lieutenant Albert Leslie Jones achieved seven victories. He was born in Warwickshire on 19 December 1897 and joined the Royal Naval Air Service in March 1916, qualifying as a pilot in October 1917. He served with 210 Squadron from 29 January 1918, and was posted to Home Establishment on 13 August, surviving the war.

He shot down two Halberstadt two-seaters on 14 May over Ypres, and three days later destroyed a Rumpler two-seater

north-east of Bailleul. Four days afterwards, on 21 May, he destroyed a balloon over Pont Ricquen and another over Estaires on 5 June to gain his 'ace' status. His sixth victim was a Pfalz D.III that he destroyed over Estaires on 28 June, and on 1 August he shot down a Fokker D.VII south-east of Ostend.

He died in Derbyshire in June 1974. Often cited as a Welsh ace, his link with Wales is uncertain.

Albert Jones

Major Hubert Wilson Godfrey Jones was also credited with seven victories. Born on 7 October 1890 in Llandeilo and a resident of Pontardawe, Swansea, he enlisted in the Welsh Regiment and fought at Suvla Bay, Gallipoli, where he was wounded and sent to London for hospitalised treatment. He received his aviator's certificate at Hendon in July 1916, and was appointed to the Royal Flying Corps on 22 July.

He achieved his first victory on 11 August 1916, flying a DH.2 with 32 Squadron when he shot down out of control a Fokker E over Rancourt. On 23 September, he destroyed a LVG two-seater over Eaucourt l'Abbaye, and 1 October saw him shoot down an unidentified two-seater above Bihaucourt, a feat he repeated twice on 16 November over Loupart Wood to achieve his status as an ace. His next victory came on 5 February 1917 when he shot down an Albatros D.I over Grévillers and his final victory came ten days later when he repeated the act.

On 21 March, his DH.2 was brought down by *Leutnant* W. Olsen and *Leutnant* W. Hilf of Fliegerabteilung 23 near Roupy. Jones survived and was hospitalised. On recovering he was posted to the Central Flying School.

He was awarded the Military Cross on 26 March 1917: 'For conspicuous gallantry in action. With a patrol of three scouts, he attacked a hostile formation of ten enemy machines. Although wounded, he continued the combat and drove down an enemy machine. Later, although again wounded, he remained with his patrol until the enemy retired.'[10]

Jones survived the war

Hubert Jones

and continued to serve with the Royal Air Force. He raced aeroplanes, cars and motorbikes, and represented Britain in the bobsleigh. He commanded the first flight from Cairo to the Cape of Good Hope, for which he received the Air Force Cross, but was killed on 14 May 1943 while piloting a Hawker Hurricane on a secret trial flight when the bomb he was carrying exploded prematurely and the aircraft crashed at Sudbourne Marshes near Orford Ness in Suffolk. He had adopted his mother's maiden name, Penderel, as his surname in 1928.

Captain Howard John Thomas Saint achieved seven victories. He was born in Ruabon, Wrexham, on 21 January 1893, and in 1911 was working as a colliery manager's apprentice. His father was a mining engineer and colliery manager.

Saint served as a chief petty officer with the Royal Naval Air Service Armoured Cars in France in 1915 and 1916. He was commissioned sub lieutenant in August 1915 and then volunteered for pilot training, joining 10 Naval Squadron on 26 July 1917.

On 9 August 1917, while flying a Sopwith Triplane, he downed an Albatros D.III over Polygon Wood, and five days later he shot another down in flames over the Houthoulst Forest. Saint was wounded in the leg on 16 August 1917, but on 21 August he shot down an unidentified two-seater one mile south of Roulers. On 25 August, he downed an Albatros D.V south of Roulers and then switched to a Sopwith Camel to achieve his fifth victory on 21 September by shooting down another Albatros D.V over Wervicq. Two days later, over Westroosebeke, he repeated the feat. His final victim was an Albatros D.V that he destroyed north-east of Dixmude on 20 October.

He was subsequently awarded the Distinguished Service Cross:

For conspicuous bravery in attacking superior hostile formations of enemy aircraft. On the 21st September 1917, he, with three

Howard Saint

other machines, attacked five hostile scouts. After getting to close quarters with one of them, he fired three bursts from his machine-gun and drove it down completely out of control. On the 23rd September 1917, while leading a patrol of eight scouts, he attacked a hostile formation of ten machines. One of these he drove down, diving vertically, out of control. He has forced down other machines completely out of control, one of them in flames; and has also shown great courage in attacking enemy troops and aerodromes with machine-gun fire from very low altitudes.[11]

After the war, he was the Chief Test Pilot for the Gloster Aircraft Company. He died in September 1976, aged 83.

Captain Dudley Lloyd-Evans had eight confirmed victories. Born in Newport, Monmouthshire in 1895, he was commissioned as a second lieutenant in the South Wales Borderers in October 1914. In 1916, he was awarded the Military Cross. His citation read: 'For conspicuous gallantry in action. He wired the portion of the enemy's intermediate line which was captured that night. Later, he led a bombing attack with great courage and initiative.'[12]

He then joined the Royal Flying Corps and, in the early part of 1918, was posted to 64 Squadron. His first victory occurred on 31 May, when flying an S.E.5a, he attacked and destroyed an Albatros D.V over La Bassée. On 25 July he destroyed a Fokker D.VII west of Aubers. On 21 August, he claimed his third victory when he destroyed another Fokker D.VII north-east of Douai. Two days later, he destroyed a two-seater LVG two-seater reconnaissance aircraft over Cantin.

His fifth victory came the following month, on 3 September, when he drove down another Fokker D.VII out of control over Brebières. He was now an ace. Two days afterwards he attacked yet another Fokker D.VII north-east of Cambrai, and shot it down out of control as well. His seventh victory came on the same day – 18 September. He downed one Fokker D.VII and destroyed another east of Havrincourt.

He survived the war and, in December 1918, was awarded the Distinguished Flying Cross. His citation read: 'A brilliant fighting pilot who has carried out numerous offensive and low-bombing patrols with marked success. He has accounted for six enemy aeroplanes, and in these combats in the air he is conspicuous for dash, determination and courage.'[13]

Lloyd Evans continued his service with the Royal Air Force after the war ended, and won a bar to his Distinguished Flying Cross in 1920 while serving in Mesopotamia. His citation for this award read:

LVG C.VI

For gallantry, skill and devotion to duty on 1 November 1920, while accompanying another machine on reconnaissance. Owing to engine trouble, the second machine, with pilot and observer, had to make a forced landing in hostile country. A party of mounted Arabs at once started firing at the observer, who was dismantling a Lewis gun. On seeing this, Flying Officer Evans landed at great peril to himself, took both officers in his already loaded machine, and, getting off with much difficulty, returned to Headquarters.[14]

He served throughout the Second World War, retiring from the Royal Air Force in September 1945. He died on 20 March 1972 in Cheltenham.

Lieutenant-Colonel Lionel Wilmot Brabazon Rees was also credited with eight victories. Born at 5 Castle Street, Caernarvon, on 31 July 1884, he was the son of a solicitor who was also an honorary colonel in the Royal Welsh Fusiliers. Educated at Eastbourne College, Lionel Rees entered the Royal Military Academy at Woolwich in 1902. He was commissioned into the Royal Garrison Artillery on 23 December 1903, and posted to Gibraltar. Promoted to the rank of lieutenant in 1906, he served in Sierra Leone in 1908. In 1912, he paid for his flight training and was awarded his Royal Aero Club Aviator's Certificate in January 1913.

In May 1913, Rees was seconded to the Southern Nigeria Regiment and served in the West African Frontier Force. He joined the Royal Flying Corps in August 1914 as an instructor at Upavon, and was promoted to captain in October 1914.

In 1915, he was appointed to the command of 11 Squadron at Netheravon, arriving in France in July 1915, and within a short time he was awarded the Military Cross. His citation read:

For conspicuous gallantry and skill on several occasions, notably the following: On 21st September 1915, when flying a machine with one machine gun, accompanied by Flight-Serjeant Hargreaves, he sighted a large German biplane with two machine guns 2,000 feet below him. He spiralled down and dived at the enemy, who, having the faster machine, manoeuvered to get him broadside on and then opened fire. Despite this, Captain Rees pressed his attack and apparently succeeded in hitting the enemy's engine, for the machine made a quick turn, glided some distance and finally fell just inside the German lines near Herbecourt. On 28th July, he attacked and drove down a hostile monoplane despite the main spar of his machine having been shot through and the rear spar shattered. On 31st August, accompanied by Flight-Serjeant Hargreaves, he fought a German machine more powerful than his own for three-quarters of an hour, then returned for more ammunition and went out to the attack again, finally bringing the enemy's machine down apparently wrecked.[15]

Flying a Vickers F.B.5 'Gunbus', he had driven down a Fokker E monoplane on 28 July, and on 31 August he destroyed an LVG two-seater near Achiet-le-Grand. The victim on 21 September was an AGO two-seater which was also driven down.

The following day, 22 September, Rees drove down an Albatros two-seater south-east of Albert and, on 30 September,

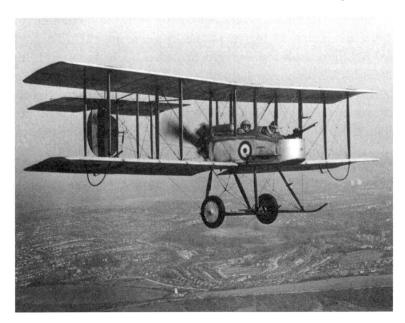

Vickers Gunbus

he captured another Albatros two-seater near Gommecourt. On 31 October, he drove down another LVG two-seater over Pys to Irnes.

At the end of 1915, he returned to England and took command of the Central Flying School at Upavon. In June 1916, he took command of 32 Squadron and returned to France in preparation for the Somme offensive; he was now promoted to the rank of major.

On 1 July, the first day of the campaign, he took off at 5.55 a.m. in a DH.2, joining what he thought was a British formation; he was attacked by German aircraft. He fired on a Roland two-seater aircraft, hitting it between the two crew members, and the machine plunged groundwards, out of control. He next attacked another Roland, hit its engine and forced it to land. Single-handedly, he then attacked five other enemy aircraft. At this point he was shot in the leg but he still attacked the formation leader. His ammunition now all expended, he drew his revolver to fire at close range, but dropped it into the nacelle. He returned to base and asked for some steps to be brought to help him get down from the cockpit as his leg was now paralysed.

For this action Rees was awarded the Victoria Cross. His citation read:

> On 1st July 1916 at Double Crassieurs, France, Major Rees, whilst on flying duties, sighted what he thought was a bombing party of our machines returning home, but they were in fact enemy aircraft. Major Rees was attacked by one of them, but after a short encounter it disappeared, damaged. The others then attacked him at long range, but he dispersed them, seriously damaging two of the machines. He chased two others but was wounded in the thigh, temporarily losing control of his aircraft. He righted it and closed with the enemy, using up all his ammunition, firing at very close range. He then returned home, landing his aircraft safely.[16]

After recovering from his injuries, he went on a War Office mission to America, and became a temporary lieutenant

Lionel Rees

colonel in May 1917. From then until the end of the war, he commanded the School of Aerial Fighting at Turnberry, Scotland.

On 2 November 1918, he was awarded the Air Force Cross and, in 1919, the OBE. He retired from the Royal Air Force in 1931 with the rank of group captain and, in 1933, he sailed single-handedly across the Atlantic in a ketch. When war broke out again in 1939, he rejoined the Royal Air Force and was appointed a wing commander. He married in August 1947, aged 62, and had three children. He died of leukaemia on 28 September 1955 at the Princess Margaret Hospital in Nassau in the Bahamas and was buried in the Nassau War Cemetery. During his working life he was known to give his pay to Service charities.

Captain William Victor Trevor Rooper had eight confirmed victories. Born in Chester on 10 May 1897, the family moved to Gresford in Denbighshire. He was educated at Bilton Grange, Rugby, and Charterhouse. When war was declared, he enlisted in the 24th (Denbighshire Yeomanry) Battalion of the Royal Welsh Fusiliers aged 17, and served as a motorcycle despatch rider until he was gazetted second lieutenant in December 1914. He volunteered for the Royal Flying Corps in September 1916 and was promoted lieutenant in May 1917. That summer he joined 1 Squadron.

Flying a Nieuport, he claimed his first victim on 28 July 1917 when he shot down an Albatros D.V over Becelaere. On

William Rooper

9 August, he captured an unidentified enemy two-seater near the Houthoulst Forest and, on 17 August, he downed a DFW two-seater over Ten Brielen, near Ypres.

In August 1917, he was promoted to captain and flight commander and, the following month, shot down an Albatros D.V over Houthoulst on 11 September, and became an ace when he destroyed in flames another Albatros D.V east of Poelcapelle on 19 September. His sixth victim came six days later when he destroyed an Albatros D.V east of Gheluvelt.

On 1 October, he downed an DFW two-seater over Houthoulst and on 5 October registered his last victory when he destroyed an Albatros D.V over Zandvoorde. Four days later, he was shot down near Polygon Wood by *Leutnant* Dilthey of *Jasta* 27. His aircraft crashed in the front-line trenches, and Rooper broke his thigh. He died later from the effects of his injuries, aged 20, and was buried in Bailleul Communal Cemetery Extension. The Chaplain wrote: 'I have never known anyone so universally liked, loved and admired as your boy, not only by his squadron, but by all who came across him,' and an officer of his flight added: 'We feel his loss enormously, but feel proud that he gave his life so gloriously to save a comrade.'[17]

One of three sons, his brother, Ralph Bonfoy Rooper, was killed, aged 23, while serving with the French Red Cross Society on 29 May 1918. His other brother survived, but lost two of his own sons on active service during the Second World War.

Helmut Dilthey was born in Westphalia on 9 February 1894 and joined the German Air Service in November 1914. He was awarded the Iron Cross Second Class on 18 June 1915, and in October 1916 the Iron Cross First Class. Under the command of Hermann Göring in *Jasta* 27, he scored six victories. He was then given command of *Jasta* 40 and downed an enemy observation balloon in June 1918. The following month he was killed in action over Lille.

Captain Franklin Geoffrey Saunders was credited with eight aerial victories. Born in Mumbles, Swansea, on 3 June 1891, he was a sub-lieutenant with the Royal Naval Volunteer Reserve when he was granted his Royal Aero Club Aviator's Certificate on 1 January 1914 after a solo flight in a Bristol biplane at Brooklands.

On 27 January he was posted to HMS Pembroke, a naval barracks at Chatham. He was commissioned as a second lieutenant in the Army on 9 September, and by late 1916 he was serving with the Royal Flying Corps.

He gained his first victory while serving with 47 Squadron in Greece. Flying a B.E.12 fighter, he forced down and captured

an Albatros two-seater reconnaissance aircraft over Lahana. This was shared with Second Lieutenant Gilbert Green.

On 18 March, he achieved his first sole victory when he shot down a Friedrichshafen G over Karasouli. Two days later, he destroyed an Albatros two-seater west of

Helmut Dilthey

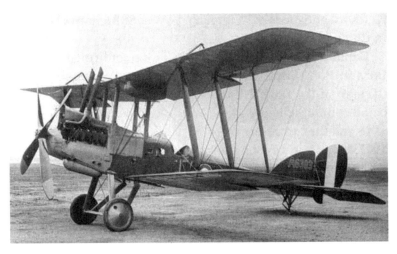

Royal Aircraft Factory B.E.12

Dovista and, on 25 June, he destroyed an Albatros D.III. For these actions he was awarded the Military Cross.

Saunders was then transferred to 17 Squadron and flew an S.E.5a fighter. His next victory was not until 22 January 1918, when he captured a DFW C at Porna. A few days later, on 31 January, he destroyed a Rumpler C north-east of Kajendra. His final two victories came on the same day – 5 February. In one afternoon he downed an Albatros D.III at Vernak Farm and shot down a DFW two-seater in flames north-west of Topolcani.

Promoted to the rank of captain, in March 1918 he was awarded a bar to his Military Cross. His citation read: 'For conspicuous gallantry and devotion to duty. On three separate occasions during a month he has fought a hostile machine, pursued it over the enemy's lines and driven it down to earth, where it was completely wrecked. He has shown the most consistent gallantry and skill in action.'[18]

Franklin Saunders survived the war and was transferred to the unemployed list. In April 1921, he returned to the active list with the rank of flight lieutenant, but left the service in June 1921. He married Kathleen Mary Jones in 1942 in

Hereford and died on 20 January 1951 at St Richard's Hospital in Chichester, aged 59.

Captain Francis Mansel Kitto had nine confirmed victories. Born in Pontypridd on 1 January 1897, he was employed on the staff of the English Electrical Company in Preston before being commissioned into the Welsh Regiment on 9 November 1916 and then transferring to the Royal Flying Corps. By early 1917, he was serving on the Western Front with 43 Squadron, with whom he was to register three victories flying a Sopwith 1½ Strutter.

His first success was on 17 March, when he downed an Albatros D.II east of Arras. On 8 April, he repeated the feat north-east of Vimy. This time his victim was an Albatros D.III. On 17 August, he shot down an Albatros D.V over La Bassée to Lens.

Kitto then transferred to 54 Squadron to fly Sopwith Camels. Here he was to register a further six victories. On 1 December, he was appointed a flight commander and promoted to captain. On 15 March, he shot down an Albatros

Franklin Saunders

Francis Kitto

D.V over Sequehart and, on 24 March, he destroyed another one over Mons and another west of Saint-Quentin. On 4 April, he took his score to seven by destroying yet another Albatros D.V south-east of Hamel.

On 22 June, he was awarded the Military Cross for his exploits. His citation read:

> For conspicuous gallantry and devotion to duty. While engaged in attacking ground targets with machine-gun fire and bombs, he observed a large party of troops, amongst whom he dropped the remainder of his bombs with the most excellent results. On a later occasion, he attacked a formation of enemy scouts, and having caused one of these to crash to the ground, he pursued another and attacked it eleven miles behind the enemy's lines, bringing it to the ground and destroying it. In addition to these, he has shot down two other hostile machines, and has shown throughout, the greatest determination and dash.[19]

On 17 June, he destroyed a Pfalz D.III south of Ploegsteert Wood and, on 4 July, he shot down a Fokker D.VII over Estrées. These were the last of his nine victories. Kitto survived the war and transferred to piloting Airco DH.9 bombers in 1919. On 24 December, he was promoted to Flying Officer. Francis Kitto died in Pontypridd Cottage Hospital on 25 June 1926, aged 28. He had been injured in a motorcycle accident in August 1925 and never recovered.

Major Ernest William Norton also achieved nine victories. Born on 14 May 1893, in Dolguan, Newtown, Montgomeryshire, he was educated at Newtown County School and then worked for a motor establishment in Welshpool.

When war broke out, he was mobilised to serve in his Territorial Force regiment, the Montgomeryshire Yeomanry, where he served as a despatch rider. On 25 May, he was commissioned as a flight sub-lieutenant in the Royal Naval Air Service and, on 29 July, received Royal Aero Club Aviator's Certificate 1476 on a Maurice Farman biplane at the Central Flying School, Upavon. He was posted to 5 Squadron at Dover, but soon afterwards was transferred to 'A' Squadron, Number 1 Wing.

While patrolling off Ostend on 23 January 1916, he dropped a 16-pound bomb on a German U-boat. In March, he was injured in the foot, leg and head whilst attacking a Zeppelin.

After recovering and being promoted to acting flight commander, he resumed service with Number 1 Wing and, on 20 October, he destroyed a German observation balloon over Ostend using Le Prieur rockets fired from his Nieuport 11. For this action he was awarded the Distinguished Flying Cross. His citation read: 'In recognition of his skill and gallantry in destroying a German kite balloon on the 20th October, 1916, under severe anti-aircraft fire.'[20]

At this period there was no suitable bullet which would set fire to a kite balloon, and it was decided to employ Le Prieur rockets, a French invention which had been successfully used by the Royal Flying Corps. The rockets were attached to the interplane struts – four on each side – and fired electrically by means of a switch, by the pilot. The method of attack was

Le Prieur rockets being fired

Ernest Norton

to approach from a height, and, when nearly over the balloon, to dive at full speed, firing the rockets so that they would travel only 300 or 400 feet. The risk of colliding with the balloon itself was an obvious and real danger.

He transferred to 6 Squadron on the Western Front and, on 8 February, registered his second victory when he drove down out of control an Aviatik two-seater over the Houthoulst Forest, while flying a Nieuport 17bis.

On 5 April, he destroyed and shot down two Albatros D.IIs west of Douai. Four days later he repeated the feat over Cambrai to claim his fifth and sixth victories. The dogfights damaged his Nieuport which resulted in a crash landing that burnt out his aircraft. Undeterred, he was soon airborne again and, on 29 April, he downed an Albatros D.III east of Honnecourt and, later the same day, shot down two more over Guise, bringing his total of victories to nine.

On 30 June, he was promoted to flight commander and to squadron commander on 31 December 1917. When the Royal Naval Air Service and Royal Flying Corps merged on 1 April 1918 to form the Royal Air Force, he was promoted to the rank of major.

Norton survived the war and continued to serve with the Royal Air Force. He was made an Officer of the Crown of Belgium in February 1919, awarded the *Croix de Guerre with Palm* by France in April, and the Belgian *Croix de Guerre* in July. In 1924, he served in Iraq, commanding an armoured car company, before returning to home duties. He served with Fighter Command from 7 September 1941, before retiring on

24 February 1944. He had taught King George VI to fly. Ernest Norton died on 23 May 1966, aged 73.

Lieutenant Samuel Parry achieved nine victories as an observer/gunner. Born in 1892 in Neath, he was living at the Shepherd's Arms, Cwmaman, Aberdare, before the war, when he enlisted in the Royal Engineers. He married Althea Lake in London on 31 October 1916. He then volunteered for the Royal Flying Corps and was posted to 62 Squadron on 28 December 1917.

Parry achieved his first three victories all in the same day. On the afternoon of 27 March 1918, flying in a Bristol F.2B, he shot down two German aircraft and destroyed another. On 12 April, he downed an Albatros D.V east of Estaires and, on 21 April, achieved ace status by shooting down two Pfalz D.IIIs between Estaires and Lille. On 3 May, east of Armentières, he downed two Albatros D.Vs and destroyed another in flames. He was killed later in the same aerial action; his pilot Lieutenant C.H. Arnison survived. Parry is buried at Huby-St Leu British Cemetery, Calais.

Lieutenant Herbert Howell Beddow had ten confirmed victories. Born in Llanelli on 19 December 1898, he joined the Royal Flying Corps in October 1917. All his victories were achieved flying a Bristol F.2B with 22 Squadron.

Pfaltz D.III

He claimed his first victory on the evening of 26 May, when he destroyed an Albatros D.V south-east of Armentières. On 8 August, he shot down a Pfalz D.III north-east of Vitry. Five days later, he downed two enemy aircraft in one morning. They were both Pfalz D.IIIs. The following day, 14 August, on landing from an observation patrol, his Bristol fighter collided with the aerodrome armoury. Both Beddow and his observer, Second Lieutenant T.J. Birmingham, were uninjured.

Two days later, Beddow again downed two aircraft in one morning – another Pfalz D.III and a Fokker D.VII – over Lille. On 22 August, north-east of Bailleul, he destroyed a Halberstadt two-seater, and five days later a Fokker D.VII was shot down out of control over Vitry. His ninth victory was another Fokker D.VII which he destroyed between Arras and Cambrai, and his final victory was the same make of aircraft which he downed on the late afternoon of 5 September over Douai.

Herbert Beddow survived the war and was killed by the Japanese in the battle for Hong Kong on 24 December 1941, aged 43, while working for the Hong Kong Education Department. By this time he had gained a Bachelor of Science degree. He was acting principal of the King's College, Hong Kong, from January 1936 to July 1937. During the fighting, the college was used as a hospital and a number of unarmed civilians were killed.

His brother Samuel had been killed on 24 April 1917, aged 22, while serving with the 17th Battalion of the Welsh Regiment on the Western Front.

Captain Robert Leslie Chidlaw-Roberts also achieved ten victories. He was born in Towyn in 1896 and joined the Royal Flying Corps in May 1915 after serving with the Hampshire Regiment. He received his Royal Aero Club Aviator's Certificate in January 1916. For several months he flew combat missions over the Western Front as an observer with 2 Squadron. After flight training, he was assigned to 18 Squadron, flying mostly night operations for eight months before joining 60 Squadron and flying as a pilot. He shot down five enemy aircraft during the Third Battle of Ypres in 1917, and doubled his total before the war's end.

On 14 September, he shot down an Albatros D.V east of Menin. Two days later, he destroyed in flames the Albatros D.III of *Leutnant* Alfred Bauerf, *Jasta* 17, south of Houthem. On 21 September, he was credited with two victories within minutes of each other. First, he destroyed an Albatros D.V, and then an unidentified two-seater. The following morning he shot down another Albatros D.V, south-east of Zonnebeke.

In an historic dogfight on 23 September 1917, he was almost shot down by Werner Voss shortly before Voss was himself shot down and killed.

Werner Voss was an outstanding German fighter pilot. Born in 1897, he served with the infantry on the Eastern Front before volunteering for the air service in August 1915. By the commencement of the Third Battle of Ypres, he had shot down 34 enemy aircraft. He was killed south of Roulers, having accounted for another 14. On 23 September 1917, over the Third Ypres battlefield, he attacked seven British

S.E.5as, driving two to the ground and damaging the rest, including the aircraft of Chidlaw-Roberts and Richard Maybery (see page 288). However, his silvery-blue Fokker Dr.I triplane was hit, and the engine cut out. He was finally shot down by Arthur Rhys Davids (see page 295).

Werner Voss

On 18 November, Chidlaw-Roberts destroyed a DFW two-seater north-east of Westrosebeke and, on 23 November, he destroyed an Albatros D.V west of Dadizeele.

On 3 January, he shot down in flames an unidentified aircraft over Comines-Menin and, six days later, an Albatros D.V over Moorslede.

He was awarded the Military Cross later in the year:

> For conspicuous gallantry and devotion to duty. He constantly attacked superior numbers of enemy aeroplanes. On one occasion he repeatedly attacked five enemy machines, driving among them and attacking each in turn at short ranges. On three other occasions he brought down enemy machines. He showed great skill and courage.[21]

His final victory was a balloon north-east of Cambrai on 29 September 1918. He survived the war and was assigned to the Reserve in March 1920. He returned to the Royal Air Force in May 1942 as a pilot officer and, on 1 September 1944, he was awarded the Air Force Cross. After the Second World War

finished he remained in the Royal Air Force, finally relinquishing his commission on 10 February 1954. He died in Winchester on 1 June 1989, aged 93.

Flight Lieutenant Harold Day achieved 11 victories. Born on 17 April 1897 in Abergavenny, he joined the Royal Naval Air Service on 28 January 1917, and was commissioned as a temporary flight sub-lieutenant in June. His first service was with 10 Naval

Robert Chidlaw-Roberts

Squadron where he flew Sopwith Triplanes. He claimed his first victory on 12 August when he shot down an Albatros D.V over Wervicq.

He fell ill on 12 September and, on his recovery, he was posted to 8 Naval Squadron the following month. Here he flew Sopwith Camels and, on 6 December, he shot down a DFW two-seater reconnaissance aircraft over Loisons, south-east of Lens. On 27 December, he shot down another DFW two-seater between Lens and Hénin-Liétard, and the following day repeated the act over Vitry. On 4 January 1918, he downed an unidentified enemy aircraft five miles north of Bourlon Wood and, two days later, destroyed another unidentified aircraft over Fresnoy.

On 22 January 1918, he shot down, out of control, an Albatros D.V over Vitry, and a week later did the same south of the River Scarpe to bring his total to eight victories. On 2 February, he claimed two enemy aircraft in one day. First he destroyed an unidentified aircraft between Douai and Ostricourt and a short while later shot down an Albatros D.V over Carvin.

Day's final victory came on 5 February when he destroyed an

Albatros D.V south of Pont-à-Vendin. He then dived on another Albatros, but his Camel was seen to break up in the air and plummeted to the ground. *Leutnant* Günther Schuster of *Jasta* 29 claimed the victory.

On 22 February, the awarding of his Distinguished Service Cross was announced. The citation read:

Harold Day

In recognition of the skill and determination shown by him in aerial combats, in the course of which he has done much to stop enemy artillery machines from working. On 6 January 1918, he observed a new type enemy aeroplane. He immediately dived to attack, and after a short combat the enemy machine went down very steeply, and was seen to crash. On several other occasions he has brought down enemy machines out of control.[22]

Harold Day was buried at St Mary's Advanced Dressing Station Cemetery, Haisnes, France.

Leutnant Günther Schuster joined the German Air Force on 23 December 1916 and claimed his first two victories in June 1917. He transferred to *Jasta* 29 on 10 September 1917, and achieved three more victories, including Harold Day. On 28 May 1918, he was appointed commanding officer of *Jasta* 17 and shot down one more enemy aircraft. He was wounded in action on 1 August 1918 and did not fly again.

Captain Arthur Gordon Jones-Williams scored 11 victories: eight flying Nieuport scouts with 29 Squadron in 1917, and three more with 65 Squadron in 1918. Born on 6 October 1898 in Vernon, British Columbia, Canada, of Welsh parents and

later living in Talybont-on-Usk, he had transferred from the Welsh Regiment in August 1916. After training with 66 Squadron, on 22 March 1917 he joined 29 Squadron.

He shot down his first enemy aircraft on 14 April, flying a Nieuport. His victim was an Albatros D.III between Neuvireuil

Günther Schuster

and Vitry. On 23 April, he downed two Albatros D.IIIs over Vitry. Jones-Williams won his first Military Cross in May. His citation read: 'For conspicuous gallantry and devotion to duty. He has continuously shown the utmost dash and gallantry in attacking superior numbers of hostile machines. On one occasion he attacked twelve hostile scouts and succeeded in destroying one and driving down another.'[23]

On 25 June, he shot down another Albatros D.III over Douai and repeated the act over Saudemont on the morning of 29 June. On 12 July, he downed an Albatros D.V over Zonnebeke-Roulers and was awarded a bar to his Military Cross.

This second citation stated:

> For conspicuous gallantry and devotion to duty when engaged in combat with hostile aircraft. On several occasions he attacked enemy formations although they were in superior numbers, fighting them in more than one instance single-handed, and showing the finest offensive spirit. He drove several machines down completely out of control, fighting until his ammunition was expended.[24]

On 20 September, he claimed his seventh victim by downing an Albatros D.III over Westroosebeke. Three days later, he did the same thing over Zonnebeke to Langemarck. He was then hospitalised and posted to a home establishment back in Britain.

In 1918, he returned to the Western Front to command a flight of 65 Squadron. On 5 September, flying a Sopwith Camel, he downed a Fokker D.VII east of Ostend. On 1 October, he destroyed a Fokker D.VII east of Roulers and on 4 October he claimed his eleventh and final victory by destroying another Fokker D.VII over Lendelede.

Jones-Williams survived the war and remained in the Royal Air Force. In 1923, he flew DH.9As in Kurdistan. As a squadron leader, he and Flight Lieutenant N.A. Jenkins made the first non-stop flight from England to India in 1929. A year later,

Arthur Jones-Williams (left) with N.A. Jenkins

both men were killed when their Fairey Napier monoplane crashed in the Atlas Mountains during a non-stop flight from England to Cape Town.

Captain Gwilym Hugh Lewis was credited with 12 victories. Born in Moseley, Birmingham, on 5 August 1897, his father was from Anglesey and his mother from Caernarvon and were both fluent Welsh speakers. Gwilym was educated at Marlborough College and then King's College, London, as was his older brother Edmund who also served with the Royal Flying Corps, and was shot down and killed on Boxing Day 1916.

Gwilym was commissioned into the 2/4th Northamptonshire Regiment in September 1915, then applied to join the Royal Flying Corps. He was encouraged to learn to fly privately, so borrowed £100 from his father and completed his Royal Aero Club course in November 1915.

Posted to France in May 1916 with 32 Squadron, he claimed his first victory on 15 July when shooting down a Fokker Eindecker east of La Bassée. On 22 September, he destroyed a Roland C.II over Bancourt. He was then posted to the Central Flying School at Upavon before joining 40 Squadron for the

279

remainder of the war, landing in France again in December 1917. On 19 December he shot down, out of control, an Albatros D.III between Lens and Pont-à-Vendin, another Albatros, a D.V, between Hénin and Liétard on the morning of 19 January 1918, before achieving 'ace' status by shooting down a Pfalz D.III over Lille on 16 February.

On 11 April, he destroyed a Fokker Dr.I east of Lens, and the following day shot down, out of control, a Pfalz D.III over Croix Barbee. Above Merville, on 20 May, he shot down another Pfalz D.III, and the following day repeated the act over Douai.

His tenth victim was yet another Pfalz D.III, this time shot down in flames east of Hulluch. On 2 July, he shot down a Fokker D.VII north-east of Lens and his final victim was an LVG two-seater which was captured on the morning of 7 July near Lens.

The award of his Distinguished Flying Cross appeared on 21 September 1918:

> It is largely due to this officer's ability and judgement as flight leader that many enemy machines have been destroyed with very few casualties in his formation. He is bold in attack, and has personally accounted for eight enemy aircraft, displaying marked disregard of personal danger.[25]

Gwilym Lewis survived the war, and after leaving the Royal Air Force, took up a career in insurance. When the Second World War broke out, he was recalled to the Royal Air Force and given the rank of wing commander. He died in December 1996 at the age of 99.

In 1990, he recorded his memories of the Great War. He described a dogfight as 'electric and very exciting. Very fast-moving.' When asked about the tactics he used he said, 'I didn't know any other tactics than getting on the tail of a chap, if possible out-manoeuvring him and killing him. I had very definite ideas under a two-seater. Under his gun if possible and

Gwilym Lewis
© Imperial War Museum

his tail was a good position.' Commenting on the Germans he stated, 'We disliked them intensely but if we captured one we brought him into the mess and gave him a drink. It was a lively game. If you didn't pot him down, he potted you and it was about the highest stakes you can play for.'

Being thousands of feet up in an open cockpit he said was 'very exciting and breezy. Extremely cold. One shouts with pain sometimes. If suddenly you saw a flight of Huns... the blood would be stimulated and the cold would go.'

He also commented on the physical strain the pilots were under:

> One's nerves were bound to get tampered with after a lot of activity, such as we had on the Somme in 1916. It was quite a strain to be fighting through the whole of that battle and right to the end. And no question about it, one does peter out. Speaking for myself, in 1918, by July, I did peter out in the air and I went to the doctor and I said, 'I've blacked out and he said "Time you went home. Off you go."'

Lieutenant Josiah Lewis Morgan achieved 12 victories. An observer/gunner ace, he flew with Hiram Frank Davison, a Canadian pilot, for 11 of those successes. Born in Porth on 5 June 1893, Morgan joined the Royal Flying Corps from the South Wales Borderers on 13 January 1918, having been commissioned in October the previous year.

He joined 22 Squadron in January, and achieved his first victory on 6 March in a Bristol F.2B when he shot down an Albatros D.V over Douai. Two days later, he achieved three victories in the same day: two Albatros D.Vs were downed between Lille and Douai, and then a Pfalz D.III was destroyed over Douai. On 13 March, he destroyed in flames another Pflaz D.III over Annoeullin, and five days later set an Albatros D.V on fire over Carvin to bring his total to six.

On 25 March, he shot down an Albatros D.V north of Havrincourt Wood and the following day he destroyed in flames a Pfalz D.III east of Albert. March 27 saw him account for two Fokker Dr.Is. One was downed over Montauban and the other destroyed south-east of Albert. On 29 March, he achieved his final two victories on the same day, an unidentified two-seater was destroyed south-east of Hangard and a Rumpler two-seater was shot down out of control east of Berviller.

He was awarded the Military Cross and his citation read:

> For conspicuous gallantry and devotion to duty when carrying out many low-flying and offensive patrols, and engaging enemy troops, transports, etc., with machine-gun fire, and inflicting heavy casualties. On many occasions he attacked and destroyed, or drove down out of control, hostile machines, and he invariably displayed a dash and determination worthy of the highest praise.[26]

On 4 April, he returned to Home Establishment to serve as an instructor at Number 6 School of Aviation, where he remained until the end of the war. In April 1919, he was transferred to the unemployed list and returned to civilian life. He died in Cardiff on 11 May 1982.

Captain Reginald Rhys Soar also had 12 confirmed victories. He was born on 24 August 1893 in Castleford, Yorkshire of a Welsh mother. Proud of his Welsh ancestry, he always used his middle name. Soar joined the Royal Naval Air Service in August 1915, and began his service with No. 3 Wing in the Dardanelles before transferring to 5 Naval Wing at

Reginald Rhys Soar

Dunkirk. In October 1916, he transferred again, this time to 8 Naval Squadron.

His first victories came on 20 December 1916 when, flying a Sopwith Pup, he shot down two Halberstadt scouts over Rémy and Fontaine. The squadron was then re-equipped with Sopwith Triplanes. On 23 May, he shot down an unidentified two-seater over La Bassée and on 12 June an Aviatik two-seater over Arras. Thirty minutes later, he captured another Aviatik north of Arras to achieve his status as an ace. On 29 June, he downed an Albatros D.III east of Lens and, on 3 July, he took on seven enemy fighters single-handed above Pont-á-Vendin and shot one of them down. Two days later, he downed another Aviatik east of Wingles.

The squadron was then issued with Sopwith Camels and, on 11 July, he captured an unidentified two-seater east of Izel. Two days later, he destroyed another unidentified two-seater over Lens to bring his score to ten victories. He then switched back to the same Sopwith Triplane and shot down an Albatros D.III over Quiéry-la-Motte on the morning of 17 July. Four days later, he repeated the act.

In August, Soar was awarded the Distinguished Service Cross:

> For courage and skill as a scout pilot. On 23rd May 1917, he
> attacked a two-seater artillery machine, and as the result of a well
> thought out attack brought the machine down out of control. On

12th June 1917, he brought down two enemy machines out of control. On 29th June 1917, in company with Flt. Lieut. Little, he attacked and brought down an Albatross scout. On 3rd July 1917, whilst leading an offensive patrol, a formation of seven Albatross Scouts was engaged, and he brought down one, out of control. On 13th July 1917, in company with Flt. Lieut. Little, he attacked and drove down out of control one two-seater machine, following it down to within 1,000 feet of the ground.[27]

In April 1918, he was promoted to Officer Commanding 'A' and 'B' Flights, 255 Squadron, based at RAF Pembroke. Rhys Soar died in Martletwy, Pembrokeshire, in 1971.

Captain Charles Chaplin Banks was credited with 13 victories. Born on 17 December 1893 in Hampstead, London, his father was later the schoolmaster and owner of Arnold House Preparatory School in Llanddulas, Denbighshire, where Charles was brought up. A schoolmaster himself before the war, Banks was commissioned into the 5th (Flintshire) Battalion of the Royal Welsh Fusiliers before joining the Royal Flying Corps in October 1916. His brother, Second Lieutenant Arthur Chaplin Banks, had been killed in France on 22 June 1916 while serving with the 2nd Royal Welsh Fusiliers.

Initially posted to Home Defence with 44 Squadron, flying a Sopwith Camel on 28 January he engaged a Gotha Bomber over London and was decorated for this action. Banks and Temporary Captain George Henry Hackwill were awarded Military Crosses in February 1918. Their citation read: 'For conspicuous gallantry displayed when they engaged and shot down a Gotha raiding London. During the engagement, which lasted a considerable time, they were continually under fire from the enemy machine.'[28]

He was then posted to 43 Squadron in France where, on 6 April, he destroyed an Albatros D.V over Guillaucourt. Six days later, he shot down another one over the Bois du Biez and, on 3 May, another east of Villers-Bretonneaux. Five days afterwards he became an ace by downing his fifth victim – a Fokker Dr.I south-east of Bailleul. On 30 May, he drove down an Albatros two-seater out of control over Flers and, on the last day of May, Banks captured at night a Friedrichshafen G two-seater, the first time this had been achieved. On 10 June, he destroyed an Albatros D.V west of Monchy, followed by the destruction of a Pfalz D.III over Ribécourt and a Fokker D.VII over Somain on 29 August.

During the first part of September 1918, the squadron converted to Sopwith Snipes. The Snipe was a heavier, stronger aircraft that the Camel, was very manoeuverable and easier to handle, with a better view from the cockpit and a faster rate of climb. In his Snipe, Banks claimed three more victories. On 27 September, he shot down a Fokker D.VII over Cambrai, repeated the feat over Quierzy on 1 October and again on 30 October over Aulnoye.

The following year, Banks received the Distinguished Flying Cross. His citation read:

A brilliant and skilful airman who has been conspicuous for his success in aerial combats. On 30 October he, single-handed, engaged five enemy aeroplanes and drove one down out of

Sopwith Snipe

285

control. In the fight his aileron controls were shot away, but by skilful handling and with cool presence of mind, he brought his machine back and made a successful landing. In addition to the above, Capt. Banks has accounted for nine other enemy machines.[29]

During the Second World War his son, Sergeant Arthur Banks, also served with the Royal Air Force. After being shot down behind German lines in Italy, he joined the partisans but was betrayed and captured by the Germans before being killed by the Italians. He was awarded the George Cross in 1946 for his courage during his captivity and this was presented to his father by King George VI.

Charles Banks died in Lewes in Sussex on 21 December 1971, four days after his 78th birthday.

Captain John Stanley Chick achieved 16 victories. Born in Pontardawe on 22 December 1897, he enlisted in the Royal Engineers as a pioneer in 1914. He transferred to the Royal Flying Corps in February 1917 and was commissioned on 3 May. He received his Royal Aero Club Aviator's Certificate after a solo flight in a Maurice Farman biplane at the Military

Charles Banks (lying down centre)

Charles Chaplin Banks
© Imperial War Museum

School, Ruislip on 27 May. In November he was posted to 11 Squadron, flying Bristol F.2 two-seater fighters.

His first victory occurred on 1 January 1918 when he brought down an Albatros D.V over Crèvecoeur. On 28 January, he downed a DFW two-seater north of Bourlon Wood and, on 12 March, came his most remarkable victories. On that day he accounted for no fewer than five enemy aircraft in a single sortie. His first victim was an unidentified two-seater south of Cambrai. Then over Caudry, he shot down four Fokker Dr.I fighters. The following afternoon he shot down an Albatros D.V south of Cambrai. Two days later, on 15 March, he destroyed in flames and shot down two Albatros D.Vs over Rumilly.

Chick was promoted to lieutenant on 1 April and, on 9 May, he drove down two Pfalz D.IIIs south of Albert. He was awarded the Military Cross and his citation read:

> For conspicuous gallantry and devotion to duty. While leading a patrol of four machines over the enemy's lines, he attacked an enemy two-seater machine, which his observer drove down completely out of control. Shortly afterwards, the patrol engaged nineteen enemy machines; he dived on to the uppermost machine, and drove it down in a series of spins and side-slips completely out of control. He then attacked two others and brought them down in the same manner, while his observer drove down another out of control. On another occasion his formation,

John Chick

consisting of five machines, attacked twenty-five enemy aeroplanes. He destroyed one of the enemy, and drove down another out of control. He set a magnificent example of courage and skill.[30]

His string of victories came to an end on 15 May when he dispatched four German aircraft. In the morning, he destroyed in flames an unidentified two-seater over Brebières and then, in a late afternoon sortie, he destroyed a Fokker Dr.I and a Pfalz D.III, and shot down a Fokker Dr.I, all south-east of Albert.

Appointed to flight commander and given the temporary rank of captain, he was injured in a crash on 26 June 1918 but survived the war. Chick continued to serve with the Royal Air Force post-war, including a spell with an aerobatics team. When the Second World War began, he was officer commanding 49 Squadron and he served throughout the war in a variety of posts, before retiring in December 1947. He died on 21 January 1960 in Colchester, aged 62.

Captain Richard Aveline Maybery was responsible for 21 victories. Born in Brecon on 4 January 1895, he was educated at Connaught House, Weymouth, Wellington College and Sandhurst where he passed out fifth in his class. Gazetted second lieutenant in September 1913 in the 21st Lancers, he was promoted to lieutenant in February 1915 and reached the rank of captain. Maybery served in India where he was seriously wounded during the fighting at Shabqadar in September 1915.

Richard Maybery

Unable to sit on a horse owing to his wound, while recovering he volunteered to help a nearby Royal Flying Corps unit with their spotting. He transferred to the Royal Flying Corps in 1916, and served as an observer and then a pilot. He joined 56 Squadron, flying an S.E.5a, and brought down an enemy machine on his first patrol on 7 July 1917 when he drove down an Albatros D.V between Hénin and Liétard. On 12 July, he destroyed an Albatros D.V over Dadizeele and shot down another over Polygon Wood four days later. On 23 July, he destroyed a fourth Albatros D.V over Moorslede, and on 27 July he drove down an Albatros D.III north-east of Roulers.

During the Third Battle of Ypres, which began on 31 July, Maybery downed 13 enemy aircraft. His sixth victory was an unidentified two-seater over Wevelgem and, on 10 August, he destroyed two Albatros D.IIIs – one south of Roulers and the other north of the Houthoulst Forest. On 22 August, he destroyed an Albatros D.V over Clerkavenhoek, and on 3 September repeated the act over Houthem, and again over Moorslede two days afterwards.

Maybery's total now stood at 11 enemy aircraft. On 10 September he downed two Albatros D.Vs in a single day – one south-east of the Houthoulst Forest and the second over Zonnebeke-Moorslede.

The announcement of his Military Cross came at the end of that month. His citation stated:

For conspicuous gallantry and devotion to duty. After attacking two aerodromes in succession at very low altitudes, and inflicting considerable damage, he attacked and dispersed a number of mounted men and then attacked a goods train. He next attacked and shot down a hostile machine at 500 feet, and before returning attacked a passenger train. On numerous occasions he has attacked, single-handed, large hostile formations and set a fine example by his gallantry and determination.[31]

On 30 September, he destroyed a Pfalz D.III west of Roulers, and on 2 October destroyed an Albatros D.V over Rollechemcapelle. On 28 October, he destroyed an Albatros D.V over Dadizeele, and three days later shot down an Albatros D.V east of Ledeghem and destroyed another south-west of Roulers. He repeated this feat on 30 November when he destroyed two Albatros D.Vs over Bourlon Wood.

On 18 December, he was awarded a bar to his Military Cross. The citation for his second award was:

For conspicuous gallantry and devotion to duty as leader of offensive patrols for three months, during which he personally destroyed nine enemy aeroplanes and drove down three out of control. On one occasion, having lost his patrol, he attacked a formation of eight enemy aeroplanes. One was seen to crash and two others went down, out of control, the formation being completely broken up.[32]

On 19 December 1917, he followed his 21st and last victory down and was hit by enemy fire, crashing near Bourlon Wood. His commanding officer wrote to Maybery's mother:

Your son had just crashed down his 20th [sic] Hun in flames, when his own machine was seen to be going down. It was very misty and the fighting was severe, and in the mist another German came from behind and above, and shot him down. Captain Maybery was, I think, the bravest and most dashing air fighter I have ever come across, and of course his career here has been brilliant. To this squadron his loss is a terrible blow; he was so brilliant, so popular, and always so cheerful. He set a wonderful example to the newer pilots; he was almost too brave.[33]

Another Royal Flying Corps officer wrote:

I don't think I ever met a man so capable – he was good at absolutely everything. He has done a tremendous lot of good in the war. I always say that he and Captain Ball and Lieutenant Rhys Davids did more harm to the morale of the German Flying Corps than any other 15 pilots we have ever had. They all, always, took on any odds – they were too brave and reckless.

The General of his Cavalry Brigade in India also wrote: 'He was one of the keenest youngsters I have ever met, and there never was a braver.'[34]

The victory was claimed by *Vizefeldwebel* Artur Weber of *Jasta* 5, although a mobile anti-aircraft battery also claimed to have shot him down.

Richard Maybery lies in Flesquières Hill British Cemetery.

Captain Peter Carpenter achieved 24 victories. He was born on 6 December 1891 in Cardiff and attended the National School in Grangetown where he stood out as a rugby player. He enlisted in the Royal Fusiliers in 1915, but broke his leg during a rugby game and was posted to Home Establishment. He applied for a transfer to the Royal Flying Corps and was posted to 45 Squadron in September 1917 after 84 hours of training.

Flying a Sopwith Camel, he scored his first victory on 20 September when he shot down an Albatros D.V east of Ypres. On 21 October, he destroyed in flames another Albatros D.V over Lille, and ten days later he destroyed an Albatros two-seater east of Le Quesnoy. On 8 November, he destroyed another one south of Passchendaele and on 15 November accounted for a Rumpler two-seater north-east of the Houthoulst Wood.

The new year saw the squadron based on the Italian front. On 10 January, he destroyed an Albatros D.III over Ceggia-Staffolo,

Peter Carpenter

and five days later another over Vazzola. On 26 January, he destroyed a third over Novesta, and on 27 February, now with 66 Squadron, a fourth over San Donà di Piave. On 11 March, he destroyed in flames his tenth victim, a Aviatik (Berg) D.I, north of Valstagna, and he followed this up by downing two more of this type of aircraft on the same day – 21 March – over Ghirano and Cimadolmo. On 30 March, he destroyed an Albatros D.II three miles south of Mansuè. April 11 saw him shoot down an unidentified two-seater over Arcade. Six days later he destroyed an Albatros D.V over Borgo, and on 31 May another west of Feltre.

He destroyed, in flames, an Albatros D.V on 9 June south of Sebastiano, and the following day he destroyed an LVG two-seater north-east of Feltre. On 15 June, he shot down another LVG south of Feltre and, later that morning, achieved his twentieth victory by destroying an Albatros D.V over Feltre. On 14 July, he destroyed an Albatros D.III west of Feltre.

The announcement of his first Military Cross followed. His citation read:

> For conspicuous gallantry and devotion to duty. Within a period of the last three months he has brought down six enemy machines, four of which were observed to crash to the ground, the remaining two being shot down completely out of control. The offensive tactics pursued by this daring and skilful officer have produced most successful results.[35]

On the last day of August he claimed his next victim – an Albatros D.V destroyed west of Staffolo. He was awarded the bar to his Military Cross just a month later:

> For conspicuous gallantry and devotion to duty. He led an offensive patrol against seven of the enemy; three were destroyed. Again he led a patrol of three machines against six of the enemy; two of them were destroyed and one driven down out of control. Later, with two other pilots, he engaged twelve hostile machines, of which three were destroyed and one driven down out of control. He shot down several machines himself.[36]

Carpenter was subsequently awarded the Distinguished Service Order:

> For conspicuous gallantry and devotion to duty. He has destroyed nine enemy machines, and driven three down out of control. He has led forty-six offensive patrols. On one occasion twelve enemy aircraft were attacked, and on another he led two other machines against nineteen of the enemy, destroying six of them. He has at all times shown a magnificent example.[37]

October 8 saw him destroy an Albatros two-seater south-west of Vado Ligure and he downed his last victim on 25 October when he shot down an Albatros D.V over Feltre.

Peter Carpenter survived the war, having flown 190 combat patrols and nine bombing raids. He was subsequently awarded the Italian Bronze Medal for Military Valor. After the war ended he founded a shipping company, but this failed during the economic depression. He subsequently worked for Legal and General Insurance until he retired. During the Second World War he served in the Middlesex Home Guard. He died on 21 March 1971 in Golders Green, aged 79.

Lieutenant Arthur Percival Foley Rhys Davids achieved 25 victories. Of Welsh ancestry, he was born in London on 27 September 1897. He attended Eton, where he was Head Boy, and won a scholarship to Oxford to study Classics. He left Eton

Arthur Rhys Davids

in 1916 and joined the Royal Flying Corps. On 7 April 1917, he joined 56 Squadron on the Western Front. On 7 May, he was flying with the famous ace Albert Ball on his first combat mission when Ball was killed. Davids' machine guns jammed and his engine cut out, but he made a forced landing and survived.

He achieved his first victory flying a S.E.5 on 23 May 1917, when he shot down an Albatros D.III east of Lens. The following day, he downed three enemy aircraft. The first was another Albatros D.III south of Douai, followed by two unidentified two-seaters, one over Gouy-sous-Bellonne and the other over Sains. He achieved ace status the next day by destroying an unidentified two-seater west of Flers. On 26 May, he shot down an Albatros D.III over Gouy-sous-Bellonne.

On 4 June, he shot down an Albatros D.V west of Moorslede, and on 7 June an Albatros D.III over Westeroosebeke. On 12 July, he downed a Fokker DV east of Roncq and then captured a DFW two-seater north of Armentières. The following day he shot down an Albatros D.V over Moorslede. On 17 July, he accounted for another Albatros D.V, this time over the Roulers to Menin Road, and on 21 July an Albatros D.III over Polygon Wood.

In July 1917, the announcement of his first Military Cross was made: 'For conspicuous gallantry and devotion. On many occasions he has shot down hostile machines and put others out of action, frequently pursuing to low altitudes. On all occasions his fearlessness and dash have been most marked.'[38]

On 3 September, he destroyed an Albatros D.V over Houthem and, two days later, achieved the remarkable feat of accounting for three enemy machines in a single afternoon; all were Albatros D.Vs. The first was destroyed east of Menin, the second north-east of Poelcapelle, and the third was shot down east of Menin. On 9 September, he downed another Albatros D.V south-east of the Houthoulst Forest.

Later that month he was awarded a bar to his Military Cross:

> For conspicuous gallantry and devotion to duty whilst on offensive patrols. He has in all destroyed four enemy aircraft, and driven down many others out of control. In all, his combats, his gallantry, and skill have been most marked, and on one occasion he shot down an enemy pilot who had accounted for twenty-nine Allied machines. His offensive spirit and initiative have set a magnificent example to all.[39]

On 23 September, he shot down the Fokker Dr.I of the German ace Werner Voss (see page 274) north-east of the Ypres Salient and also shot down an Albatros D.V in the same area. The following day he shot down, in flames, an unidentified two-seater south of the Houthoulst Forest and, on 28 September, shot down an Albatros D.V over Comines to bring his score to 22 enemy aircraft. The first day of October saw him shoot down two Albatros D.Vs over Westroosebeke and, on 11 October, he achieved his 25th and final victory by downing another Albatros D.V north-east of Becelaere.

Davids also received the Distinguished Service Order in October 1917: 'For conspicuous gallantry and devotion to duty in bringing down nine enemy aircraft in nine weeks. He is a magnificent fighter, never failing to locate enemy aircraft and invariably attacking regardless of the numbers against him.'[40]

Twelve of his 25 victories took place in the skies above the battlefield of Third Ypres. On 27 October 1917, his aircraft was shot down by *Leutnant* Karl Gallwitz of *Jasta Boelcke*. The Germans returned his personal effects but his grave was lost and he is remembered on the Arras Flying Services Memorial.

Karl Gallwitz was born in August 1895 in Sigmaringen, Germany. Originally posted to the Russian front where he claimed two balloons, for which he was awarded the Iron Cross First and Second Class, he briefly joined *Jasta* 29 before serving with *Jasta Boelcke* for the remainder of the war. He walked away from a crash in April 1918 and survived the war, having shot down British aces Robert Kirby Kirkman and John Herbert Hedley, in addition to Rhys Davids, to bring his total to ten victories.

He was later a professor of agricultural machinery at the University of Göttingen, teaching there from 1936 to 1965. He died in Göttingen on 17 May 1984, aged 88.

Captain Dennis Latimer scored 28 victories. Born in Withington in Shropshire on 31 August 1895, his family moved to Tywyn in Merionethshire when he was a small child and lived there for many years. Latimer joined 20 Squadron early

Karl Gallwitz

Dennis Latimer

in 1918 and gained his first victory on 13 March while flying a Bristol fighter, when he shot down an Albatros D.V between Comines and Wervicq. On 21 April, he downed another north of Wervicq and, on 8 May, accounted for four enemy aircraft in a single day.

His first victim was another Albatros D.V which he destroyed in flames south-east of Wervicq and then, later that afternoon, in the space of a few minutes, between Comines and Wervicq, he destroyed in flames a Fokker Dr.I and shot down two more.

On 14 May, he destroyed an Albatros D.V over Wervicq and, a short while later, captured another near Zillebeke. The next day he shot down a Pfalz D.III north-west of Lille and destroyed a Fokker Dr.I between Comines and Ypres. He destroyed a Pfalz D.III above Comines in the early morning of 18 May, and later that same morning destroyed another north-east of the Nieppe Forest and shot down another over Merville. On 20 May, he destroyed in flames an Albatros D.V north-east of Merville and destroyed another over Coucou airfield.

A Pfalz D.III was destroyed over Comines on 1 June, and he repeated the feat on 9 June as well. Eight days later he shot down a Fokker D.VII over Boesinghe and, on 30 June, destroyed a Pfalz D.III over Comines. He scored his twentieth victory by shooting down a Fokker Dr.I over Menin on 1 July.

Around 9 a.m. on 14 July, he shot down two Fokker D.VIIs south-east of Ypres and destroyed another five days later north of Comines. August 14 saw him destroy two Pfalz D.IIIs over Dadizeele, and his final victories came a week later on 21 July when he destroyed three Pfalz D.IIIs over Menin, Dadizeele and Gheluwe, respectively.

On 16 September, his award of a Military Cross was announced: 'For conspicuous gallantry and devotion to duty on offensive patrol. He and his observer in four days' fighting destroyed 7 enemy machines and drove down three. They did magnificent service.'[41]

Five days later came the announcement of his Distinguished

Flying Cross: 'When leading an offensive patrol, this officer displayed great skill and bravery. Having shot down a scout in flames, he immediately engaged a second, which he destroyed after a short combat. In addition, he has accounted for four other machines.'[42]

On 22 August, his aircraft was shot down near Westroosebeke by *Leutnant* Willi Nebgen of *Jasta* 7. Latimer survived the crash and became a prisoner of war but his observer, Lieutenant Tom Cecil Noel, was killed, aged 20.

Dennis Latimer died on 12 January 1976 in London.

Captain James Ira Thomas Jones was credited with 37 victories. He was born illegitimately at Woolstone Farm, near St Clears in Carmarthenshire, on 18 April 1896, and had a bad stutter, which he was supposed to have acquired after being rolled down a hill in a barrel as a child.

In 1913, while working as a clerk, he enlisted in the 4th Battalion of the Welsh Regiment – a Territorial Army unit. When war broke out, he was in London studying wireless and cable telegraphy. He then joined the Royal Flying Corps as an air mechanic, and was posted to France in July 1915.

He volunteered for flying duties as an observer and, in early 1916, was flying combat missions as an observer/gunner in B.E.2s.

He was awarded the Military Medal in May 1916 for rescuing two wounded gunners under artillery fire while working at a wireless interception station near the front line. In January 1917, he was awarded the Russian Cross of Saint George.

James Ira Jones

He began his pilot training in August 1917 after receiving his commission, and was posted to 74 Squadron where he began a friendship with the noted ace Captain Edward 'Mick' Mannock.

Jones gained his first victory on 8 May 1918 when flying an S.E.5a. He destroyed in flames an unidentified two-seater enemy aircraft over Bailleul-Nieppe. In his diary he described what happened:

> At 6.25 p.m. I spotted a two-seater coming towards Bailleul from the direction of Armentières at about 4,000 feet. I was then at 3,000 feet, over Hazebrouck. The sun was behind me, nice and large. I climbed quickly to 8,000 feet towards Merville, then back towards Bailleul. Hun 'Archie' warned the enemy of my approach by sending up a series of puffs. Apparently he did not see it. It would not have mattered if he had done. I had made up my mind to get him, even if I had to ram the sod.
>
> I got up to point-blank range before firing. Then I let him have it. Almost at once he commenced smoking. There was a faint glow. Then a lovely bonfire as he went earthwards. I followed him down to the ground, firing all my bullets at him. I then flew round him as he burned fiercely on the ground near Nieppe. I knew the enemy in the vicinity were firing hard at me. I did not care. My soul was satisfied.[43]

On 12 May, he shot down an Albatros D.V north of Wulverghem. Five days later, on the morning of 17 May, he destroyed in flames a Hannover two-seater over Merville-Estaires and shot down an Albatros two-seater over Merville. The following day, he destroyed in flames another Albatros two-seater over Nieppe, and on 19 May he destroyed a balloon north-west of Armentières. On 22 May, he destroyed in flames a Pfalz D.III over Le Quesnoy and, later that day, shot down another one over Fromelles. Four days later, on 26 May, he destroyed a Pfalz D.III north of Armentières, and the following day downed two enemy aircraft: an Albatros two-seater was destroyed north-east of Nieppe Forest, and a short time later he shot down a Halberstadt two-seater over Neuf-Berquin.

On 30 May, he again downed two German aircraft in a single day. First he destroyed a LVG two-seater east of Bailleul and then a Halberstadt two-seater south-east of Bois du Biez. The following day he repeated the feat. First to fall was a Pfalz III which was destroyed over Ploegsteert Wood and then shortly afterwards, another Pfalz III was downed over Comines. On 1 June, he destroyed a Pfalz III east of Dickebusch Lake and, on 18 June, he destroyed a DFW two-seater north of Bailleul. Three days later he destroyed in flames a LVG two-seater over Ploegsteert Wood and, on 25 June, he shot down a Halberstadt two-seater over Steenwerck and a Fokker D.VIII over Estaires, which gave him his twentieth victory.

June 27 saw him destroy in flames a Hannover two-seater over La Couture and, two days later, he destroyed a Fokker D.VII over Comines. On 1 July, he destroyed a Rumpler two-seater over Tourcoing. On 24 July, Jones downed three DRW two-seaters in one day, over Merville and east of Kemmel. The following day he destroyed in flames another one south-east of Neuve-Église and the next day destroyed another west of Bailleul.

July 30 saw another astonishing set of victories when he again downed three enemy aircraft in a single day. Just after noon, he destroyed in flames a Rumpler two-seater over Cassel-Ypres. A few minutes later, a LVG two-seater was destroyed over Merville. Later in the day he downed a Fokker D.VII east of Armentières. These took his total to 31.

His award of the Distinguished Flying Cross was announced on 3 August. His citation read: 'In eleven days this officer attacked and destroyed six enemy aeroplanes, displaying great courage, skill and initiative.'[44]

On the same day, he shot down a LVG two-seater south-east of Merville and the following day destroyed a Hannover two-seater west of Estaires. August 6 saw him shoot down two Fokker D.VIIs over Sailly-sur-la-Lys, and on 7 August he registered his last two victories on the Western Front. First he destroyed a LVG two-seater five miles south-east of Estaires, and later destroyed an unidentified two-seater east of the Houthoulst Forest.

In September 1918, Jones was awarded the Military Cross. His citation read:

> For conspicuous gallantry and devotion to duty. This officer, one of an offensive patrol, engaged and shot down in flames a two-seater which fell to earth. Ten days later, on offensive patrol, he shot down a Hannover two-seater, which crashed. The next day, when patrolling, he pursued, overtook and shot down an Albatros two-seater. During the same flight he met a Halberstadt two-seater and killed the observer, who either jumped or fell overboard, but had to break off as his ammunition was finished. The next day, he shot a balloon down in flames. Three days later he got a good burst with both guns on a Pfalz scout, both wings coming off. He has driven two others down out of control.[45]

A few days later, he was awarded a bar to his Distinguished Flying Cross. The citation read:

> A gallant officer who in the last three months has destroyed twenty-one enemy aeroplanes. On one occasion he attacked a Halberstadt two-seater which was escorted by two scouts. On his approach the scouts deserted the two-seater, which he shot down in flames. He then pursued the two scouts, one of which he destroyed.[46]

In November, Jones was awarded the Distinguished Service Order. His citation read:

> Since joining his present Brigade in May last, this officer has destroyed twenty-eight enemy machines. He combines skilful tactics and marksmanship with high courage. While engaged on wireless interception duty, he followed a patrol of nine Fokker biplanes, and succeeded in joining their formation unobserved. After a while two Fokkers left the formation to attack one of our

artillery observation machines. Following them, Captain Jones engaged the higher of the two, which fell on its companion, and both machines fell interlocked in flames.[47]

Jones survived the war and, during this time, he also survived a reported 28 flying accidents. After the Armistice was signed, he volunteered to fight in Russia against the Bolsheviks. He continued to serve with the Royal Air Force until he retired on 9 July 1936. In August 1939, he was recalled as Chief Signals Officer at Training Command Headquarters. In 1940, he was flying an unarmed Hawker Henley near Swansea and he attacked a Junkers Ju 88 bomber with a Very pistol. After the war he returned to St Clears and worked in the Ministry of Pensions. He died on 30 August 1960, aged 64, after a fall in his home at Aberaeron and was buried at Cana Chapel cemetery, near Bancyfelin.

Lieutenant-Colonel Raymond Collishaw was the highest-scoring ace with links to Wales, being credited with 59 victories during the Great War, and another in Russia in 1919. He was born in Nanaimo, British Columbia, on 22 November 1893, his father having been born in Wrexham. His mother was from Newport and had been raised in Pantygog in the Garw

Valley. He later named one of his aircraft 'Black Maria' after his aunt in Pantygog. On leaving school at 15, he worked as a cabin boy. In late 1915, he applied to the Royal Naval Air Service and, in the meantime, paid for his own flying lessons in England. He joined the Royal Naval Air Service in January 1916 and flew Sopwith 1½ Strutters

Raymond Collishaw

with No. 3 Wing. He achieved his first two victories on 25 October when he destroyed and shot down two enemy scout aircraft over Lunéville.

Collishaw was shot down on 27 December, but survived and was posted to 3 Naval Squadron in February 1917, flying a Sopwith Pup. On 15 February, he shot down a Halberstadt D.II over Bapaume and on 4 March repeated the act. He was then transferred to 10 Naval Squadron to fly Sopwith Triplanes and achieved his status as an ace on 28 April by destroying an Albatros D.II over Ostend. Two days later he did the same thing east of Courtemarck. On 9 May, an Albatros D.III was shot down east of Dixmude, and three days later a seaplane was destroyed over Ostend. On 1 June, he destroyed in flames an Albatros D.III south of Wervicq, and the following day achieved his tenth victory by shooting down an unidentified two-seater over St-Julien. On 3 June, he destroyed in flames an Albatros D.III over Roubaix and another over Lille the next day.

Collishaw claimed two more victories on 5 June by shooting down in flames an Albatros two-seater over Wervicq and another one north-west of Poelcapelle. The following day he surpassed this feat by accounting for three Albatros D.III aircraft over Polygon Wood. On 7 June, he shot down another Albatros D.III between Menin and St-Julien.

On 9 June, Collishaw was again shot down. In his autobiography he recorded what happened:

> I took off from Droglandt at 0500 hrs with a two-flight patrol
> detailed to cover the area east of Ypres, and we had hardly
> crossed the lines when we ran into a formation of Albatros D.IIIs.
> As usual, they were below our altitude, and we dived on them,
> going down from 17,000ft. I got on the tail of one of them and,
> although the German pilot went into a series of tight turns, my
> Triplane was able to turn even more tightly. It looked like another
> sure victory, and I had just got his tail into my sights, and was
> about to open fire, when a devastating stream of bullets smashed
> into my cockpit. They came at me from out of the sun. His

attack left me unscathed, but shattered my controls. I was quite helpless.

I could do nothing at all to control my machine, which fell off on one wing and then went into a hair-raising series of cartwheels and wild swoops and dives. I was absolutely terrified at first, but this gave way to a dulled sort of resignation, and I can recall thinking rather wistfully how nice it would be to have a parachute.

We had been at around 16,000ft. when my machine was damaged, and the descent took some 15 minutes, although it seemed much longer than that. We fell closer and closer to the ground and, just before smashing into a hillside, the Triplane took it in its mind to try one final swoop, and that saved me. We hit with a tremendous crash and the Triplane folded into a mass of wreckage, but I was left intact with no more than bruises and a determination that never, never again would I let anyone come at me out of the sun.[48]

He was soon flying again in another Sopwith Triplane and on 15 June, dispatched four enemy aircraft: a two-seater between St-Julien and Houthem, another one over Menin, and two Albatros D.Vs over Moorslede. On 17 June, another

Collishaw's Sopwith Triplane

Albatros D.V was accounted for over Roulers, and seven days later another one over Moorslede. His 25th victory came on 2 July when he destroyed an unidentified two-seater over Poelcapelle Station.

Collishaw's most remarkable day came on 6 July 1917 when he downed no fewer than six enemy aircraft in the space of ten minutes. All were Albatros D.Vs and were shot down over Dêulémont and Menin.

On 11 July, an Albatros D.V was shot down over Moorslede and another on 12 July over Polygon Wood. He himself was shot down again on 15 July but was unhurt. He was awarded the Distinguished Service Cross on 20 July:

> In recognition of his services on various occasions, especially the following: On 1st June 1917, this officer shot down an Albatross Scout in flames. On 3rd June 1917, he shot down an Albatross Scout in flames. On 5th June 1917, he shot down a two-seater Albatross in flames. On the 6th June 1917, he shot down two Albatross scouts in flames and killed the pilot in a third. He has displayed great gallantry and skill in all his combats.[49]

Also on 20 July, an Albatros D.V was destroyed between Menin and Messines and, on 21 July, two more were downed over Passchendaele. July 27 saw him dispatch two more north of Menin and over Polygon Wood respectively. The following day he was ordered home on leave and, on 11 August, Collishaw was awarded the Distinguished Service Order:

> For conspicuous bravery and skill in successfully leading attacks against hostile aircraft. Since the 10th June 1917, Flt. Lieut. Collishaw has himself brought down four machines completely out of control and driven down two others with their planes shot away. Whilst on an offensive patrol on the morning of the 15th June 1917, he forced down a hostile scout in a nosedive. Later, on the same day, he drove down one hostile two-seater machine completely out of control, one hostile scout in a spin, and a third machine with two of its planes shot away. On the 24th June 1917,

he engaged four enemy scouts, driving one down in a spin and another with two of its planes shot away; the latter machine was seen to crash.[50]

He was back in France in November and took command of 13 Naval Squadron, flying Sopwith Camels. On 10 December, an Albatros two-seater was driven down over Dunkerque and his 40th victim was an Albatros D.V over Ostend on 19 December. In January 1918, he was posted back to 3 Naval Squadron but ordered not to fly in combat. This squadron became 203 Squadron when the Royal Air Force was formed on 1 April and, by June, he was once more permitted to fly. He went on to achieve 19 more victories – all in the same Sopwith Camel.

On 11 June he downed two Pfalz D.IIIs east of Outtersteene and west of Armentières. Four days later he destroyed a Fokker D.VII over Ervillers and another one on 26 June north of Noyon. On 30 June, another Pfalz D.III fell out of control over Houthoulst Wood. The same fate befell two DFW Mars two-seaters north-east of Dixmude on 4 July, and on 20 July two more fell south-east of Merville and over Miraumont. Collishaw's 50th victory came on 22 July when he destroyed an unidentified two-seater over Dorignies and later that day destroyed an Albatros D.V over the River Scarpe.

Collishaw was awarded the Distinguished Flying Cross at the start of August:

> This officer is an exceptionally capable and efficient squadron commander, under whose leadership the squadron has maintained a high place in the Army Wing. He has carried out numerous solo patrols and led many offensive patrols, on all occasions engaging the enemy with great bravery and fearlessness. Up to date he has accounted for forty-seven enemy machines, twenty-two in the last twelve months.[51]

On 9 August, a DFW Mars two-seater was destroyed north-east of Locon and, the following day, he downed two Fokker

D.VIIs west of Bray-sur-Somme. On 15 August, a Fokker D.VII was destroyed south of Damery and 5 September saw him capture one at Inchy-en-Artois.

He received a bar to his Distinguished Service Order in September:

> A brilliant squadron leader of exceptional daring, who has destroyed fifty-one enemy machines. Early one morning he, with another pilot, attacked an enemy aerodrome. Seeing three machines brought out of a burning hangar, he dived five times, firing bursts at these from a very low altitude, and dropped bombs on the living quarters. He then saw an enemy aeroplane descending over the aerodrome; he attacked it and drove it down in flames. Later, when returning from a reconnaissance of the damaged hangars, he was attacked by three Albatross Scouts, who pursued him to our lines, when he turned and attacked one, which fell out of control and crashed.[52]

On 24 September, he destroyed a Fokker D.VII at Épinoy and two days later achieved his final victories of the war when he destroyed two Fokker D.VIIs over Lieu-Saint-Amand.

Raymond Collishaw was the fourth highest-scoring Allied ace of the war, behind René Fonck, Billy Bishop and Edward Mannock. He served in the Royal Air Force after the war ended and fought in Russia in 1919 where he was credited with another victory – his 60th. He retired from the Royal Air Force in 1943 with the rank of Air Vice-Marshal and died on 28 September 1976.

CHAPTER SEVEN

One Welsh Airman's War

'I fly because it releases my mind from the tyranny of petty things.'
Antoine de Saint-Exupéry

OVER 9,300 AIRMEN and women died during the Great War
and thousands more were wounded or injured. Hundreds
of those casualties were from Wales. In order to give some
indication of the experience of the Welsh airmen who served
on active duty in many different countries, one airman's story
is herewith told in more detail.

Donovan Baldwin Griffith was the son of Baldwin and Mary
Fanny Griffith of Bron Awel in Ruthin. His father was the town
clerk, and Donovan was born in Ruthin on 22 January 1899. He
was educated at the local grammar school and his education
success was reported in January 1915:

> The Grammar School reopened on Tuesday after the Christmas
> holidays. Mr H. Moore, one of the masters in the school, has
> obtained Commission in an Irish Regiment and has left to take up
> his new duties. All the Assistant Masters who were in the school
> when the war broke out have obtained commissions in the Army
> and are now on active service. A splendid example of patriotism.
> The Headmaster has fortunately been able to replace them with an
> excellent staff and the school work has not suffered. In the list of

Candidates who successfully passed the Oxford junior examination at the Cardiff Centre is the name of Donovan Griffith, a pupil in the Grammar School.[1]

Donovan attested for military service in Wrexham on 1 November 1916, aged 17 years and ten months, his headmaster at Ruthin School providing a 'certificate of moral character'. He gave his occupation as that of a student and was posted to the 61st Training Reserve Battalion. He was just over five foot tall. Mobilised on 9 March 1917, by which time he was employed as a clerk, he was posted for training at Kinmel Park in north Wales and subsequently posted to the 221st Infantry Battalion.

On 9 March, his father wrote a letter to the Army regarding his son:

> The bearer is my son referred to in my letter of the 3rd instant, and, as desired in your letter of the 4th, he is asking to see you personally. I should be very grateful if you would kindly have him posted to the 65th Battalion commanded by Colonel Beresford-Ash. I am informed that Colonel Field's Battalion, referred to in my previous letter, is filled up and that boys are now being posted to the 65th Battalion. My son will be pleased to explain the reason for his request if you desire it. Thanking you for your courtesy. Believe me, yours very truly, Baldwin Griffith.[2]

Despite this plea, Donovan's request was not granted, so he volunteered for flying duties in July and was posted to the Royal Flying Corps Cadet Unit at Denham in Buckinghamshire on 13 August 1917. On 7 November, he was discharged and appointed to a temporary commission as a second lieutenant on probation. The confirmation of his appointment as a flying officer came in the *London Gazette* on 23 April 1918.

After 85 hours' flying time, he was posted to 209 Squadron in June 1918 and flew Sopwith Camels. The squadron had been involved in the famous engagement with *Jasta* 1 on 21 April 1918 in which Manfred von Richthofen was killed.

Manfred von Richthofen's Dr.I

These are his flying Log Book entries from his arrival in France, and give an insight into the life of a young pilot on the Western Front in 1918:

1918		
20 June	45 minutes	Practice noting landmarks.
21 June	30 minutes	Practice.
22 June	20 minutes	Practice.
23 June	30 minutes	Practice.
24 June	2 hours	Amiens to Abbeville. Aerial Sentry.
25 June	55 minutes	Aerial firing at target.
26 June	45 minutes	Learning lines etc.
26 June	15 minutes	Landed at 205 Squadron. Smashed a tail skid.
26 June	15 minutes	Returned to Squadron OK.
27 June	2 hours	Amiens to Abbeville. Aerial Sentry. Nothing to report.
27 June	25 minutes	Aerial firing.
28 June	2 hours 20	Amiens to Abbeville. Aerial Sentry. No Huns seen.
28 June	50 minutes	Target practice. Right hand gun gave no stoppages. Too much tension on spring.
29 June	45 minutes	No. 2 ASD to 209 Squadron. Bringing back new machine.

29 June	3 hours	Albert to Villers-Bretonneux. Patrol. Met some Huns. Saw Foster bring one down. Lost patrol and came back by myself.
30 June	1 hour 40	Villers-Bretonneux. Saw one enemy aircraft. Foster dived but he got away. 3 two-seaters attacked and driven east.
30 June	1 hour 30	2 two-seaters attacked indecisively.
30 June	1 hour 15	Patrol with 'C' Flight. Two enemy aircraft observed. Retired east.
1 July	40 minutes	1 enemy aircraft seen. Retired east.
1 July	1 hour	Captain Foster's engine went dead, so I carried on alone but saw no enemy aircraft.
3 July	1 hour 10	Patrol. Villers-Bretonneux to Albert for enemy aircraft. None observed.
4 July	65 minutes	Hamel. At 6.15 a.m. north of Hamel 2 bombs dropped on carrying party. At 5.20 a.m. 1 bomb on active machine gun post and later one direct hit observed on dug-out. Bombs dropped from 400 ft. 650 rounds fired at trenches while low strafing. One round through aileron and two through plane.
4 July	75 minutes	At 11.20 four bombs dropped on building east of Warfusee-Abancourt. Men emerging from buildings attacked with machine-gun fire. Hun archie very active. One bullet through right lower plane and main spar.
5 July	90 minutes	Patrol after wireless enemy aircraft Barbie to Albert. No enemy aircraft seen.
6 July	30 minutes	Attacked on two-seater south of Sailly-Laurette and fired about 200 rounds, then engine went 'dud' and I made for home. Engine finally gave out when about 20 feet up near Pont-Noyelles but managed to land safely.
7 July	75 minutes	Foster and self. 8 enemy aircraft observed between Bray-Rosieres.
7 July	25 minutes	Hesdin to Squadron delivering new machine.
8 July	70 minutes	Int WEA. One two-seater observed over Chignolle but was lost in mist. Engine not very good.
8 July	75 minutes	May and Scadding. Int WEA. No enemy aircraft seen.
9 July	60 minutes	LOP. (Scadding, May, Harker and Porter). No enemy aircraft seen.
10 July	75 minutes	I WEA. 1 two-seater observed off Cayeux. Thomas leading.
10 July	20 minutes	Practice bomb-dropping.

12 July	110 minutes	LOP. (May, Scadding, Harker and Walker). One two-seater observed and driven east from Bray. I was too far away to fire. 1 two-seater observed by Harbourmieres. 2 trains going south from Flaque dump. I crashed the bus on landing.
13 July	40 minutes	Hesdin to Squadron delivering new machine. Weather dud.
13 July	25 minutes	Machine test.
14 July	120 minutes	Low patrol. Dropped 1 bomb on Cappy and returned and landed with 3 in rack.
14 July	15 minutes	Practice and machine test.
15 July	125 minutes	Low patrol. Dropped 4 bombs on Maricourt Wood. AA fire very heavy. Piece of shrapnel through cowling.
16 July	60 minutes	Hutments at Foucaucourt aerodrome attacked with bombs and machine guns. 1st hit edge of road, 2 and 3 near huts and 4 direct hit on most westerly hut. Fired at KB and huts. Enemy machine-gun fire very good. 80 machines took part.
16 July	90 minutes	Bombs dropped on La Flaque dump from 10,000 feet. Results not observed owing to bad visibility.
17 July	130 minutes	Squadron bombing and HOP. Bombs dropped on Rosieres and observed to burst near railway station.
18 July	150 minutes	Flight bombing and HOP. Bomb dropped on Fricourt n. Albert. 3 enemy biplanes and 2 enemy triplanes observed above us. Coming back lost formation and landed at Candour. Arrived back alright.

That was Donovan's last entry in his log book.

At 4.15 a.m. on the morning of 19 July, he took off on a special mission and was seen over Cappy aerodrome at 4.45 a.m. His Sopwith Camel was hit by gunfire from Flakbatterie 82 over a German aerodrome and shot down. Donovan was declared missing in action. Lieutenant Scadding, referred to in Donovan's log book above, was also shot down by flak but survived and spent the rest of the war in a German prisoner of war camp.

Captain Robert Mordaunt Foster (see above in the log book entry) was credited with 16 victories. He survived the war, served throughout the Second World War, and retired as Air Chief-Marshal Sir Robert Foster, KCB, CBE, DFC.

Donovan Griffith

Donovan's father finally received confirmation of his son's death six months later in January 1919:

The Late Lieut. Donovan Griffith
Mr Baldwin Griffith has lately received information that his son, 2nd Lieut. Donovan Griffith, RAF, who was reported missing on the 19th of July last, was killed on that day. A letter from the Captain of the Squadron states: 'At the time we were bombing and shooting up an enemy aerodrome at dawn, this being carried out at about 200 feet. Fifteen machines and pilots started out and two did not return, one being 2nd Lieut. Griffith, the other 2nd Lieut. Scadding, the latter having been reported a prisoner of war. This work we were engaged in was of a very hazardous nature and I am of the opinion that this officer was shot down and killed by machine-gun fire from the ground. The aerodrome we were strafing was at Cappy on the Amiens-Albert front, and we were stationed at Bertangles.' This is confirmed by a letter from the International Prisoners of War Society at Geneva, which states that '2nd Lieut. Donovan Griffith was brought down east of Hamel and

Ruthin War Memorial

buried there.' His Major writing to his parents shortly after he was reported missing said, 'We are all very sorry indeed to lose your son, who was a very stouthearted little pilot and was beginning to do good work. I only wish we had as good officers as he was as reinforcements.'[3]

Donovan Griffith was buried in Villers-Bretonneux Military Cemetery, aged 19, and his grieving parents dedicated a memorial to their son in the form of a painting in St Peter's Church in Ruthin, painted by his artist sister, Mignon. It depicts the three Marys at Christ's sepulchre against a backdrop of the Clwydian Range, north Wales. The accompanying inscription reads: 'To the Glory of God and in proud remembrance of their son Lieut. Donovan Baldwin Griffith RAF who fell in action in France July 19 1918, aged 19 years, and lies at Villers-Bretonneux. This painting is dedicated by Baldwin and Mary F. Griffith of Bryn Rhos, Ruthin.'

The Last Airman of the Great War

'We dedicated ourselves to death.'
Hubert Williams

THE LAST ROYAL Air Force pilot of the Great War to die was Hubert Williams, who passed away, aged 106, on 20 September 2002, in a nursing home in Cardiff, the city in which he was born on 9 November 1895.

Hubert joined the Royal Engineers and was trained in the Salisbury area, eventually joining 26th Division in France. He transferred to the Royal Flying Corps in 1915, attracted by the superior pay, and was sent to the de Havilland training school in northern France. The school mirrored the French system of pilot training. The trainee was seated in a glider attached to a winch by a rope. If he could control it satisfactorily he was ready for the next step. Hubert passed on his second attempt, and graduated to a skeleton aircraft with a small engine. He was allocated ten hours of training, but passed in seven.

The final stage of his training was three hours flying a de Havilland aircraft around a circuit. He moved on to fighter training and flew a Sopwith Camel attacking and bombing German trenches during the Battle of the Somme from an aerodrome at Avignon. He recalled his experiences later:

I was keen to get cracking to stop the enemy coming into the country. We knew we might die but we were prepared to die for our country. I can remember the bombing, the shrapnel, shells going off all around, the guns flashing. It was terrible. There was smoke everywhere. I could hear people screaming and there was masses of blood. I lost a lot of my friends. I can remember waving to one colleague as we were flying and the next second he was a ball of flames. He had been shot down by a German plane and I expected the same thing to happen to me at any second.[1]

In his words, 'We dedicated ourselves to death.'[2]

When he was 22, he was posted to Macedonia and took part in bombing raids on enemy positions in the Grande-Couronne and Petit-Couronne mountains. Bombing involved banking the aircraft to allow the bomb on one side of the aircraft to be released, and reversing the banking to allow the bomb on the other side to be dropped. He learned quickly, when flying through anti-aircraft fire, to head for the last shell burst, knowing that the next one would not burst there.

He did not carry a parachute, and his aircraft was shot up seven times, but each time he managed to return to base. Repairs to his aircraft were carried out by the ground crew, using linen cloth and glue. On the eighth occasion he was hit by anti-aircraft fire. The shell burst broke one of his struts and fractured one of the ailerons. He turned for home but, the next thing he knew, was waking up in a hospital in Malta, suffering from malaria and the effects of gas poisoning. He had been pulled unconscious from the wreckage by local villagers, and it was nine months before he was well enough to return home. He was then sent to work in the Plymouth area as a staff officer, but resigned after two years and returned to civilian life.

Hubert Williams rejoined the Royal Air Force during the Second World War and trained Polish pilots to fly, reaching the rank of Squadron Leader. After retiring from the Royal Air Force, he ran a successful electrical business in Cardiff for 42 years. His flying days were not over, however, as on his

Hubert Williams

hundredth birthday he took the controls of Concorde during a flight to New York and, at 102, he received the *Légion d'honneur* from the French government.

He said of his time as a pilot, 'I'm no hero. I just consider myself a remarkably lucky man to have survived.'[3]

Hubert Williams was indeed a fortunate man. Given the inherent flaws in both men and machines, the fortunes of war and the height and speed at which the pilots and observers were endeavouring to kill the enemy before they themselves were killed, it is remarkable that so many did survive.

They were men of a bygone age who believed in the cause for which they were fighting, and had a strong will to survive. They came from a variety of backgrounds and occupations and fought high above the battlefields, often with terrible consequences. The men and women of the ground crews and support services provided the resources for the fliers to carry out their duties in the sky. They were vulnerable to enemy air attacks, shelling and disease, and died in large numbers in a catastrophic war.

Endnotes

Chapter 1: 1914 and 1915

1 *Llanelli Star*, 5 September 1914.
2 *Abergavenny Chronicle*, 27 November 1914.
3 *London Gazette*, 1 January 1915.
4 *South Wales Weekly Post*, 28 November 1914.
5 *South Wales Weekly Post*, 23 January 1915.
6 *London Gazette*, 1 January 1915.
7 *Labour Voice*, 19 May 1917.
8 *London Gazette*, 12 December 1919.
9 *Glamorgan Gazette*, 19 February 1915.
10 *Western Mail*, 1 April 1915.
11 *Haverfordwest and Milford Haven Telegraph*, 19 May 1915.
12 *Carmarthen Weekly Reporter*, 25 June 1915.
13 *The Times*, 9 July 1915
14 *Wrexham Advertiser and North Wales News*, 17 July 1915.

Chapter 2: 1916

1 *The Times*, 23 February 1916.
2 Sambrook private papers, courtesy of Llangwm Local History Society.
3 *Western Mail*, 6 July 1916.
4 Lane, Frederick W., *A Great Adventure in East Africa*, Exeter, 2015, pp. 135–6.
5 Walmsley, L., Flying and Sport in East Africa, London and Edinburgh, 1920, pp. 67–8.
6 *The Aeroplane*, 10 May 1922.
7 *Haverforwest and Milford Haven Telegraph*, 9 August 1916.
8 *The Shirburnian*, 1916.
9 De Ruvigny, *Roll of Honour 1914–1918*, Uckfield, 2009, p. 210.
10 Ibid.
11 *Brecon and Radnor Express*, 5 October 1916.
12 Franks, Giblin and McCrery, *Under the Guns of the Red Baron*, London, 2000, p. 14

13 *Flight*, 5 October 1916.
14 *Flight*, 29 March 1917.

Chapter 3: 1917

1 *Aberdare Leader*, 13 January 1917.
2 *Cambrian Daily Leader*, 22 January 1917.
3 *Carmarthen Journal and South Wales Weekly Advertiser*, 16 February 1917.
4 *Hull Daily Mail*, 17 February 1917.
5 *Ampleforth Journal*, 1917.
6 De Ruvigny, op. cit., p. 138.
7 Ibid.
8 Ibid.
9 Ibid.
10 In Franks, Giblin and McCrery, op. cit. p. 104.
11 *Western Mail*, 14 April 1917.
12 *Brecon Radnor Express*, 26 April 1917.
13 *Flight*, 19 April 1917, p. 381.
14 Franks, Giblin and McCrery, op. cit., p. 111.
15 Ibid., p. 114.
16 *Carmarthen Journal and South Wales Weekly Advertiser*, 24 May 1918.
17 *Western Mail*, 11 July 1917.
18 *Llanelli Star*, 5 May 1917.
19 Air 1/1219/204/5/2634, National Archives.
20 *Chester Chronicle*, 19 May 1917.
21 www.dnw.co.uk/auction-archive/lot-archive/lot.php?deptment=Medals&lot_id-161606.
22 *Western Mail*, 22 May 1917.
23 www.southwalesargus.co.uk/news/11433258.
24 De Ruvigny, op. cit., p. 74.
25 Ibid.
26 Liverpool Scroll of Fame, courtesy of Liverpool Record Office.
27 Ibid.
28 Ibid.
29 *Cambrian News*, 18 May 1917.
30 *Haverfordwest and Milford Haven Telegraph*, 23 May 1917.
31 *Cambrian News and Merionethshire Standard*, 24 August 1917.
32 *Brecon and Radnor Express*, 7 June 1917.
33 *Brecon County Times*, 14 June 1917.
34 *Western Mail*, 29 October 1914.
35 Courtesy of Guy Griffiths.

36 *Brecon and Radnor Express*, 21 October 1915.
37 Ibid.
38 Ibid.
39 *The Abingdonian*, July 1916.
40 *London Gazette*, July 1916.
41 *Llanelli Star*, 23 June 1917.
42 *North Wales Chronicle and Advertiser for the Principality*, 29 June 1917.
43 *Western Mail*, 21 June 1917.
44 *North Wales Chronicle and Advertiser for the Principality*, 6 July 1917.
45 Courtesy of Brian Pocock.
46 Ibid.
47 *Birmingham Daily Gazette*, 28 June 1917.
48 www.visittenby.co.uk/culture/the-great-war-they-did-their-bit-by-doing-their-best.
49 De Ruvigny, op. cit., p. 145.
50 *The Times*, 7 August 1917.
51 *Western Mail*, 10 August 1917.
52 Ibid.
53 *Western Mail*, 11 September 1915.
54 De Ruvigny, op. cit., p. 67.
55 *Liverpool Echo*, 20 August 1917.
56 Air 3/2/4773, National Archives.
57 AOM 273/11, National Archives.
58 *The Times*, 31 August 1917.
59 *Brecon County Times*, 6 September 1917.
60 *Cambrian Daily Leader*, 29 August 1917.
61 Henshaw, T., *The Sky Their Battlefield 2*, London, 2014, p. 123.
62 *Western Mail*, 10 November 1917.
63 *Gloucestershire Echo*, 26 October 1917.
64 *Llanelli Star*, 20 October 1917.
65 *The Roath Roamer*, courtesy of the Glamorgan Archives.
66 Service Record, National Archives.
67 *Western Mail*, 1 December 1917.
68 *Labour Voice*, 15 December 1917.
69 *Western Mail*, 15 December 1917.
70 *Western Mail*, 31 December 1917.
71 *Herald of Wales*, 5 January 1918.

Chapter 4: 1918

1   www.keble.ox.ac.uk/about/post/keble-and-the-great-war/roll-of-honour-1914-1918.
2   Courtesy of Ben Sloper.
3   *Western Mail*, 15 January 1918.
4   De Ruvigny, op. cit., p. 52.
5   *The Breconian*, April 1918.
6   *Western Mail*, 18 March 1918.
7   *Yorkshire Post and Leeds Intelligencer*, 3 May 1920.
8   *London Gazette*, 15 June 1917.
9   *Western Mail*, 26 March 1918.
10 www.stmaryshaverfordwest.org.uk/documents/stmaryshaverforwest.pdf.
11 Alyn James private papers, courtesy of Tim Butcher.
12 Ibid.
13 *Spirit of the Air*, 1 April 1918.
14 Hyde, H.M., *Sir Patrick Hastings, his life and cases*, London, 1960, p. 60.
15 www.the-saleroom.com/en-us/auction.categories.
16 Franks, Giblin and McCrery, op. cit. p. 191.
17 *Llanelli Star*, 6 April 1918.
18 *Aberdare Leader*, 2 October 1915.
19 *Aberdare Leader*, 13 April 1918.
20 *Barry Dock News*, 19 April 1918.
21 Unknown Yorkshire newspaper, undated.
22 *London Gazette*, 24 May 1917.
23 *Merthyr Express*, 25 May 1918.
24 *London Gazette*, 16 September 1918.
25 *Nottingham Evening Post*, 23 May 1918.
26 *Toronto Evening Telegram*, 11 July 1918.
27 *Cambrian News*, 7 June 1918.
28 *Brecon and Radnorshire Express*,11 July 1918.
29 *London Gazette*, 22 June 1918.
30 *London Gazette*, 8 February 1919.
31 *Western Mail*, 22 July 1918.
32 *London Gazette*, 11 March 1916.
33 *Liverpool Echo*, 5 July 1918.
34 *Western Mail*, 5 August 1918.
35 *South Wales Weekly Post*, 14 September 1918.
36 *Western Mail*, 14 August 1918.
37 *Heroes in Hell*, John Gwilliam, privately published.

38 *Western Mail*, 26 August 1918.
39 *Western Mail*, 3 September 1918.
40 *Western Mail*, 7 September 1918.
41 *Glamorgan Gazette*, 5 July 1918.
42 *Cambrian Daily Leader*, 12 September 1918.
43 *Cambrian News*, 20 September 1918.
44 *London Gazette*, 9 January 1918.
45 *Western Mail*, 18 September 1918.
46 www.findagrave.com/cgi-bin/fg.cgi?page=gr&GRid=15752406
47 *Doncaster Chronicle*, 20 September 1918.
48 *North Wales Chronicle and Advertiser for the Principality*, 20 September 1918.
49 *London Gazette*, 15 April 1916.
50 Paul Kemp Private Collection.
51 Paul Kemp Private Collection.
52 Ibid.
53 *The Pembroke and County Guardian*, undated.
54 *Western Mail*, 12 October 1918.
55 *Cambria Daily Leader*, 4 June 1918.
56 *Amman Valley Chronicle*, 15 August 1918.
57 *Essex Newsman*, 19 October 1918.
58 McCrery, N., *Final Wicket*, Barnsley, 2015, p. 464.
59 www.ancestry.co.uk/family-tree/person/tree/67799502/person/34423279806/gallery
60 *Western Mail*, 23 October 1918.
61 Ibid.
62 *London Gazette*, 4 November 1918.
63 http://ourheritagewarmedals.co.uk/ww1.htm.
64 *Western Mail*, 7 August 1915.
65 *Flight Magazine*, 14 November 1918.
66 *Cambrian News*, 15 November 1918.
67 Citation for Military Cross.
68 *Carmarthen Journal*, 27 December 1918.

Chapter 5: 1919 to 1921

1 *London Gazette*, 8 February 1919.
2 *London Gazette*, 16 August 1917.
3 *London Gazette*, 18 November 1919.
4 *London Gazette*, 8 February 1919.
5 *Labour Voice*, 15 February 1919.

Chapter 6: The Welsh Flying Aces

1 *Edinburgh Gazette*, 28 August 1915.
2 *London Gazette*, 3 December 1918.
3 Ryan, R.W., *From Boxkite to Boardroom*, Moose Jaw, 1982.
4 *London Gazette*, 8 February 1919.
5 Wallace Smart, private diary. Courtesy of Ben Smart.
6 Ibid.
7 *London Gazette*, 23 April 1918.
8 *London Gazette*, 17 April 1917.
9 *Dundee Evening Telegraph*, 25 February 1927.
10 *London Gazette*, 26 March 1917.
11 *London Gazette*, 2 November 1917.
12 *London Gazette*, 21 December 1916.
13 *London Gazette*, 3 December 1918.
14 *London Gazette*, 7 June 1921.
15 *London Gazette*, 29 October 1915.
16 *London Gazette*, 4 August 1916.
17 De Ruvigny, op. cit., p. 172.
18 *London Gazette*, 24 August 1918.
19 *London Gazette*, 22 June 1918.
20 *London Gazette*, 1 January 1917.
21 *London Gazette*, 5 July 1918.
22 *London Gazette*, 22 February 1918.
23 *London Gazette*, 18 July 1917.
24 *London Gazette*, 17 September 1917.
25 *London Gazette*, 21 September 1918.
26 *London Gazette*, 26 July 1918.
27 *London Gazette*, 11 August 1917.
28 *London Gazette*, 8 February 1918.
29 *London Gazette*, 7 February 1919.
30 *London Gazette*, 13 May 1918.
31 *London Gazette*, 27 September 1917.
32 *London Gazette*, 18 December 1917.
33 De Ruvigny, op. cit., p. 122.
34 Ibid.
35 *London Gazette*, 16 August 1918.
36 *London Gazette*, 16 September 1918.
37 Ibid.
38 *London Gazette*, 18 July 1917.
39 *London Gazette*, 17 September 1917.
40 *London Gazette*, 18 March 1918.

[41] *London Gazette*, 16 September 1918.

[42] *London Gazette*, 21 September 1918.

[43] Jones, I., *Tiger Squadron*, London, 1956, pp.107–8.

[44] *London Gazette*, 3 August 1918.

[45] *London Gazette*, 16 September 1918.

[46] *London Gazette*, 21 September 1918.

[47] *London Gazette*, 2 November 1918.

[48] Quoted in Franks, N., *Sopwith Triplane Aces of World War 1*, Oxford, 2004, p. 83.

[49] *London Gazette*, 20 July 1917.

[50] *London Gazette*, 11 August 1917.

[51] *London Gazette*, 3 August 1918.

[52] *London Gazette*, 21 September 1918.

Chapter 7: One Welsh Airman's War

[1] *Denbighshire Free Press*, 23 January 1915.

[2] Service record, National Archives, WO339/113911.

[3] *Denbighshire Free Press*, 11 January 1919.

Epilogue: The Last Airman of the Great War

[1] *Western Mail*, 20 September 2002.

[2] *Front Line* article by Peter Gorman, January 1997.

[3] Ibid.

Bibliography

De Ruvigny, *Roll of Honour 1914–1918*, Uckfield, 2009.

Franks, N., *Jasta Boelcke*, London, 2004.

Franks, N., *Sopwith Triplane Aces of World War I*, Oxford, 2004.

Franks, N., Bailey, F. and Duiven, R., *The Jasta War Chronology*, London, 1998.

Franks, N., Bailey, F. and Duiven, R., *Casualties of the German Air Service*, London, 1999.

Franks, N.L.R., Bailey, F.W. and Guest, R., *Above the Lines*, London, 1993.

Franks, N. and Giblin, H., *Under the Guns of the German Aces*, London, 1997.

Franks, N. and Giblin, H., *Under the Guns of the Kaiser's Aces*, London, 2003.

Franks, N., Giblin, H. and McCrery, N., *Under the Guns of the Red Baron*, London, 1998.

Front Line, The Western Front Association South Wales Branch Newsletter, January 1997.

Gwilliam, J., *Heroes in Hell*, privately published, undated.

Henshaw, T, *The Sky Their Battlefield II*, London, 2014.

Hobson, C., *Airmen Died in the Great War 1914–1918*, Suffolk, 1995.

Hyde, H.M., *Sir Patrick Hastings, his life and cases*, London, 1960.

Jones, I., *Tiger Squadron*, London, 1956.

Kennett, L., *The First Air War 1914–1918*, New York, 1991.

Lewis, B., *Swansea in the Great War*, Barnsley, 2014.

McCrery, N., *Final Wicket*, Barnsley, 2015.

McInnes, I. and Webb, J.V., *A Contemptible Little Flying Corps*, London, 1991.

O'Connor, M. and Franks, N., *In the Footsteps of the Red Baron*, Barnsley, 2004.

Revell, A., *Brief Glory*, Barnsley, 2010.

Ryan, R.W., *From Boxkite to Boardroom*, Moose Jaw, 1982.

Shores, C., Franks, N. and Guest, R., *Above the Trenches*, London, 1990.

von Richthofen, M., *The Red Fighter Pilot*, Florida, 2007.

Also by the author:

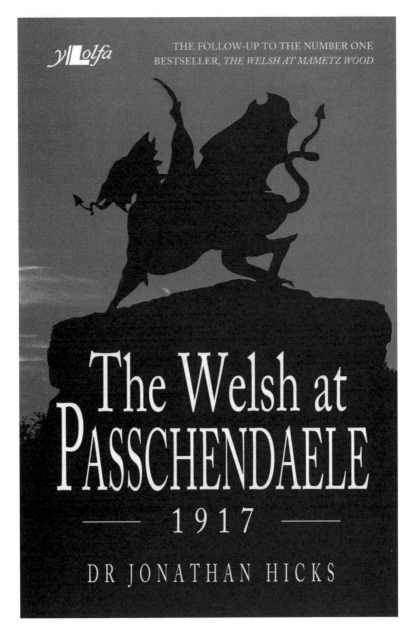

y Lolfa

THE FOLLOW-UP TO THE NUMBER ONE
BESTSELLER, *THE WELSH AT MAMETZ WOOD*

The Welsh at
PASSCHENDAELE
— 1917 —

DR JONATHAN HICKS

£14.99

The Welsh at Mametz Wood

The Somme 1916

DR JONATHAN HICKS

£12.99

JONATHAN HICKS

THE DEAD of MAMETZ

The most dangerous
enemies were on
his own side

THE FIRST THOMAS OSCENDALE NOVEL

£8.95

DEMONS
WALK AMONG US

The follow-up to *The Dead of Mametz*

Jonathan Hicks

y Lolfa

£8.95

Wales and the First Air War 1914–1918 is just one
of a whole range of publications from Y Lolfa.
For a full list of books currently in print, send
now for your free copy of our new full-colour
catalogue. Or simply surf into our website

www.ylolfa.com

for secure on-line ordering.

TALYBONT CEREDIGION CYMRU SY24 5HE
e-mail ylolfa@ylolfa.com
website www.ylolfa.com
phone (01970) 832 304
fax 832 782

Ask for a print quote!
01970 832 304